My sister forever!

TOP

of the

MOUNTAIN

a story about real love

Wa

TOP

of the

MOUNTAIN

a story about real love

Wade J. Carey

Top of the Mountain
a story about real love
Copyright © 2017
by Wade J. Carey

Library of Congress Control Number:
ISBN: 1544888708
ISBN: 978-1544888705
For more information on author Wade J. Carey, visit http://flamingsword.us
Printed in the United States of America by CreateSpace

Cover artwork by: Rachel Bostwick
Cover image by: Elissa S. Carey
Edited by: Cheryl Tengelsen
Interior layout by: Rachel Bostwick

Certain stock imagery for the following chapter headings are used by permission from www.bigstockphoto.com: Prayer of Salvation, Biblical Verses Used.

I JOHN 4:8

"Whoever does not love does not know God, because God is love."

I JOHN 2:15

"Do not love the world or anything in the world. If anyone loves the world, love for the Father is not in them."

EPHESIANS 5:5

"For of this you can be sure: No immoral, impure or greedy person—such a person is an idolater—has any inheritance in the kingdom of Christ and of God."

PROLOGUE

Cottondale, TX
October, 1942

A mid-morning autumn breeze exhaled dry wisps of summer's final breath upon the lovely hamlet of Cottondale. The amazing tranquility of this rural landscape was ironically, its most distinct feature. This sleepy little north Texas town—a mere forty miles northwest of Ft. Worth—lollygagged through another one of its stunningly bucolic days.

On this gentle morning, ten year old Rachel Green sat under a huge shade tree on the west side of Jerry's General Store, near the center of the community. The store sat placidly on a quiet country road. A typical, slightly rusted tin roof topped the old building, which was wrapped in aged, dark wood and fronted with a large covered entryway. Intermittently festooned across the building's perimeter were various tin signs with product advertisements from the World War II era.

Joining Rachel was her classmate and best friend in the world, Harvey Gordon. Rachel and Harvey's special friendship dated back as far as either of them could even remember. Due to the fact that Cottondale's only school had closed just a few years previous, Rachel and Harvey had to make the daily weekday trek to the nearby town of Paradise for their classes.

But not today. Today was Saturday.

By virtually all standards, Rachel was a beautiful young lady. Her bright red hair and somber green eyes were nothing less than striking.

Her parents often encouraged her that she was beautiful enough to move to Hollywood one day to become a famous movie star. Rachel's outward appearance contrasted greatly with her friend Harvey, who was quite ordinary for a slightly chubby, shy boy with brown hair and no real distinguishing physical features.

While Rachel's family was as close to middle class as one could be during the savages of the Second World War, Harvey was the son of a poor farmer and didn't have much—materialistically speaking. Despite their economic differences, however, Rachel and Harvey enjoyed a unique and special bond as they grew up together in their lovely home town.

As the twosome quietly relaxed on some large rocks under the notably sprawling tree next to the store, Harvey asked, "Hey, Rachel. How come your daddy likes to come here on Saturday mornings? It's not like I'm complaining or nothing. I was just wondering."

Rachel looked over at her friend and shrugged. "I'm not real sure, Harvey. I'm just glad he comes and picks you up so we can spend some time together. You know, outside of school."

"Me too."

They both smiled and were quiet for a few moments.

Rachel continued, "Come to think of it, I think my daddy is waiting on Blaine's father to come meet with him about some kinda business deal."

Harvey's shoulders visibly shrank. There was that dreaded name again—Blaine. Young Blaine Billings was the same age as Rachel and Harvey, only he lived in nearby Paradise. Born into money that was largely driven by his hard-charging entrepreneurial father, Blaine's outlook on life was one of expectation and privilege. Unfortunately, humility was nowhere to be found in him. Blaine was handsome and rich—an enviable combination to most people.

"Oh, Blaine's coming, huh?" Harvey said, not able to mask his disappointment. "I guess I was hoping it'd be just you and me today."

No sooner had these rueful words left Harvey's lips than he spotted a wall of dust stirring up about a mile down the road. It was obvious that a car was approaching. As Rachel and Harvey gazed in the distance at the rapidly approaching vehicle, young Harvey couldn't help but to feel like this was a seriously bad omen. His overwhelming sense was that his life's greatest enemy was suddenly invading his quiet world, destroying his peace and interrupting this wonderful day he was spending with his true love.

Even at the young age of ten years old, Harvey was well beyond his years in wisdom and discernment. What he may have lacked in notable physical appearance was more than made up for by having a grounded intelligence and the ability to learn very quickly. He was also very spiritually attuned to his faith in Jesus Christ for such a young man.

Being a straight-A student and the son of a poor farmer, Harvey had very little time to spend on the normal childhood activities in life—except when it came to Rachel. Between his schooling and chores on the farm, Harvey stayed so constantly busy; he had little time to focus on himself. Despite the fact that Rachel lived so close to his family's homestead, Harvey often longed to one day go see the world outside of Cottondale so he could make his mark in it. He very much felt like he was destined to leave this place to find his destiny in some big city somewhere. Of course, he desperately wanted to bring Rachel with him. He actually couldn't picture his life without her being a big part of it.

As the shiny black, almost new, Buick Roadmaster came to a screeching halt in front of the store, the dust proceeded to settle down. Then, the driver's side door opened and a handsome man in his mid-thirties hopped out. Soon thereafter, the passenger door opened and the Billings men—both the younger and the elder—moved towards the front door of the store.

Rachel and Harvey instinctively stood up. Rachel then waved at Blaine, whose quizzical expression fell into a sneer when he saw his two classmates under the tree. The young interloper was there for one reason and one reason only—to see Rachel.

Blaine's father marched purposefully towards the front door of the store as Blaine's path diverted towards the tree, where his beautiful prize awaited him to rescue her from such a poor, loser like Harvey.

When Blaine made it to their spot, he turned around and pointed back at his father's automobile.

"So how do y'all like daddy's new car?" he said.

Rachel grinned as Harvey looked down, trying to mask his contempt.

"It's real nice," Rachel said. "What kind is it?"

"It's a new Buick," Blaine said proudly.

"How did your daddy get a new car? I hear they're real hard to get these days."

Blaine grinned. "I reckon it's because my daddy's such an important man. Only those who are important in the war effort can get new automobiles these days, you know."

"So when did he get it?" she asked.

"It was one of the last ones made back in February this year," Blaine bragged. "Daddy said they're not making many new cars for a while; you know, until we win the war and all."

"That's nice," Rachel said.

She started twirling her hair.

Rachel then elbowed Harvey to show his manners.

"Oh yeah," Harvey said. "It's a really pretty car, for sure."

Blaine sported a satisfied look. Since he had now taken what he considered to be a superior position over Harvey, a blanket of smugness settled into his attitude.

"So what're y'all doing?" Blaine asked.

"We're just waiting for my daddy to have his meeting with yours," Rachel said.

"Oh," Blaine said. "I saw Mr. Green at the doorway to the store when we pulled in. Why do you think they're meeting today?"

"Do you think it has something to do with the war?" Harvey added.

Blaine ignored him and focused his gaze on Rachel.

"I'm pretty sure they have some important money business to discuss," Rachel said. "Daddy's bank in Bridgeport is supposed to help Mr. Billings do some kind of work project … I think…."

Blaine nodded slowly. "That makes sense. My dad doesn't tell me too much, except to teach me things about how this world works. I guess since he's so important, he needs money from the bank for something."

"Probably so," Rachel agreed.

"So are y'all coming to the big homecoming lunch at church tomorrow?" Harvey asked Blaine.

Blaine shook his head. "Dad says he's too busy to mess around with silly things like church. He's too busy staying focused on making money and helping our country defeat Hitler."

For some reason, Harvey felt bold. "Y'all should still come to church, Blaine. We've been studying the gospel of Luke this month—"

"For your information," Blaine said hotly. "I don't need religion and I don't need you telling me what to do."

Harvey shook his head. "Don't be so dramatic, Blaine. I was just trying to be friendly."

Blaine snorted.

Rachel understood what was going on—a covert battle for her affection. She quickly made her decision and patted Harvey on the shoulder and walked towards Blaine, saying, "Hey Blaine, let's go check out the new candies Mr. Jerry has inside for a minute."

Blaine smiled at his apparent victory.

"Don't worry—we'll be back in a bit," she said to Harvey.

"Oh, okay…." Harvey said, dejectedly.

He sat back down on a rock.

A familiar blanket of rejection descended upon Harvey. It was hard for anyone—let alone a ten-year old boy—to deal with seeing arrogant people always seem to win. Deep in his heart, in a place he rarely showed the world, Harvey was terrified that the one thing he wanted more than anything else—to one day marry his beloved Rachel—would somehow elude him. Worse yet, the idea of Blaine taking her away from him tore his little heart to shreds.

Because of the hardships that so often emanate from his blue collar status in life, Harvey always knew he was born to serve others. But the one thing he had prayed for so strongly in his young life was that God would bless him with the woman of his dreams to be his wife one day. To Harvey, this wasn't a very big request for God to fill. He very much clung to this tenuous hope.

After an agonizing fifteen minutes of waiting, both Rachel and Blaine exited Jerry's General Store, followed by their fathers. By the tone of their muffled voices and the general laughter that ensued, things seemed to have gone pretty well inside. Interestingly, Rachel was carrying a bag of candy.

But it was something else that suddenly caught Harvey's attention. Something he couldn't believe he was seeing with his very own eyes: Blaine took Rachel's hand and held it as they moved towards Mr. Billings' car.

Oh no!!! he thought.

Rachel's father looked directly at Harvey and waved him over as the others got into the Buick. Much to Harvey's dismay, once he reached the front of the store where Mr. Green was waiting, Blaine, his father, and Rachel started driving off; back in the direction from whence the car had approached. Rachel waved at Harvey with an uncomfortable grin from the car's window. Harvey reluctantly waved back.

Harvey's dismay was apparent, so Mr. Green quickly said, "I'm sorry, Harvey. But Rachel is going over to a gathering at Blaine's house in Paradise today."

"But ... why—?"

"Everything is okay, young man. It's just that we have some important business to attend to with Blaine's father at their house."

Harvey's facial expression betrayed his severe disappointment. Mr. Green picked up on this and said, "Listen, son. Let me give you a little bit of advice. The sooner you accept your station in life, the sooner you'll find peace and contentment. You can't fight who you are."

Harvey looked up and said, "I don't understand—"

"You don't need to understand, Harvey. Just listen to me. Ole Jerry inside has agreed to take you home for me because I need to follow Mr. Billings to his house. That means I can't take you home today. But Jerry will take good care of you, I promise."

Harvey frowned.

"Go on, now. Jerry is waiting for you inside. When I picked you up this morning, I told your folks I might need Jerry to take you home for me today—depending on what happened in my meeting."

Mr. Green patted Harvey on the shoulder. "Everything will be okay, young man. Trust me."

Reluctantly, Harvey turned on his heels and proceeded inside as Rachel's father departed.

As the screen door smacked close behind Harvey, the various rustic aromas of sassafras, molasses, fresh bread, and stick candy from the old general store gently surrounded him in a familiar way. He could hear Mr. Green get into his car and begin to drive away. The sounds of grinding gravel under his tires signaled that Harvey was now all alone with the bald, thin-framed owner of the store, who appeared to be in his late fifties.

Jerry looked up from behind the counter when he saw his visitor and declared, "Well hello, Harvey! C'mon over here and let's have a little chat."

Harvey really liked the old man. Actually, everyone did. He headed towards the counter, plopped down on one of the stools, and then looked up at the proprietor as if the world was about to end.

"What's with the sour look?" said Jerry.

Harvey shook his head. He hesitated to share his frustration out of fear that verbalizing it would somehow make it worse. He felt that by keeping it to himself, he could still cling to a sliver of hope that he was over-reacting to Blaine's invasion.

"Let me guess," Jerry continued. "You're upset because Blaine drove off with *your* girl. Am I right?"

Harvey was a terrible liar, so he couldn't even muster an ounce of strength to internalize it anymore.

"I'm afraid so, sir," he mused.

Jerry nodded once. "Would you mind terribly if I gave you some friendly advice?"

"No sir, I wouldn't mind that at all."

"Now I'm not going to give you some selfish advice like what Mr. Green just tried to give you outside. I'm talking about something very important; something that will help you to grow closer to the Lord."

"How did you—?"

"Never mind about that, son. Please just listen to me. The first thing I want to tell you is that true love may indeed take both people involved, but real love always starts with God. And I mean *always*."

Harvey nodded his understanding.

Jerry continued, "Let me share a verse with you I'm sure you've heard many times before. But this time, I want you to listen to it very, very closely. It's *John 3:16 ... For God so loved the world that he gave his one and only Son, that whoever believes in him shall not perish but have eternal life.*"

"Yes sir, I've heard that many times at church."

"Indeed you have. But today, I want you to really think about the fierce, real love it took for God to give His only Son to the world. That, my friend, is exactly what real love is all about—sacrificial love."

"What exactly do you mean by that?"

"Jesus Christ became flesh out of His intense love for His people and to save humanity from its sin. Whether one likes it or not, all people are born sinful and must overcome their self-focus in order to survive this temporary world through Jesus. Sadly, folks like Mr. Billings and Mr. Green are overcome with their desire to be the god of their own world and pursue what they really love, which is money.

13

Their love of money is to the exclusion of God—I mean, the *real* God."

"Well, that ain't right," Harvey said. "You know something? We had to memorize the Ten Commandments in Sunday school, and—"

"You're on the right track with that," Jerry interrupted. "But for today, I'd like you to focus on the first two of those commandments. In particular, the first one. Can you tell me what the first two commandments are?"

"Yes sir. They're in *Exodus 20:3-4* ... *'You shall have no other gods before me,* and *'You shall not make for yourself an image in the form of anything in heaven above or on the earth beneath or in the waters below.'*

"Very good. Although you don't hear about it very often, virtually everything in the Bible centers on that one basic premise—that there is only one God, and one God alone. Not only that, but only the real God deserves worship."

"I understand."

"Do you, now?"

Harvey was thoughtful for a few moments.

"Yes sir," he said, shrugging. "At least, I think I do."

Jerry grinned. "What I mean, Harvey, is that all humans are born thinking they're the god of their own world. As a result, they often try to block the real love of God their Father, who created them and sustains them."

They were both quiet for a few more moments.

"Hmmm. I don't know, Mr. Jerry. Maybe I'm just not supposed to be a big shot like Mr. Billings and Blaine. They seem to have it so easy in life."

Jerry shook his head. "That's only on the surface, son. Below the surface, men like that have a spiritual ugliness that's both sad and somewhat nauseating."

Harvey suddenly blurted, "Then how come Rachel doesn't love me like she loves Blaine? I just don't get it."

Unsurprised, Jerry replied, "Because Rachel is caught up in a type of humanism."

"Humanism—what's that?"

Jerry sat down on a stool behind the counter to get closer to Harvey's line of sight. The older man looked intently at his young friend, and with a gentle voice said, "Humanism is basically the belief that human desires are more important than God's desires—or His will."

"Ahhh, c'mon. That's just dumb."

Jerry shrugged. "Perhaps so, but that doesn't stop people from following that sinful principle. To them, it feels good—at least, for the moment it does."

Harvey shook his head. "Maybe if I was rich and handsome, Rachel would love me and marry me one day."

Jerry reached across the counter and patted Harvey on the shoulder before saying, "Let me give you another important verse to think about, young man. You weren't born rich, but you do have your whole life ahead of you. And believe it or not, your struggles will ironically forge you into a powerful man one day. You need to listen to me because I've gotten pretty darned good at seeing things like this."

Harvey reluctantly grinned.

Jerry continued, "Here's the verse … *1 Corinthians 1:26* … *Brothers and sisters, think of what you were when you were called. Not many of you were wise by human standards; not many were influential; not many were of noble birth.*"

"Well, no. I wasn't born noble, that's for sure."

"Perhaps not, but you were certainly *reborn* noble when you surrendered your life to Jesus Christ at church a few months ago."

Harvey visibly brightened. "Something just came over me that day at church and it was so neat. I didn't know you were there that day."

"I sure was," Jerry said proudly. "Watching folks genuinely surrender their life to Jesus Christ is just about my favorite thing in the whole wide world."

A huge smile emerged on Harvey's face.

Jerry nodded and continued, "Anyway, I have one more thing for you, before I run you back home."

"What's that?"

"As a Christian, you shouldn't merely pursue things in life that somehow make you feel better. That's what Rachel and Blaine now do. Instead, you should pursue eternal things which make you a better follower of Jesus Christ. In the end, that is what's truly important."

Harvey was quiet for a few moments as this sunk in.

Jerry continued, "Rachel and Blaine are on a worldly path which will only lead to incredible pain. They think they're pursuing their dreams, but what they're actually pursuing is their destruction. Listen, you may not believe me now, but please trust me on this. I didn't get this old by being a fool."

"I understand, sir."

"I've got one more thing for you, Harvey."

"What's that?"

"I'd like you to never forget that real love *always* starts with the Lord. Without God, no one will ever find real love because it just doesn't exist outside of Him."

Harvey nodded. "Yes sir. I'll try to remember that."

Jerry stood back up. "How about me letting you sample some of our newest candy sticks before we saddle up in my old white Ford truck out back and I run you home? Would that be okay with you, my young friend?"

"That'd be great, Mr. Jerry. The candy sure sounds good, and I'd really appreciate a ride home. Thanks."

PART I

LONGINGS OF THE HEART

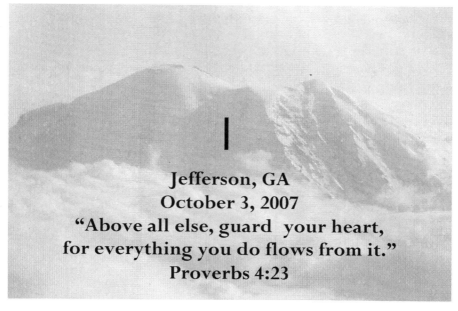

I

Jefferson, GA
October 3, 2007
"Above all else, guard your heart,
for everything you do flows from it."
Proverbs 4:23

The old woman rapidly blinked her eyes as they begrudgingly crept open on what she felt would be another miserable day in her life full of regrets. As she laid there staring at the ceiling, the crushing heartache that was the keynote of her seventy-five years on Earth seemed to be squatting on her heart like a herd of elephants. She desperately wanted to feel serenity in what were possibly her final days, but she could no longer even imagine what peace looked or felt like anymore.

Rachel's beautiful red hair had slowly changed over the years into a faded, silver-gray. The once lovely figure of her younger years had now been replaced with a gaunt and broken down version, which had little resemblance to what she had boasted about for much of her life. The cancer that was rampaging throughout her frail body was clearly winning the war, and all medical treatments would likely be ending soon.

Her end was near. She just knew it.

Rachel heard a rapid *knock-knock-knock* at the door to her old home, followed by the rattling sound of a key being inserted into the lock. She remained still. A few moments later, the beaming face of her beloved niece, Vanessa Hunter, who lived nearby, greeted her somber day. Vanessa was in her late thirties and had short, brunette hair and a medium build.

"Good morning Aunt Rachel," Vanessa said cheerfully.

Rachel cracked a small grin that looked more like a wince. "Good morning, sweetheart. Thanks for stopping by today."

"I wouldn't dare miss a chance to visit my favorite aunt."

"Don't you mean to say, you don't want to miss seeing me in my death bed, right?"

Vanessa shook her head. "Now, now. You have no idea how much time God still has left in store for you."

Rachel shook her head. "Like I've told you before, I really have no idea who God is. He sure hasn't done much for me in my life."

"Oh, I suppose you've had your ups-and-downs, for sure. But you mustn't forget—Jesus died for your sins and He wants you to come to Him for forgiveness and be a part of His eternal kingdom. That's far from being a trivial issue in your life. I'm afraid you can't put off God any longer—especially now."

Rachel shook her head. "If Jesus really loved me, he wouldn't have let me experience so much pain in my life. You're my favorite niece and I certainly appreciate you taking such good care of me. But I just don't believe all of that 'God is love' stuff. Based on my life, it just doesn't make any sense; it just doesn't fit."

"Actually, that depends on what you mean by love," Vanessa said. She sat down on a chair next to Rachel's bed. "Real love is genuine, you know."

"What do you mean by that?"

"Honestly, it seems to me that the human version of love is self-centered and incomplete. On the other hand, God's version of love is based on the fact that it starts with Him and involves sacrifice. That's what I mean by real love—it's more a matter of the will than a mere human feeling or emotion."

"Humph," Rachel snorted as Vanessa pulled out her Bible.

"Part of why I stopped by today was to read a few verses to you, Aunt Rachel. I believe they'll greatly encourage you if you allow them to. Do you mind?"

Rachel shrugged. "I suppose so. I can't really stop you, can I?"

Vanessa grinned. "So speaking of real love, let's start with this passage: *Romans 5:8 ... But God demonstrates his own love for us in this: While we were still sinners, Christ died for us.*"

"What's that supposed to mean?"

"First off, I'm afraid it means the false idea of love you appear to believe in needs to die a quick and definitive death. To be brutally honest, your misconception about real love has become a type of false idol in your life."

Rachel shook her head in frustration.

Vanessa continued, "With Hospice perhaps being summoned here to take over care for you in the next couple of weeks, your days on Earth may become few. Please forgive me if this sounds morose, but it's very important that you hear me out today."

"Now this may surprise you, but honestly, what you're saying doesn't sound too ugly or mean. Especially if it's the truth."

Vanessa nodded. "Okay, good. With your overall situation in mind, I think your false ideas about real love need to die—and soon. Time is of the essence."

Rachel suddenly sat up in bed and blurted, "Don't you think I know I'm dying? Why do you keep saying that???"

Vanessa raised her hands in a defensive position and motioned for her aunt to lie back down on her propped-up pillow.

"I love you, Aunt Rachel. I'm only trying to help."

The old woman sighed and was quiet for a few moments.

"You and your husband Wyatt have always been so kind to me," Rachel said. "As you know, after my fourth husband and I divorced years ago, I moved here to Jefferson to be near you. Y'all have graciously let me live in this house for free, and I'll always appreciate you for that."

Vanessa grinned. "Oh, it's true we could've rented-out this old house and perhaps made a few bucks a month, but helping you was the very least thing we could do. Besides, this house has so many bad memories for Wyatt; I have no idea why he wanted to purchase it years after his mother Abbie moved to Florida. It's not like he has good memories of his childhood home."

"Yes, I remember you telling me the story of Wyatt's father leaving his mother when he was only a year old. I suppose that's not the most pleasant thing to reminisce about."

"No, it's not. But listen; based on your situation, I have a few other passages I think might make sense to you. Is it okay if I share them with you?"

"I grew up in church, honey, and that never seemed to work. But if you want to read me something, then be my guest. Beggars can't be choosers, you know."

"While it's true you grew up in church, you never *became* the church," Vanessa said. "So here goes: *Isaiah 40:29 … He gives strength to the weary and increases the power of the weak.*"

"I do feel very weak."

"Then you should allow God to strengthen you."

Rachel shook her head. "I've tried—"

"Please … let me finish."

Rachel nodded as Vanessa continued, "Next, I have for you *Proverbs 15:13 … A happy heart makes the face cheerful, but heartache crushes the spirit.*"

"Now *that* makes sense to me. A crushed spirit is exactly how I feel these days. Not to mention all of the heartache I've endured over the years."

"To finish out my message to you, here is *Ecclesiastes 7:29 … This only have I found: God created mankind upright, but they have gone in search of many schemes.*"

Rachel looked directly at Vanessa and said sadly, "I suppose you want to throw my sordid past up in my face, huh? Are you going to blame me for all of my so-called schemes?"

Vanessa shook her head. "In order to share my message with you today, I need to bring up a few important things from your past. No, I'm not throwing anything in your face. But in order to make my point, we need to discuss Blaine…."

Tears welled up in Rachel's eyes.

Vanessa continued, "You've admitted to me before that your obsession with Blaine absolutely ruined your life. Do you still feel that way?"

Rachel nodded reluctantly. She then said, "I always thought that if I achieved my goal of true love with a successful man like Blaine, then I'd live happily ever after. But as you know, the story of my life doesn't look anything like that … not at all."

"No, but it could have. Although Blaine died last year, the real love in your life only lives about forty minutes south of this very spot. Have you ever considered that?"

"Who—Harvey? Don't be silly, Vanessa. Harvey and I have always just been good friends—almost like brother and sister. I never really felt romantically towards him."

"Who said anything about romance?"

"Isn't that what real love is?"

Vanessa shook her head. "Romance is certainly a part of real love, but it cannot sustain it for the long-term. Real love requires something much more substantial to be part of the mix than mere romance."

"I've always felt that the most important thing in the world was love," Rachel said. "Harvey and I love each other, but not in that way."

"In what way? In the impermanent way of passionate feelings? I'm afraid that's not what real love is. If my husband Wyatt only loved me that way—only romantically and without sacrifice—then our marriage would have crumbled many years ago."

Rachel sighed. "Just like my four miserable marriages."

"Exactly. Like you said, you told me as a girl the most important thing in the world is love and having a good heart. But you weren't talking about God's version of sacrificial love—*agape* love."

"What exactly is agape love? I vaguely remember—"

"Agape love is exactly what I hinted at a minute ago. Love without sacrifice is woefully incomplete and often capricious. Far too often, I'm afraid that's what the flawed, human version of love is."

"What do you mean by the 'human version' of love?"

"Quite simply, love without God just doesn't work."

"Well, why not?"

Vanessa stared deeply into Rachel's eyes, "Because human love isn't eternal. Only God's love is eternal."

Rachel fell into deep thought for a few moments. After swimming around the depths of her feelings, she asked, "Do you really think Harvey has loved me all of these years?"

"Without question, yes. Deep down, you know it to be true."

"But Harvey married a nice lady and had two wonderful children. He was successful in his career and made a lot of money. Why in the world would he love an old wretch like me? I mean; we still see each other a few times a year, but we're just friends. That's all."

Vanessa sighed and said, "When you were children, based on what you've shared with me over the years, I believe Blaine intentionally kept you and Harvey from finding real love together. Yes, you were only ten years old when you claim you fell in love with Blaine—"

"Oh, things were different back in the forties," Rachel said. "Ten years old back then meant something completely different than what it means today. I mean; folks often got married even before turning eighteen back in those days. It wasn't odd at all for kids to talk about one day getting married when we were so young."

Vanessa nodded. "I suppose you're right. You were the one who lived through those times."

"I did, but let's get back to Harvey. I have to admit, this is very interesting."

"Let's do."

"Let me ask you this—did he send you here to see me today or something? I know you've somehow kept in touch with him."

Vanessa shook her head and grinned. "No, he didn't send me here today. Of course not."

"Oh."

"Yes, he's always been like an uncle to me, but we haven't conspired together or anything."

"Then what? Why are you bringing him up all of the sudden?"

"I'm trying to help you find peace, Aunt Rachel. After your doctor's appointment next week, if your cancer isn't in remission, they may be calling Hospice to care for you. That means they have nothing left they can do. Time may be running out."

"I understand—"

"Listen, Wyatt and I have visited Harvey's son's church down near Monroe a few times before, and we're thinking of joining it. Harvey's son is quite a good preacher, you know. We're growing very fond of him."

"Is he now? Harvey told me many years ago how proud he was of his son becoming a pastor."

Vanessa took Rachel's hand and said, "In order to share with you what I believe God wants me to say to you today, let's take a stroll through your personal history. Now I don't mean for it to sound judgmental at all. But rather, I'm hoping it will be spiritually illuminating. Do you mind?"

Rachel shrugged. "Oh, I suppose not."

"Good. You were born in 1932 in a small town in Texas, northwest of Ft. Worth. When you were ten years old, you left Harvey at an old general store and spent the day at Blaine's house. It was there that Blaine told you he wanted to marry you one day."

"Yes, that's true. And I was *soooo* flattered that such a handsome and rich boy said he loved me."

"But Blaine never committed to you, did he?"

"Well, the circumstances—"

"Circumstances—*nothing!* That man strung you along for most of your life. It started on that day you left Harvey at the store, and continued through the time when you finished high school and Blaine dumped you for some rich girl who he could take advantage of. Blaine was never there for you, Aunt Rachel. Never."

"You're wrong. Blaine and I had something—"

Vanessa shook her head emphatically. "You had a dysfunctional relationship with Blaine. It's time for you to finally admit it. Tragically, I believe that false relationship has always stood in your way of truly knowing Jesus Christ."

"Oh, you're just being protective of Harvey," Rachel snorted.

"No, actually I'm being protective of *you.*"

"How so?"

"Throughout your life, you never guarded your heart," Vanessa said. "You always bought into Blaine's lies that he loved you and would marry you one day. I'm sorry, but Blaine was nothing but a worldly man and a pathological liar."

The truth of Vanessa's words slowly began to erode Rachel's pride. She remained silent as her niece continued.

"Didn't you notice that when you finished high school and he went off to college and rarely saw you, that maybe he wasn't actually in love with you? Didn't it occur to you that perhaps Blaine had cast a shadow in your life that was robbing you of real love and happiness?"

The old woman sighed again. "I don't know, perhaps you're right."

"You know I am. Throughout your life, you knew Blaine was a selfish man who only thought of himself. From what you've confessed to me in the past, Blaine was absolutely obsessed with sexual conquests and money. You even admitted that y'all had several affairs during the time he was married to that rich woman."

Rachel looked down. "And I'm very ashamed of that."

"Just think about it. Blaine was in the oil business until the crash back in the seventies. Then, he moved to the Atlanta area from Texas with his rich wife and started his career over. All the while, you were in and out of marriages, trying to make Blaine jealous—but it never worked."

"All of that is true, dear. I even followed him to Atlanta, just to be near him in case he ever did leave his wife."

"But he never did—did he?"

Rachel was surprisingly calm at this point. She admitted, "No, I suppose Blaine never planned to leave his wife. All I could do was watch as they travelled the world together and lived it up. For some reason, as far as I know, they never had any children—and neither did I. Oh, they had lavish homes, enjoyed incredible meals, owned many expensive cars, and lived quite the extravagant lifestyle. All the while, I was sitting there, hoping Blaine would leave his wife and he and I would live happily ever after."

"That wasn't real love, was it?"

Rachel sighed. "No, I suppose not."

Vanessa calmed down and slowly said, "I'd like to read another passage to you. It's *Philippians 4:13 … I can do all this through him who gives me strength.*"

Rachel shook her head. "Why would God love a sinful woman like me? Why in the world would he care about someone who has lived her life without regard to Him whatsoever?"

"Actually, none of us are worthy," Vanessa said. "That's why we need God's grace to be saved. It's not about our actions. It's about His overwhelming love and grace."

"Then why doesn't God love me enough to allow me to experience real love?"

Vanessa smiled. "He did give you real love."

"How?"

"God gave you His only Son to die for your sins. Not only that, but God gave you Harvey—but you rejected him due to the false image you had about what real love is."

Rachel looked away, staring out the window. "Are you telling me I've been wrong for the past seventy-five years? Are you telling me that on that one particular Saturday morning back in 1942, I made a terrible choice by leaving Harvey for Blaine? Can all of my misery in life be traced back to that one simple mistake by a young girl?"

Vanessa cupped both of her hands over Rachel's left hand. Rachel had tears in her eyes again as Vanessa said, "It wasn't just that bad decision, dear. It was the false image—or false idol—you had stuck in your head about what real love is. You rejected Harvey a million times over the years due to that great lie—"

"What great lie?"

"The great lie that the world's image of love is real love."

Rachel wiped the tears from her face. "I don't know, sweetheart. I just don't know."

"Promise me you'll at least think about what we've discussed today. I just can't stand the idea of you slowly dying, but not truly knowing who Jesus Christ is and surrendering your life to Him. You absolutely must remember that real love starts with Jesus."

"And who exactly *is* Jesus? To be completely honest, I don't think I've ever really given Him a chance at my heart. I suppose I've never really been all that interested."

"That's because the world with all of its false idols stood in your way, blocking God's light. But that can change—it *should* change."

"But why is Jesus so important?" Rachel mused.

"Jesus Christ was prophesied to be called *Immanuel* in *Isaiah 7:14*. The meaning of Immanuel is 'God among us' or 'God with us.' If you stop and think about it, that's a pretty big deal."

"In what way?"

"God became flesh because God is all about real love. That's what I mean. You've lived your life without Jesus, Aunt Rachel. We both know that. But I'd like you to consider repenting and literally changing the spiritual direction of your heart. This is the most important thing in the world—especially now."

Rachel sighed. "I'll think about it, Vanessa."

"Good. Can I make you a cup of tea?"

"Of course you can, my dear. Of course."

"I'll be right back," Vanessa said.

"Please wait. I need to say something to you."

"What's that?"

"Thank you for being brave and sharing your faith with me."

Vanessa smiled. "That's my job ... and my pleasure."

2

Monroe, GA
October 3, 2007
"Let no debt remain outstanding, except the
continuing debt to love one another, for
whoever loves others has fulfilled the law."
Romans 13:8

Autumn's first brisk evening in north Georgia gently settled upon the city of Monroe, which sits due east of the sprawling metropolis of Atlanta. Many years ago, Harvey had carefully researched this area and decided to settle here. He did this in an effort to be reasonably close to the big city where most of his business transacted, but where he wouldn't be so close to the perils of city life. After all, Harvey was still a country boy at heart.

Staring out into the wooded area behind his large, fenced backyard, Harvey was enjoying the peaceful ambiance of his screened-in back porch. The dark wicker chair he sat in sported a bright red and yellow floral pattern in its puffy cushion. This clashed with Harvey's faded old blue jeans and dark sweater. The excess weight which had plagued Harvey for much of his life was finally gone, so his physical appearance was quite good for a bald man in his mid-seventies. Some might even say he was thin.

Sitting next to Harvey was his beloved son, Harvey Junior—or PJ, which stands for "Pastor Junior." PJ had been affectionately called 'Junior' during his early life. When he became an ordained minister many years later, the affectionate term "PJ" was laid on him by several of his seminary buddies after they graduated together. Unlike his father, PJ had never struggled with his weight, still had a full head of now graying hair, and was very much beloved by his mostly older congregation.

"We couldn't have picked a nicer evening to visit," Harvey told PJ, who sat right next to his dad. "I'm glad you were able to take a Wednesday night off this week. This is typically a pretty busy night for pastors."

"It sure is," said PJ. "But I've been slowly shifting our normal Wednesday night service into smaller Bible study groups throughout the week. I feel there's much more intimacy in a smaller group setting."

"True. Hey, whatever gets people studying God's Word is good by me. Without the Bible's encouragement over the years, I would have never been able to get through my life without feeling completely brokenhearted and totally without hope."

"Oh, I get that, dad. But honestly, I'm afraid you ended up brokenhearted anyway."

Harvey looked quizzically over at his son, "What do you mean by that?" he said. "Your mom died five years ago, and I think I've adjusted to this final phase of my life pretty darned well."

PJ held up his hands in a defensive gesture. "Oh, don't get me wrong. When you lost all of that weight after mom died, it was quite impressive. You've also done an amazing job of keeping it off. Mom would have been so proud of you."

"Your mother was always into all of that health-stuff. It's kind of sad that the woman who loved natural things so much was unable to see her husband finally get rid of those excess pounds."

"Yeah, but I feel that mom loved nature a little *too* much. In fact, it was pretty much her religion, wouldn't you say?"

Harvey shook his head in disappointment. "How true. My saddest thing in life is that your mom never became a follower of Jesus Christ like you, me, and your little sister Jane. I mean; all of those years, and she could never see herself loving Jesus as her Lord and Savior."

"Oh, she loved Him all right—but not in the right way. Mom saw Jesus as merely another admirable religious figure in her own Universalist belief system. Sometimes, I wonder how I became a pastor with her various humanistic beliefs being infused so prominently into my childhood."

"That's where I came in," Harvey said. "I made sure both you and your sister saw the truth of the Gospel of Jesus Christ. I always felt like that was my primary job—just like my folks did for me."

PJ reached over and gently squeezed his dad on the shoulder. "I suppose you're right, dad."

After a few moments, Harvey continued, "I'm sad to say, your mom basically cobbled together her own totem pole of religious beliefs. She picked a few things from several different religions and created her own, unique belief system. To be honest, it never made any sense to me."

"I suppose you're right," PJ lamented. "Hey, that actually reminds me of a neat passage I'm using for my next sermon."

"Let's hear it."

"Okay. It's right here in *2 Kings 17:33* ... *They worshiped the Lord, but they also served their own gods in accordance with the customs of the nations from which they had been brought.*"

Harvey nodded. "That sounds like my Eunice, all right. While I understand the human yearning to search for real truth, I have no idea how she could have so consistently rejected the message of God's real love. I hate to say it, but she essentially moved God aside and built an altar unto herself."

PJ nodded. "In all my days in the ministry, I've never been one to play the game of predicting who will be in Heaven one day. I feel like that's God's job. But I saw nothing in mom that would lead me to believe she ever repented of her sins and trusted alone in Jesus Christ."

"Unfortunately, I agree. Does that make you as sad as it makes me?"

"Profoundly so. Her own false religious beliefs became the biggest de facto false idol in her life."

Harvey looked over at PJ and said, "Well, you know what I always say ... *Satan makes idols beautiful in our own eyes.* I'm afraid idols are a type of spiritual attack that stirs up a person's pride. It's nothing new, of course."

"Nope, it sure isn't. Actually, I've often preached to my congregation that false idols block God's light and essentially replace the need for Him in our lives. That's why the Bible warns about them so often."

"It sure does," Harvey said. "And by the way, idol worship isn't just in the Old Testament. People still do that today, but in myriad ways."

"You got that right."

"Anyway, if my folks had neglected to tend to my spiritual growth in Christ when I was but a wee lad, the world of money I ended up working in would have likely chewed me up and spit me out—spiritually speaking, of course."

"Yeah, dad. I remember your stories of moving to New York City from Cottondale after college to apply your talents in investment banking. That's actually where you met mom."

Harvey chuckled. "Your mother was such a big city girl. Looking back on it, I really can't fathom why she ever agreed to move to little ole Monroe, Georgia, after we got married. Perhaps she liked our joint vision of a quiet lifestyle of her being a homemaker so she could raise you and Jane."

PJ shrugged. "This was a wonderful home to grow up in. Even though you worked all the time, mom took good care of Jane and me."

"She sure did. But please remember—I had to endure the burden of providing a good living for my family. Banking wasn't always an easy profession, you know."

They were quiet for a few moments before PJ asked, "Why did you get into banking and finance in the first place? It really doesn't seem to be your cup of tea."

Harvey was quiet. He sighed before saying, "If we're being honest, I became a banker to impress Rachel. I thought that if I moved to the Big Apple and got a big-time job, she'd consider moving there to be with me and would forget about Blaine. I desperately wanted to get her away from him."

"Really?"

"Unfortunately, yes. But as you know, my little ruse didn't work. It's a good thing God had other plans for me."

PJ nodded. "That's pretty honest, dad."

"That's the only way to be—especially at my age. Anyway, when I met your mom, everything changed. It was really nice to have a woman who wanted to be with me for a change."

"I imagine so."

They were quiet again.

Harvey shook his head. "It's funny. Rachel's dad was also in the banking business over in Bridgeport, Texas, when we were kids. I suppose I misfired when I thought Rachel would be impressed with my profession. It's sad, but I tried so hard to be the man I thought she wanted me to be. I know it may seem silly, but that's how it actually happened."

"Yeah, but I'll bet you made much more money in your career than Rachel's father did. In fact, you became pretty darned wealthy. Ultimately, that paid for me to go to seminary. By the way, thank you again for that."

Harvey nodded. "You're welcome, son. And I did, indeed, make good money in my career. On the other hand, I'm afraid Rachel's father was only involved in local banking, while I was largely on the investment side. So no, Mr. Green probably didn't make as much money as I did in his career—not that it was a contest. Anyway, I feel very grateful to have had the successful career God blessed me with. I really do."

"I see. So why did you think getting into banking would impress Rachel?"

"Although it was mis-guided, I felt like she wanted to be with a successful man like her daddy. Since Blaine had long since stolen Rachel's heart, I felt like the only thing I could do in high school and in college was to win her over with something familiar that would get her attention. I guess you could say it was my attempt at a hail-Mary pass."

"Didn't it occur to you that Rachel might want a man *unlike* her father?"

"Actually, no," Harvey said. "It didn't. I wanted her to love me so desperately; very little logic ever entered my brain when it came to Rachel Green."

PJ chuckled. "Well … if you had ended up marrying her, I sure wouldn't be around today. So I guess I'm grateful she didn't love you back."

Harvey laughed as he lightly smacked the arm of his chair. "Right you are, son!"

After a few moments, PJ said, "So how is the old gal doing these days? She still lives up in Jefferson, right? I see her niece Vanessa sometimes. Her husband Wyatt seems like a good guy."

"Yes, Rachel still lives up in Jefferson. Listen, although I totally gave myself over to loving Rachel when I was young, I really did love your mother. Although we were in completely different worlds spiritually, I enjoyed every minute I was married to her. She was a good woman and a great mother. I hope you understand that."

PJ looked concerned. "Of course, dad. But you and I both know our real family members are the true followers of Jesus Christ. I mean; I hope I'm somehow wrong and mom surrendered to Christ before she died. But like I said, I just don't see any evidence of that."

"One can only hope, son. One can only hope."

"Speaking of mom, did she ever fully grasp your apparent obsession with Rachel?"

"*Obsession?* That's a mighty strong word."

PJ shrugged and said nothing.

"Yes," Harvey admitted. "Your mom knew I harbored latent feelings for Rachel. However, she never seemed to be intimidated by it. Did she ever say anything to you about it?"

"No sir, she didn't."

"Good. I'd hate it if I had hurt your mom's feelings over a silly situation like my pipe dream of marrying Rachel."

Harvey took a sip of his coffee as PJ stretched his arms out.

"Do you still feel that way at all?" PJ asked, gently. "I mean; do you still love Rachel?"

Harvey shook his head. "Yes and no. Although I still feel some pain from all of her rejection over the years, I'm really not interested in anything romantic with her at our age. The only thing I'm concerned about with Rachel is her salvation."

"Really? When was the last time you saw or spoke to her?"

Harvey looked down. "I suppose it's been a while."

"Listen, dad. Another thing I have in my notes for Sunday's sermon is simply this: Real love is consistent."

"In what way? What do you mean by that?"

"In your situation, even though you felt disappointed that Rachel chose a worldly man like Blaine Billings, you still showed her great friendship and a type of *agape* love over the years."

"That's because real love is more about commitment than mere feelings. Feelings are fleeting; true commitments last."

"Amen. And love without sacrifice isn't real love."

Harvey nodded enthusiastically. "I had to swallow my pride with Rachel countless times and accept the sad fact that she had a penchant for consistently choosing poorly when it came to men. When she would end up with one of the many bums she dated and married over the years, I'd always wonder, *why would you go for this clown instead of choosing me???*"

"I don't know, dad. Maybe her self-esteem was so low; she never thought she'd be good enough for you."

"I sincerely doubt that," Harvey said, sitting up in his chair. "I think she just couldn't shake the false image of what success in life is—and that probably came from her parents. Rachel was quite the looker back in her day, you know. I think her folks probably filled her head with ungodly nonsense."

PJ shrugged. "You may be right. And now that we're talking so honestly about this subject, let me say that in a really odd way, I admire you for not totally writing Rachel off in your life. I mean; you could have never spoken to her again, but you remained friends with a woman who thoroughly rejected you as a man. I'm sure that wasn't an easy thing to accept."

"That's not quite it, son. Rachel's feelings were her own choice. Hey, who was I to interfere with her freedom to choose who she wanted to date or marry?"

"Oh, c'mon dad. We're both men. The natural thing to do when you get rejected by a woman is to run away. Yes, we're both Christians, but we're also both human beings and have feelings."

Harvey shook his head. "It wasn't so much that Rachel rejected me. What bothered me was that she continuously chased mirages of love instead of the real thing. I was actually more disturbed by Rachel's obsession with a nitwit like Blaine than I was brokenhearted about her lack of feelings for me."

PJ nodded. "Either way, by remaining in her life, you showed her the truth of Christ's real love and helped her through her incessant mistakes. I think that was a completely admirable thing to do."

"Thanks, son. I actually have a passage that nicely sums up why I chose to not blow Rachel off years ago."

"Oh—?"

"Yes. I learned this back in the day from an old grocery store owner named Jerry. One afternoon, Jerry showed me *1 Corinthians 10:24 ... No one should seek their own good, but the good of others.*"

"Sage advice, dad. Ole Jerry must've been a good Christian man."

"He was the best," Harvey said. "Other than my folks, Jerry had the biggest impact on my faith as a boy."

"Hey, this whole scenario reminds me of a great biblical story."

"Which story is that?"

PJ quickly flipped through his Bible. "It's the story of the prophet Hosea and his adulteress wife, Gomer. Here is the passage I have highlighted: *Hosea 3:1 ... The Lord said to me, 'Go, show your love to your wife again, though she is loved by another man and is an adulteress. Love her as the Lord loves the Israelites, though they turn to other gods and love the sacred raisin cakes.'*

"Wow. That's spot-on, son. God loved the Israelites so much— He was willing to tolerate their constant spiritual adultery; so to speak."

"That's what real love is, dad."

"Amen to that."

PJ nodded. "So what else can you tell me about Jerry the grocery store owner? I don't remember you speaking of him before."

"Well, what do you want to know? Jerry actually helped me deal with my ongoing heartbreak over Rachel quite a bit."

"In what way?"

"Whenever I saw him at the store, or occasionally at church, Jerry gave me some Psalms to stew on. Trust me; those verses were like the proverbial chicken soup for my soul."

"Do you remember any of the verses?"

"Of course," Harvey said, flipping through his Bible. "I have them marked for easy reference when I'm feeling down."

PJ tilted his head in curiosity. "You still read the verses you learned from an old grocery store owner that many decades ago?"

"Yes."

"And it was driven by your unrequited love for Rachel?"

Harvey shot a coy glance at his son. "I'll never tell."

"Ah, so you *do* still love Rachel, don't you?!?!?"

Harvey shook his head. "I love the idea of Rachel finding Jesus Christ before she dies. That's what I love."

PJ chuckled. "So what say-you about these Psalms?"

"Okay. I'll read these passages in the order Jerry gave them to me to read. Here's the first one: *Psalm 27:14 ... Wait for the Lord; be strong and take heart and wait for the Lord.* Next, there's *Psalm 34:18 ... The Lord is close to the brokenhearted and saves those who are crushed in spirit.* And the last one is *Psalm 30:5 ... For his anger lasts only a moment, but his favor lasts a lifetime; weeping may stay for the night, but rejoicing comes in the morning.*"

"Very interesting. It seems he had those in a specific order for a good reason."

"Indeed. They're pretty much like a mathematical formula that leads to healing."

They were quiet for a few moments.

"So what else did Jerry share with you?" said PJ.

"Ole Jerry was the first person to share with me the basic spiritual makeup of our universe. He was actually very good at presenting a big-picture view of how things work in this world...."

"Go on."

Harvey nodded. "He explained to me a shockingly simple concept, which is the most basic thing about God. Jerry said that all people are born feeling this way."

"And that is—?"

"Whether we realize it or not, Jerry said that our initial sinful, human sense of God is that He is some kind of cosmic Santa Claus who is supposed to give us our every desire in this life. It's truly a genie-in-a-bottle, human construct."

"I see," PJ said. "And we both know how wrong that is. This is God's world, not ours."

"Exactly. Jerry also said that there are only two types of belief systems in this world—faith in God through Jesus Christ, and various types of humanism."

"Humanism?"

"That's it," Harvey said, nodding. "He really didn't elaborate on it, but Jerry started teaching me this back in 1942—well before you were born."

"That's interesting, dad. Hey, switching gears here ... maybe you should call Rachel and try to dismantle her belief in humanism one more time. She's been pretty sick for awhile, hasn't she?"

"Yes, she sure is. She's been fighting cancer for some time now. I think I'll give her a ring to see if I can maybe stop by there tomorrow."

"Great idea, dad."

3

**Jefferson, GA
October 4, 2007
"I pray that the eyes of your heart may be
enlightened in order that you may know the
hope to which he has called you, the riches of
his glorious inheritance in his holy people."
Ephesians 1:18**

Sitting dutifully in the middle of Rachel's small dining room was a rickety, oblong table, which was covered with a simple brown tablecloth. The old covering just barely reached over the perimeter of the table's frayed wooden edges. Rachel sat on one of the short sides of the ancient relic on the right. She was eagerly awaiting Harvey to bring her some hot tea from the adjacent kitchen.

When Harvey entered the room with two piping hot mugs, Rachel smiled and said, "Thanks so much for stopping by today, Harvey. You're a real sweetheart for coming to see an old woman—and an even bigger one for preparing our tea. Truth be told, you've always been a true gentleman."

Harvey grinned as he sat down on the opposite side of the table.

"Ah, it was nothing," he said. "I'm just glad I called you last night so we could finally get together today and get all caught up. It's been far too long since we've seen each other."

"It sure has."

"And to be completely honest with you, I'm also a little concerned about your health."

Rachel shook her head. "As well you should be. Like I said last night, I'm sorry I'm not quite well enough to have driven to meet you somewhere today. I'm just so tired all the time."

Harvey nodded. "I'm very sorry about that, Rachel. Getting old really stinks."

"It sure does, but it beats the alternative."

"Perhaps you're right."

"So anyway, how's your own health these days? You look so young and spry. You were always a late bloomer, Harvey. And shoot; since you've trimmed down so nicely, you look fantastic!"

"Thanks, but appearances can be deceiving."

"Whatever do you mean?"

"Well, dear," Harvey began. "All of my health-markers are in the good range, except for one."

"Oh—?"

"It seems that I've developed a little bit of a heart murmur in the past year or so. Oh, it's not anything to be alarmed over—at least not yet. But my doctors have instructed me to come in every few weeks or so for a checkup. They want to ensure it doesn't get any worse."

"Oh, Harvey. I'm so sorry. You be sure to do what your doctors tell you to do. After all I've been through in my wretched life, the last thing I want to do is see my oldest friend become worse off than I am."

Harvey sighed. He knew what his mission was today, and he was largely uncomfortable with it. The night before, PJ had given Vanessa's phone number to Harvey, and he contacted her after setting the appointment with Rachel. Vanessa had advised him that her Aunt Rachel was feeling mostly glum, so he shouldn't expect much during their visit. However, Harvey wasn't seeing that at all in Rachel—at least thus far.

Nonplussed, he dove in.

"Rachel, I want to talk to you about something very serious today. Now this is a conversation we've occasionally had in the past. But with your serious health concerns, I wouldn't feel right if I didn't discuss it with you at least one more time."

Rachel nodded. "Because I'm so sick, I suppose you want to talk about Jesus. Am I right?"

Harvey reflexively relaxed a bit. "You are. But instead of only sharing Scripture with you as I've done in the past, I'd like to also try something else."

"Oh—what's that?"

"I'd like to begin by illustrating the way I see your spiritual situation with an analogy from a movie we both like very much. I really feel like this will help you understand what I'm trying to say."

"What movie are you speaking of?"

"I remember a great scene from the 1972 film, <u>The Poseidon Adventure</u>? Do you remember that movie?"

"Of course, Harvey. I remember it well."

"Good. Now after the boat capsized, do you remember the warning Gene Hackman's character gave to that group of people who were marching towards the wrong end of the ship in an attempt to escape?"

"Wait a minute … I think so. Was he the Reverend?"

"He sure was. Do you remember when the good Reverend tried to warn those who were walking in the wrong direction—I believe it was towards the bow? He was desperately trying to tell them they were going the wrong way. It was actually a very poignant moment in the movie. I've always remembered it."

Rachel nodded excitedly. "I do remember that."

"Good. That's exactly what I've been trying to make you understand for all of these years. While you've been chasing your dreams in the world, I've been travelling the other direction by pursuing a more difficult road in finding my identity in Christ. No offense, but to me, you've always been going the wrong way, Rachel. In this analogy, I'm Gene Hackman, trying to warn you."

Rachel reluctantly nodded her agreement. "At this point, I can't argue with that very well, can I?"

Harvey was surprised. He shook his head.

"No, you truthfully cannot."

"Don't look so surprised, Harvey. I've been thinking about a lot of spiritual things since Vanessa stopped by yesterday."

"Okay then, good. So I have a question for you. Were you aware that the Bible calls followers of Jesus Christ *royalty?*"

"Really? No, I'm not familiar with that. Can you explain?"

"The passage is actually right here," Harvey said, pulling out his Bible. "It's *1 Peter 2:9 … But you are a chosen people, a royal priesthood, a holy nation, God's special possession, that you may declare the praises of him who called you out of darkness into his wonderful light."*

"I've never heard of such a thing," said Rachel. "Can you repeat that again?"

Harvey did so.

"I declare," she said. "That's something I've never heard in the few times I've attended church since we were kids back in Cottondale. So what exactly does that mean?"

"According to that and other passages, it means that committing your life to Christ means you become a co-heir of the entire universe with Him. As Peter said in that passage, Christians actually become part of God's *royal priesthood*. If you ask me, that's a pretty incredible honor."

"That sure does sound wonderful," Rachel said. "But what does that have to do with me? As you know, I've never been very religious."

"And I hope you never do become religious," Harvey retorted. "What I'm talking about here is *faith*, not religion."

"Is there a difference?"

"Of course there is. But please bear with me. I really have some important things I need to share with you today. And please also know this—I'm very grateful that you're hearing me out. I have a lot on my heart and I simply must get it off my chest."

"Oh, Harvey. You've always had a lot on your heart—and a lot you've always wanted to say to me. For the life of me, I just can't understand why you've always been so shy about sharing your intimate feelings with me. You actually have the warmest heart of any person I've ever known throughout my entire life. Did you know that?"

Harvey gulped. "No." This unexpected warmth threw him a little off his game. "Let's get back to that in a minute," he said. "What I want to share with you next is something ole Jerry from the general store in Cottondale told me many years ago. Do you remember the old fella?"

"Oh, yes," Rachel exclaimed. "He was soooo sweet."

"He sure was. Jerry actually helped me in countless ways when I was a young man."

"I'm not surprised."

"Anyway, Jerry explained to me that so much of the Christian faith boils down to one essential concept. This precept towers in importance over the rest of everything else in the Bible. In fact, this concept is the absolute pinnacle of understanding God. Virtually everything in the Christian faith cascades downward from this one simple thing."

"Well, don't keep me in suspense."

"It's the first commandment."

"Uhmmm—?"

"The first commandment states that we shall have no other god before the real God...."

Harvey paused.

Rachel nodded. "Please, dear. Do go on. I'd like to understand exactly what you're saying."

"Let me read you another few passages. I think they'll help."

"Go right ahead."

"The first one is about love: *1 John 4:10* says ... *This is love: not that we loved God, but that he loved us and sent his Son as an atoning sacrifice for our sins.*"

"Vanessa said something like that to me just yesterday. So you're saying—"

"I'm saying that everlasting love starts with God. You see, real love runs deeper than mere emotions. It's actually more of a decision than a feeling."

Rachel sighed. "But when it gets down to it, I *do* believe in God, Harvey. That's what I've been trying to tell you all of these years. I do believe in Him."

Harvey reached across the table and took Rachel's hands. "I have to be honest, Rachel. I spoke to Vanessa last night, and she warned me that you were feeling pretty negative about everything. Because of that, I was somewhat dreading coming by to speak with you about God, today. I was afraid you'd kick me out or something."

Rachel smiled. This surprised Harvey. "Yes it's true, Harvey. I've been very negative, here lately. But after Vanessa said some honest things to me yesterday, I've had a chance to really think about my life—especially about you and me. In doing so, I've had a lot of unique and strange thoughts. It may sound odd, but so many realizations have been raining down on me since she left yesterday."

"Oh—what kind of realizations?"

Rachel sighed. "Well, here goes. Vanessa told me she felt that you were actually the true love of my life."

Harvey reeled at this. He had come here today to go on the spiritual offensive, so very few things would be able to throw him back on his heels. This was definitely one of them—his relationship with Rachel Green.

He cleared his throat. "Well ... what did you say about that? Do you think it's true?"

Harvey was afraid to hear her answer.

A coy look spread across Rachel's face. "I'm not sure yet. Honestly, I'd hate to think that I've wasted my whole life chasing so many dreadful men—especially Blaine Billings. But the thought of you and I together seems so—"

"Hang on," Harvey said, nervously. "Let's get back to that in a minute. I don't want us to get ahead of ourselves."

Rachel nodded her agreement. She could sense Harvey's trepidation.

He continued, "So what I wanted to tell you today is that the path that may seem right in the world actually has nothing at the end of it but pure and utter pain. In fact, to love the world means you're actually consorting with God's enemy, who is called Satan. Now I'm not going to go into all of that right now, but I do want to share this important verse with you. It's in *1 Corinthians 10:20* ... *No, but the sacrifices of pagans are offered to demons, not to God, and I do not want you to be participants with demons.*"

"I declare, Harvey. Did you say *demons?* Are they really real?"

"You bet they are. And everything you do in your life that doesn't honor God is of the world. That is, it's of the world of Satan and his demons."

Rachel shook her head. "I'm afraid you're losing me on this. I don't understand."

"Please bear with me. The sin of focusing on one's self automatically excludes God from the picture. This is actually the pivot point for every single person who has ever been born. In other words, we all have a critically important spiritual choice to make—to become a true child of God and love and serve Him, or to engage in self love and serve our self. When we serve our self, we automatically serve the world."

"What exactly do you mean by *pivot point?*"

"What I specifically mean by 'pivot point' is sin. You see, in its most basic essence, sin is the choice to serve yourself rather than God."

"But—"

"My dearest, Rachel. You're a special creation of the Lord, but I'm not sure you've ever fully realized that. I can't say I'm one-hundred percent sure about this, but a long time ago when we were kids, I believe you made the choice to conform to a false image of the world and what it had to offer. Now I don't know if it was because of your upbringing, or if it was because of your own personal choice. Perhaps it was a combination of those and other things. But as I see it—and honestly, you can take this or leave it—it seems to me that for all of your life, you've been building steps to your own throne, not to God's. At least not the real God."

Rachel folded her arms. "Are you implying that I've loved myself more than anyone else?"

"Yes."

"Is there anything wrong with that?"

"There certainly is."

"Humph," Rachel snorted. "So why did you find such a good relationship with Jesus Christ and I didn't? Explain that to me."

"In my opinion, I believe it's because I was simply available. If I'm being completely honest here, I think you drowned out God's holy voice over the years by constantly filling his ears with your own motives in life. Those selfish desires were nothing but cleverly disguised false idols."

Rachel was quiet for a moment. "If it's like normal, I suppose you have a passage to back that up? That seems to be your modus operandi."

Harvey chuckled. "I do. It's in *James 1:14 ... but each person is tempted when they are dragged away by their own evil desire and enticed.*"

After a few moments, Rachel blurted, "Why didn't you fight for me, Harvey? Part of me has always wondered why you didn't just stand up to Blaine and show him *you* were my true love. I know you felt that way."

"Would it have mattered???"

Rachel was quiet for a few moments. "I honestly don't know the answer to that question."

"Unfortunately, I do. Listen, Rachel. From the time you drove off with Blaine that awful Saturday morning when we were ten years old, you've been searching for your self-esteem in the world instead of the Lord. I think it's about time for you to admit you've been chasing a mirage; a false idea about what real love is."

Tears slowly began to descend down Rachel's face.

"I'm not trying to hurt your feelings," Harvey continued, softly. "I'm just trying to say, I believe the real love God designed for you and I ended up dividing us. If you'll notice, we've lived completely opposite lives on totally separate paths. But somehow, God has sustained our friendship."

Rachel shot him a painful look. "You don't need to rub it in. I know what a failure I've been."

"Oh c'mon, Rach. Although it's uncomfortable, I'm stepping out of our normal course of conversation today for a simple reason—I'm very concerned about your eternal soul."

"I suppose you're right. I won't even consider arguing the fact that you've always been so kind to me. Honestly, I've often wondered why."

"Actually, I've tried to be kind to everyone throughout my life."

"Are you going to deny that you have special feelings for me???"

Harvey paused for a moment. "No, I won't deny that on a day like today. I guess we're long overdue to put all of our cards on the table."

"We sure are, and I'm glad we're finally doing it. Your kindness to me has been perhaps the most consistent thing in my seventy-five years on this Earth. I'll never forget you for that."

Harvey nodded. "Thanks. Actually, I believe being kind to others is the mortal enemy of their self-love. Honestly, it would have been easy for me to have written you off many years ago as someone who didn't want me. Instead, I chose to be your friend so I could watch over you."

Rachel looked straight into Harvey's eyes. "It saddens me to say this, but the real love you've shown me is the closest thing to love I've ever had. Everyone else who claimed they loved me always wanted something in return."

Harvey looked down for a moment. "Listen. Not to sound melodramatic or anything, but I believe what I'm about to tell you is perhaps the most important thing you'll ever hear."

"At this point, there's no use in being shy anymore."

"Fair enough—I won't hold back. Here's what I feel: I think you need to focus on God's love for you, instead of your love for God. If you do this, you just may learn to love Him. You see, real love is a choice. The battle you've been fighting all of your life with God is that you've consistently wanted God to acquiesce to you, not vice versa."

"None of what you're saying lines up with what I've always thought true love is."

Harvey shook his head. "Like all of us, you must commit to loving the Lord, but I'm afraid your self-will has always stood in the way. It's been very much like a dark storm over your entire life. For you to understand what real love is, you need to give God an open heart to work with. When you focus primarily on yourself and your feelings, you've made yourself the de facto god of your own world. When this happens, it's extremely difficult to hear God's holy voice ... or feel His incredible love."

"But why is that? What you're saying just doesn't feel right."

"Hold on, now. You need to remember that feelings are often like smoke on the wind—they'll just float away after burning hot for a short while. On the other hand, God's love for us is uncaused—it just *is.*"

"But why is that?"

"It's because God is eternal. And because He is eternal, His love is eternal. Mere human beings like you and I will never be able to fully understand this concept."

"But Harvey, I'm an old woman who's lived my life for myself. How can God ever forgive me for keeping Him off to the side for so long?"

"Ahhh, so you do realize that you've had God on the back-burner?"

Rachel nodded. "Yes."

"Okay, then. That's good. Let me continue by reading you a couple of poignant passages that'll help you understand what God's sacrificial love is all about."

"Please do."

Harvey paged through his Bible. "The first one tells us that we are indeed *very* special to our heavenly Father. It's in *Psalm 139:13 ... For you created my inmost being; you knit me together in my mother's womb."*

Rachel wiped away a couple of tears.

"I don't know who wrote that," she said. "But does God really love me that much? Does He know me that well?"

"Of course He does, which leads me to the crux of the problem we've been discussing today. At one time or another, we're all faced with this choice. The passage is in *Romans 12:2 ... Do not conform to the pattern of this world, but be transformed by the renewing of your mind. Then you will be able to test and approve what God's will is—his good, pleasing and perfect will."*

"So what is God's will for me? Can you answer me that?"

"To discover God's will, you must first love Him with all your heart and soul, and you must also love your neighbor as yourself. That's the starting point."

"So where do I come into the picture?"

"Exactly!"

"What do you mean by that?"

"Self-love is not real love, Rachel. Listen, for all of your life, you've been trying to select a single grain of sand here and there on an immensely beautiful beach. In reality, God is offering you the *entire* beach. Why would you reject His generous offer for something so small, fleeting, and insignificant as your own desires?"

Rachel looked down and took a sip of her tea, which was now only lukewarm.

"I honestly don't know the answer to that," she said.

"I think I do—"

"Where do we go from here, Harvey?"

Harvey beamed at this. "Miss Rachel, I'd like to officially ask you out on a date. What do you say?"

Rachel blushed. "Why Harvey, are you serious?"

"Indeed I am."

She tilted her head. "Why did it take all of these years for you to finally ask me out on a real date?"

"Oh, I came close a couple of times, but Blaine always seemed to know how to get in the way. I hate to admit this, but he intimidated me."

Rachel shook her head. "He was not a nice man."

"Sadly, I agree. Do you remember that time on my birthday when we were thirteen? You know, when we sat under that big tree next to Jerry's store and played with my little dog, Pumpkin. Do you remember that?"

"Of course. By the way, what kind of dog was Pumpkin?"

"She was a miniature schnauzer mix. I really miss her."

"I do too. Anyway, did you come close to asking me out on a date that day?"

"I did, but I chickened out."

Rachel nodded. "Thanks for admitting it wasn't all my fault."

"Of course it wasn't. But listen. It's never too late. So how about this? Why don't I come pick you up Saturday night at five pm? We can go get some barbeque down at Edwin's BBQ in Winder. That's my favorite place to eat these days. The owner is the only one I know who has Bible verses in his menu and Bible tracts at the register."

"That sounds wonderful! I can't wait. We can have some of their lovely fried squash and ranch dressing. That's always been something we've enjoyed throughout the years whenever we've gotten together as friends for a meal."

"We sure have, Rachel. That sounds great. Listen, I'll get out of your hair. Do you need me to do anything before I go?"

"Thanks, but no. Someone from a local church group is actually coming by tomorrow to help me with some chores around here."

"Great, then," Harvey said, standing up.

He moved around and gave Rachel the biggest hug he could muster. She embraced him as well. For the first time in many decades, they both felt like kids again.

"I'll see you on Saturday," Harvey said.

Rachel smiled. "I can't wait."

On this day, a spark of real love between them was finally ignited.

4

Jefferson, GA
October 5, 2007
"Do not forget to show hospitality to strangers, for by so doing some people have shown hospitality to angels without knowing it."
Hebrews 13:2

A barely audible buzz from the ancient doorbell to the old house awoke Rachel with a start. The old woman rolled over and looked at her nightstand clock, which reflected 9:38 am in bright red numbers.

She had overslept.

As Rachel dragged herself up from a wonderful slumber, the first thing she noticed was that she felt surprisingly refreshed. In fact, she couldn't remember the last time she had slept that well—or that deeply. This was an unusual surprise, as sleep had been her enemy for many years now. Today, however, felt like a brand new chapter in her life. She felt an odd sense of anticipation.

Rachel headed towards the door as the bell buzzed once again.

When Rachel opened the front door, there before her stood a man of medium height and medium build. She reckoned he was somewhere in his fifties. His face was rugged and a bit haggard, but also friendly and comforting—in an intangible way. His gray goatee and gray hair gave him a manly appearance, but his kind mannerisms put Rachel immediately at ease.

"Hello, Rachel. My name is Mick. I'm from the local ministry alliance. I'm here to help you with a few yard chores today—and anything else you might need."

"Good morning, Mick. Please forgive my appearance. I'm afraid I overslept this morning—"

"No problem, ma'am. And don't let my pony-tail throw you off. It's just my thing—no big deal."

Mick turned his head to the side so she could see.

Rachel grinned and nodded.

"Anyway, may I come in?" he asked.

"Please do."

Mick stepped inside the smallish, old house.

Rachel walked slowly behind her guest, continuing to size him up.

"May I get you some coffee or something?" she asked.

"That would be very nice," Mick said, turning towards her. "But since you just awoke, how about if I make some coffee for you, instead?"

Rachel ran her fingers through her frazzled hair and said, "Well, that would be very kind of you, Mick. I need to change into some proper clothing anyway. Please excuse—"

"No worries, Miss Rachel. In my line of work, I'm not really into fashion shows. I'm just glad to see you feeling a bit perky this morning."

Rachel smiled. "Very well, then. The coffee is in the cupboard above the sink, and the coffee maker is on the counter. I'll be back out in a few minutes."

"10-4, ma'am. Please take your time."

After about ten minutes, Mick and Rachel were sitting in the living room on couches opposite of each other. The windows were now open and a coolish breeze made its way into the house on this partially sunny, autumn day.

"So before I tell you what I need you to do in the yard today," Rachel began. "Please tell me about yourself, Mick. I don't want you to feel like a servant or anything. You're obviously here to help me, and I'm very grateful."

"Ah, no worries, ma'am. There's really not much to tell you about myself. I'm not married and I've dedicated myself to serving the Lord in any way I can. It's actually a joy to be able to help folks in Jackson and the surrounding counties on behalf of Jesus Christ."

"That's wonderful. Say, do you mind if I ask you some questions about your faith in the Lord? I've been talking with my niece and an old friend the past couple of days. Although it's been great talking with them, I actually have some more questions."

"Sure thing. But first, I need to disclose that I'm not an ordained minister."

"That's okay."

"That said, I've studied the Bible frontwards and backwards for all of my life. I actually have a lot of it memorized."

"Oh, that's impressive."

Mick shrugged. "I believe the Bible to be the true Word of God. I also feel that it's intertwined with His power like your veins and arteries carry the life-giving blood throughout your body."

Rachel nodded quickly. "I was primarily in nursing throughout my working career. In our bodies, the power is definitely in the blood."

"And that's where the saving power of God is—in the blood of Jesus Christ."

"Hmmm. I find that intriguing. So let me ask you this. Are there any passages you consider to be at the top of your list about who Jesus Christ is? I've found myself wondering a lot about Him lately."

"As a matter of fact, I do," Mick said proudly. "Let me start with this old fave: *Hebrews 4:15 ... For we do not have a high priest who is unable to empathize with our weaknesses, but we have one who has been tempted in every way, just as we are—yet he did not sin.*"

"So what does that mean?"

"It means that Jesus Christ physically entered the world to save humanity. In addition, He did it in a way so that His example will always be a part of God's eternal kingdom. You see, where mankind has always failed when it comes to resisting temptation and sin, Jesus showed the world that only God in the flesh can resist sin. But that doesn't mean Jesus wasn't tempted—He was clearly tempted like all of mankind is tempted every day."

"I see—"

"In other words, Jesus was lowered into an imperfect body out of God's love for the world. Because Jesus paid the price for mankind's sin, a reconnection between God and humans became possible. Jesus is referred to as the 'first fruits' of life, death, and resurrection—that means He leads the way. His sacrifice for us makes Him our perfect

High Priest. Jesus is most definitely the only way to God, and He is the only one who can forgive sin."

"That's interesting. But honestly, it's also a little confusing."

Mick nodded. "I understand."

"My friend Harvey told me yesterday he didn't think I've been following God's true will for my life. Instead, he thinks I've been following my own will."

"Do you think he's right?"

Rachel sighed. "Actually, I do."

Mick nodded again. "Well, since we've just met, I can't speak to the truth of your friend's claim. However, someone following their own way is definitely a common human affliction. Let me give you an interesting passage that states a powerful message. It's very much applicable to every person. It's in *1 John 2:17 … The world and its desires pass away, but whoever does the will of God lives forever.*"

Rachel nodded. "It seems I've been focusing on the wrong image of what life and God are all about. It's honestly very embarrassing, Mick."

"You shouldn't be embarrassed—you should consider asking Jesus for forgiveness for your sins. We in the business call this the beginning of *repentance,* which means you literally change direction from the world and turn towards God."

"Honestly, I'm a little confused. The heart strings of my faith have been tugging at me lately, but I'm afraid my days on Earth may be few."

"I'm sorry to hear that."

Rachel looked directly into Mick's eyes. "My senses also tell me you're something more than just a pleasant fellow from a local ministry group. Does that sound like the ramblings of a demented old woman?"

The moment of truth had arrived for Mick. As a holy angel of God, he always knew how to follow God's instructions. Rachel was demonstrating a changing heart, so he immediately shifted into a joyous direction which he had taken countless times over the years with people.

"Miss Rachel, one day, I think a book should be written titled, The Cult of Me. The reason why is that the natural human propensity is to trust in yourself or others to the exclusion of your heavenly Father. In many ways, people often build their own false cult of an untrue reality. Actually, many years ago, the prophet Jeremiah had some wise words on this subject: *Jeremiah 17:5 says ... This is what the Lord says: 'Cursed is the one who trusts in man, who draws strength from mere flesh and whose heart turns away from the Lord.* Does that make any sense to you?"

"Yes, I believe it does. Both my niece Vanessa and my friend Harvey have been saying pretty much the same thing to me for the past couple of days. To be honest, I've never stopped to think about how foolish it was to favor people and their opinions about life over what God has to say. Does that sound crazy?"

"It's only crazy if someone continues to think trusting in humans is somehow better than trusting in God. This is confirmed in *Isaiah 2:22,* which says ... *Stop trusting in mere humans, who have but a breath in their nostrils. Why hold them in esteem?*"

"That's interesting."

"What I'm basically saying is that every human being must make a choice between the various forms of humanism and the One who carried the title of Immanuel, who is Jesus Christ. Basically, it's either God or man. It's your choice."

"That's beginning to make a lot of sense. As I look back on it, I can see that I've been having a tug-of-war with God all of my life. Unfortunately, I've always wanted my way instead of His."

Mick nodded. "Please remember that God doesn't exist for mankind, and mankind doesn't exist for itself. Everyone exists for God and His purposes. After all, it's His world."

Rachel suddenly appeared sullen. "Because I've been chasing after what I thought was right, I think I may have wasted my life. Harvey and Vanessa both talked about false idols, but I'm not sure I fully understand what they are."

"Oh, I think you'll figure it out pretty quickly," Mick said. "But essentially, false idols act as an eclipse in your life, blocking God's light and His real love."

"But why didn't God just knock them down for me?"

"Because God doesn't force Himself on anyone. Listen, idolatry isn't talked about nearly enough in churches today, but it's the fountainhead of virtually all sin. Once you toss in pride, you've got yourself a spiritually lethal concoction—false idols riding along the river of pride through the center of your soul."

"If that's true, I can now see why I've never found real love in my life. In fact, real love has always seemed to elude me—just beyond my reach. Unfortunately, I've always blamed others for it. That is, until today. When I look at it logically, it seems that it was my own fault after all."

"Real love is dedicated, Miss Rachel. Do you realize that Harvey has been dedicated to you in a similar way to how God has been dedicated to His rebellious people over the ages?"

"How do you—?"

"I'll get to that in a moment," Mick said. "Can you please just trust me on this? I'm only here to help—I promise."

Rachel nodded. "Sure. What have I got to lose?"

"Thank you. What I want to share with you next is that there are four Greek words for the word love—three of them are used in the Bible, but one of those three is only used sparingly."

"Why do Greek words matter?"

"Because that's the language the New Testament was written in."

"Oh."

"The four different words for love in Greek have different meanings. This is a key concept because they'll help you understand what real love is better than merely using the English word, *love.*"

"I understand."

Mick nodded. "Good. What I have to say is this—I think you may have made the mistake of placing all of your feelings about love on the wrong word; the wrong meaning."

"Wait—now I'm confused."

"Let me go ahead and give you the four words—agape, philia, storge, and eros."

She chuckled. "That sounds Greek to me."

"Nice one," Mick said, chuckling. "But seriously, agape love is a sacrificial love; philia love is friendship love; storge isn't used often, but it's a family type of love; and then there's the troubling one, eros. Eros love is passionate love."

"Let's see, so you have sacrificial, friendship, family, and sexual love. Did I hear that right?"

"You sure did."

"At first blush, I can see where I spent most of my life chasing after eros love."

"That's a natural human propensity."

"Actually, as I consider this, it seems I defined true love as the powerful attraction I had towards certain men."

"Like I said—"

"No, that's definitely what I've always considered real love to be. I guess that's where I made my mistake."

"Yes, my friend," Mick said. "You're on the right track. Please tell me what else your heart is telling you about this."

"Well, let's see. When I was a girl, I felt a strong attraction to a boy named Blaine. Now deep down, I knew Blaine wasn't right for me. Truthfully, after speaking with him for about two minutes, you could easily see how much he was all wrapped up into himself—like he was living in some kind of cocoon or something. Anyway, for some reason, I felt compelled to chase after him."

"You did all of that when sweet ole Harvey was standing right there next to you, waiting to love you the right way."

Rachel was quiet as a spiritual wave swept through her soul. After a few moments, she asked, "Just who are you, Mick? I've had a good but *certainly strange* feeling about you since I opened the door and saw your face. You're telling me things about my life that a complete stranger couldn't possibly know. Should I be afraid or something?"

"No, Miss Rachel," Mick said, shaking his head. "You have nothing to fear. I'm an angel of the Most High God. I've actually been sent to minister to you today. Are you surprised to hear this?"

Rachel looked out the window, behind Mick, for a few moments. Mick remained quiet as his newest client grasped the incredible moment she was experiencing.

"I don't know if you're a crazy person," Rachel began. "But even if you are, I'm enjoying our conversation. So just in case I'm not hallucinating—or even dead—let's continue our discussion."

Mick shrugged. "Now would be a good time for a pearl of wisdom from the book of Proverbs. This one is from *Proverbs 16:9 ... In their hearts humans plan their course, but the Lord establishes their steps.*"

"Let's see how that applies to me," Rachel thought out loud. "I planned to live my life as Mrs. Blaine Billings, but the Lord had something else in mind for me. I'm assuming you think Blaine wasn't God's will for my life, right?"

"That's correct. I don't feel that Blaine was God's plan for you. In your heart, can you now look back and see where God consistently blocked you and Blaine from ever getting married?"

Rachel sighed again. "Now that y'all—you, Vanessa, and Harvey—have been beating me senseless with that concept, I can't really deny it anymore."

"Let me ask you this ... what do you think your life would have been like if you had turned your heart towards Harvey instead of Blaine?"

"But that's not what I felt back then. I seriously doubt it would have worked out with Harvey."

"In the past two days, you've probably heard that real love is more of a decision than a feeling, right?"

"Right."

"Now this may be an extreme example, but despite what you've likely seen in the movies, throughout history, many arranged marriages have been successful and ultimately happy. While it's true that deciding to love someone is probably not the best plot for a chick-flick, it does show the commitment end of what marriage is. It also demonstrates the decision it takes to *agape* love someone."

"But your so-called chick-flicks demonstrate the power of—"

"They largely demonstrate the emotional aspects of eros love, which actually comes and goes. You cannot depend on eros love to take care of you when you're old and fighting cancer at seventy-five, Rachel. Only the other loves—agape, storge, and philia love can do that."

"Are you saying I've somehow been lied to?"

Mick nodded. "Both your selfish heart and Satan's world of lies have deceived you, Miss Rachel. That's the bad news. The good news is that it's not too late to surrender your life to Jesus Christ and spend eternity with Him."

Rachel had a quizzical expression cross her face. "Do you think Jesus will forgive me for my selfishness, Mick? Is He really that wonderful?"

"Yes, Jesus is that incredible. But like I just said, He won't force Himself on anyone. You must remember that coercion isn't in any way a component of real love."

"Let me think about this for a minute. Everything is happening so quickly."

"I understand. Listen, while you're rolling that around, allow me to point out something you may have not realized."

"Please do."

"Now that the spiritual reality of your situation is settling into your soul, have you ever considered the idea that the Lord may have sent

Harvey as a type of missionary to the Atlanta area long before Blaine or you ever considered moving here?"

"Really?"

"Absolutely, yes. Even though you rejected what appears to have been God's plan for you to choose Harvey over Blaine, the Lord was watching over you and sent ole Harv here, knowing you'd follow Blaine here one day. You see, God is always several steps ahead of both people and the evil plans of demons. And God's will is always accomplished—no matter what."

Rachel shook her head. "This is a lot to take in."

Mick continued, "While you're thinking about that, please also consider the fact that today is not the first time I've been in this very living room, giving someone some spiritual advice. I've actually been here before."

"What—with whom?"

"This house used to be owned by Wyatt's mother, Abbie Hunter. Do you remember that?"

"Of course. I've heard that Abbie hasn't been feeling very well herself, here lately. Anyway, when did you come here to see her?"

"Forty years ago; back in 1967. Actually, I've been working in and around this area for quite some time now."

"In order for you to have been here forty years ago, you'd have to be much older than you appear, unless—"

"Unless I'm an angel, just like I said."

The unique nature of her spiritual situation weighed heavily on Rachel's shoulders as the tectonic plates of her soul continued to shift.

"But Mick, I still believe Harvey should have been bolder in expressing his love for me. If he had done so, I think he might have saved me from living a selfish life apart from God."

Mick shook his head. "No ma'am, Rachel. It's *you* who should have sought out Jesus Christ instead of constantly following yourself. You were searching for real love, but you were actually looking in the wrong direction. For the past sixty-five years, real love was standing right next to you in the person of Harvey Gordon."

Rachel wept as the dam of her self-focused prison burst wide open. Mick moved over to her couch and held her hand.

"What's happening, Mick???" Rachel said. "I don't understand; *I'm afraid."*

"Don't be afraid, Miss Rachel. This is a wonderful moment. In fact, this is the most important moment of your entire life."

"Are you serious?"

"Yes, I'm very serious."

"So what's happening?"

"Let me explain it to you this way. Your spiritual life is just like a mountain. This is actually true of every single human being. All of your priorities in life are stacked-up on this mountain, but at the very top is the upper tip of the mountain. Can you picture that?"

She nodded.

"Good. The first commandment states that you must have no other gods before the real God. Are you with me?"

She nodded again.

"If your life is being lived righteously, Jesus Christ is at the very top of that mountain; so to speak. Every single thing in this world that blocks the view of the top of your mountain is a false idol. In other words, if God isn't at the top of your spiritual mountain—if you can't see Him being number one in your life—then clouds of idols are in the way, blocking His truth, His light, and His real love."

After a few moments, Rachel wiped the tears from her face. "I'd like to change my ways. Is it too late?"

"No, it's not too late. All you need to do is genuinely ask Jesus for forgiveness of your sins and trust alone in Him for your salvation. Would you like me to help you with that?"

Rachel shook her head. "If you don't mind, I'd like to have some private time with the Lord. I have a lot to think about—and a lot to confess to Him."

Mick gave her hand a light squeeze and then stood up. "Very well, then. I'll be just outside, trimming your hedges and doing a little raking, as per your request. If you need me, just holler."

"Will do. Thanks, Mick."

"And one more thing," the angel continued. "I want to give you a passage to think about. It's in *Ecclesiastes 7:1* ... *A good name is better than fine perfume, and the day of death better than the day of birth.*"

"So what does that mean?"

"Oh, I'll just let you ponder that as you talk to God. Please let me know if you need anything."

"I will," Rachel said.

Mick stepped outside as the old woman had a heart-to-heart talk with her Savior. As the angel worked in her yard, Rachel could see the clouds of the world disappearing as she confessed her sins. By the time she had finished her prayers, the eyes of her heart could clearly see the truth of Jesus Christ. For the first time ever, she could see Jesus at the top of her spiritual mountain.

Several minutes later, as she sat on her old couch all alone, the once broken heart of the old woman now had a brand new spiritual heart. Everything in her life was now fully attuned to Jesus Christ. Everything had now changed during these few blessed few moments.

Then, without any warning, Rachel's heart stopped beating on Earth for the very last time....

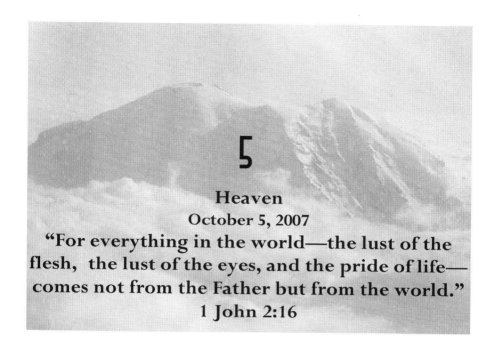

Heaven
October 5, 2007
"For everything in the world—the lust of the flesh, the lust of the eyes, and the pride of life—comes not from the Father but from the world."
1 John 2:16

Rachel finally became accustomed to the immensity of Heaven's brightness as the arrival celebration at the forest lodge on the edge of Heaven began to wind down. So many of the people who had greeted her upon her arrival at the lodge today to meet Jesus Christ were merely acquaintances down on Earth. This was due to Rachel's focus on the world and not on God's kingdom. But now, these people very much seemed like family. Although Rachel felt indescribably amazing, she wondered how she could have ignored all of these wonderful people she had met over the course of her lifetime.

After exiting the fallen world earlier that day, many things had rapidly taken place as Rachel passed from her temporary existence into her permanent life. Upon taking her last breath on Earth, angels had escorted her through a spiritual realm to Heaven's gate, while others showed her the way to the nearby forest lodge. After meeting Jesus Christ in person, she fell to her knees and wept tears of utter joy.

Rachel now stood in the middle of the celebration hall, amazed that she had been transported to such a wonderful place.

"Greetings, Rachel," a vaguely familiar voice said, quickly gaining her attention. "Now that you're finishing up here, we need to move to the next meeting on your agenda."

Rachel spun around and saw the familiar face of an old friend from many decades ago.

"*Jerry?!?!?!?*" she exclaimed.

"That's me."

Rachel immediately embraced the old general store owner.

"Well, I can't say I'm surprised to see you here," she said. "You're probably the kindest man I've ever met—except for maybe Harvey."

Jerry smiled. "Thank you, dear. And I must say; you look as youthful as ever since you shed your temporary earthly body."

"Thanks. It actually feels like an immense weight has been lifted off of my shoulders. For all of my wasted years down on Earth, I so much wish I hadn't been afraid to die. This place is absolutely wonderful."

"It surely is," Jerry agreed. "But I need to tell you something very important."

"Oh—what's that?"

"Do you remember that nice fellow named Mick?"

"Of course. He was the last person I saw before I died. He was actually instrumental in helping to open my eyes towards Christ."

"Right. Well, do you remember him telling you he was an angel?""Absolutely," Rachel said, nodding. "At first, I wasn't so sure. But now, I can see he really was an angel."

Jerry grinned coyly. "As am I."

Rachel's eyes grew big. "Really? Are you serious?"

"I certainly am. Angels have been surrounding you for a long time now, and it appears you didn't even know it. But please know this— people don't become angels when they arrive here in Heaven. Angels are angels, and people are people. That's the way it always has been and the way it always will be."

"That's interesting—and soooo lovely. It's funny; I had no idea just how close God was to me. Unfortunately, I kept rejecting His overtures until near the end. I sure wish I had lived my life for Jesus Christ."

"Getting here is what matters the most."

"That sounds right to me," Rachel said. "But I can't help but to wonder what changed things for me this week. I shudder to think about the alternative."

"I think you already know the answer to that question."

"Oh yeah—Harvey showed up. You know, he and I have talked about Jesus on countless occasions over the years. Although I never got angry with him for discussing his faith with me, to be honest, I was never really that interested in what he had to say—until just recently."

"Harvey has an immense heart, Rachel. He loves you in a way that all people should love each other. It's my guess that Harvey's patience and perseverance with presenting you with the Gospel finally sunk in. That, my friend, is an excellent example of real love."

She nodded. "Perhaps so, but I'll always give thanks to the real source of my salvation—Jesus Christ—for not giving up on me. I neglected to bring this up with the Lord a few minutes ago. I should have thanked Him more than I actually did."

"Oh, I'm sure you'll have your chance again very soon," Jerry said. "Come, now. If you don't mind, I'd like you to take a walk with me. I think you'll find the next item on your agenda to be very illuminating."

"So you're now my tour guide?"

Jerry laughed. "In a manner of speaking, yes."

"That sounds great."

The angel gently took Rachel's arm as they exited the forest lodge. They walked down the six steps and began heading to the right; away from the direction Rachel had approached the building from.

"The important thing is that you finally sought out the Lord," Jerry continued. "And I'm happy to say, you found Him."

"Indeed I did."

"Okay, then. Now that you're a bona fide citizen of Heaven, we'll need to begin your new life with some education. After all, you didn't exactly spend much time down on Earth as a follower of Christ. Basically, we need to work on your spiritual acuity."

"That makes a lot of sense. I can't wait to learn more."

"Good. I'd like to now share three verses with you as we make our way to an important banquet, where you're the guest of honor. These verses are my traditional way of beginning a lesson with someone. I guess you could say it's my way of doing business. Anyway, the first one is in *Proverbs 8:17… I love those who love me, and those who seek me find me.*"

"It was so nice to hear Vanessa and Harvey read Bible verses to me before I died. I never realized how much truth was contained in what I previously felt was just an ancient old book."

65

Jerry nodded. "Yes, that's one of Satan's favorite lies. We run into that nonsense all the time down on Earth."

"I see. So tell me something, Jerry. Now that you mention it, what's the deal with Satan and his demons? I really didn't have time to get into that subject before I entered Heaven. Come to think of it, Harvey mentioned something about demons just yesterday."

"It's really pretty simple. Satan and his demons constantly do their level best to harass people with temptations in an effort to block them from finding the real love of God ... among other evil things they do."

Rachel shook her head. "Temptations and false idols seem to be a regular theme in my brief but ongoing education about the Lord."

"That's because temptations which turn into idols are nothing but false gods in some way, shape, or form. You see, God lovingly created many things in your life to be enjoyed and used properly. However, people elevate some of these secondary things to idol status. In effect, this ruins God's intended purposes. In some cases, certain things that become false idols are just plain ole destructive and have no purpose at all in God's kingdom."

"Do you have an example of that?"

"I have many, but let's wait until we get to the banquet. It's been especially set up for your arrival."

"How exciting!"

"So speaking of idols, here's a good passage: *1 Corinthians 8:4 ... So then, about eating food sacrificed to idols: We know that 'An idol is nothing at all in the world' and that 'There is no God but one.'*"

"Indeed, there's only one true God. It honestly feels like God called out to my heart during the last couple of days. I distinctly remember everything about my soul changing, seemingly all at once. My faith felt completely different than it ever had before. I guess you could say it finally felt real."

Jerry nodded. "I've known you since you were a young gal, Rachel. While it broke my heart when you chose Blaine's way of the world back when you were young, I always hoped you'd repent and turn to Christ."

"So you knew Blaine was a scoundrel, huh?"

Jerry shrugged. "I knew he was well on his way to becoming one, for sure. It makes me sad that he never repented of his sins and turned to Jesus."

"Oh...."

Rachel fell into deep thought as they strolled through a richly appointed forest pathway. After a few moments, she said, "So you're saying that since I haven't seen Blaine, I suppose he never turned to Jesus before he passed?"

Jerry nodded. "It's always a tragedy when someone chooses the world over God."

"I see. Well, anyway … do you know what's strange, Jerry?"

"What's that?"

"Today almost feels like it's my birthday. I feel as giddy as I did when I was a school girl."

Jerry grinned. "In a spiritual sense, it *is* your birthday."

"Oh—how so?"

"Down on Earth, birthdays are celebrated on the day you're physically born. Up here, however, it's different. You see, we celebrate your spiritual birthday in two ways. The first way is on the day you surrender your life to Jesus Christ down on Earth. That's the day your spirit and soul are born again. Later on, when you physically die, your redemption into God's eternal kingdom is fulfilled. This is your true birthday. Is this making any sense?"

"It is," Rachel said, nodding. "I believe that even though I lived most of my life apart from Jesus, I always had His sparkle of hope in my soul."

"And for good reason," Jerry said. "It's because real love is always imbued with hope. If you think about it, without God's gift of hope, life is completely dysfunctional."

"I agree. You know, Harvey has always lived a good life. As a dear friend and sometimes confidant, he's always been a great encourager."

"He sure has."

"On the other hand, I lived a very worldly life, so I suppose I deserved all of the terrible heartaches I experienced. But for Blaine … well … he seemed to always get what he wanted. I always felt like he got away with living for himself in virtually everything he did."

Jerry shook his head. "Blaine's godship only lasted until the day he died. Then, I'm afraid, his worldly way of living ended rather abruptly."

"How sad."

"It sure is. As it relates to Harvey, it's important for you to understand that living a good life by loving the Lord doesn't mean you'll have material health and wealth on Earth. Truth be told, as a follower of Jesus Christ, Harvey could have just as easily had many financial and/or health struggles throughout his life."

"Really?"

"Absolutely. On the other hand, those who don't love God—like Blaine—they really don't win in the end if they don't repent of their sins. Right now, things on Earth will always pass away, but God's kingdom lasts forever. That's a huge distinction."

"I see."

"Listen, God is always overjoyed with wonderful moments like today—where you began your eternal life in His presence. In other words, your day of physical death is actually your forever birthday. Although it's impossible for any of us to fully understand how God works, the more you seek Him out, the more He reveals Himself to you."

"Hmmm," Rachel murmured. "So whether you find material success on Earth, or whether you're one who struggles, everyone who loves Jesus wins and gets to spend the rest of eternity with Him. Is that right?"

Jerry nodded. "It is. You must remember that God will judge each person through the blood of Jesus Christ. Material success has nothing directly to do with salvation."

As they rounded a stretch, within proximity now was an end to the forest and the beginning of a bright opening through the trees. Rachel and her angelic escort continued towards it.

"Okay," Rachel said. "So what other verses do you have for me?"

"The last one for now is in *John 6:44* … *'No one can come to me unless the Father who sent me draws them, and I will raise them up at the last day.'*"

A warm wave swept through Rachel's soul as she said, "I can't wait to see Jesus again."

"Your wish is my command," Jerry said, grinning. "Voila…."

A luminous radiance burst into sight as they exited the forest area. There, before Rachel and Jerry, stood the most beautiful mountain in all of existence. Rachel naturally stopped walking and gawked at the snow capped peak, which was barely discernable through its surrounding cloud cover. Moving downward from the top one could see numerous types of ecosystems, including green forested areas, rocky crags, flowing water, and numerous trails. The mountainside was also dotted with some occasional buildings; all of which blended in with the mountain as if they were a natural part of it.

The largely triangular-shaped mountain was at once magnanimous, yet still had a great peace and majesty about it. The brightness that enveloped the area surrounding Jerry and Rachel appeared mostly as light blue, with brilliant streaks of various shades of blue-green, yellow and a mellow violet.

As Rachel's gaze panned to the bottom of the mountain, she focused on something that made her do an immediate double-take. There in front of her was a rectangular wooden banquet table with a dozen women seated at it. All of the ladies were looking directly at them.

Rachel and Jerry moved forward.

When they reached the head of the table, the faces of the twelve ladies came into clear focus. Although it was an incredibly diverse array of women, Rachel had no idea what to expect next.

Emerging from behind some trees near the other end of the table was a welcome sight—Jesus Christ. The Lord smiled at Rachel and motioned for her to sit down. She did so as Jerry took a seat to her right, next to one of the ladies.

"Once again, welcome Rachel. How do you like my beautiful mountain?"

Rachel smiled and said, "It's incredible, Lord. But can you tell me why we're gathered here? I'm very curious and Jerry wouldn't say."

"This mountain is what I often use to teach someone the spiritual lessons they missed out on during their earthly life. Every one of these ladies has an interesting story to tell. I very much desire for you to hear their testimonies."

Jesus opened his hands in a way that made it clear He was talking about every lady at the table.

"All of you were once daughters of Adam," Jesus continued. "But you're now an important part of my eternal kingdom. You were once estranged because of sin; now you're joined with me forever."

"Wow," said Rachel. "Do all of these ladies have a story like mine?"

Jesus nodded at Jerry.

"Well, sort of," the angel said. "It's more like this ... every one of these ladies had a major false idol in their life, and they all overcame their sin and saw the truth of the Gospel of Jesus Christ. What all of you have in common is that most of you died on Earth not long after your heart changed and you surrendered your life to Jesus. So not only do these ladies have some things to teach you, they were also sitting in your exact seat sometime in the past."

Rachel's brow furrowed. "Is this some kind of classroom or something? Am I going to learn something important from their stories?"

"Essentially, yes," Jerry said. "Every lady was tempted by something in their life—a powerful false idol—and every lady eventually found their way to the foot of the Cross to find forgiveness."

"This sounds *very* interesting," Rachel said. "I can't wait to hear—"

"And we can't wait to share our stories with you!" the petite blonde next to Jerry said quickly. "By the way, my name is Lillie."

"Hello, Lillie. It's nice to meet you."

"Before I explain how all of this works," Jerry began. "I'd like to explain the big picture of this program about real love—"

"This is a lesson about *love*?" Rachel interrupted. "I thought this was a lesson about false idols."

Jerry shook his head. "You may find this to be surprising, but idols are nothing but impediments to experiencing real love in your life. In order to have any kind of sensible explanation about what love is from God's perspective, we must show you not only how idols block the love of God, but how Satan uses them in combination; sort of like a nasty stew the devil cooks in his evil spiritual cauldron."

"This all so interesting. Please go on, Jerry."

"Since we're at a table with so many ladies, I'd like to continue my explanation with a powerful story of women from the book of Ruth. This verse is from *Ruth 1:16 … But Ruth replied, 'Don't urge me to leave you or to turn back from you. Where you go I will go, and where you stay I will stay. Your people will be my people and your God my God.'*"

"Since I'm starting us off with the opening segment today," Lillie added. "I'd like to add that like Ruth, we'll be by your side forever, Rachel. Those of us on the mountain are honored to demonstrate these important lessons about the Lord when ladies like you arrive here. We were all just like you at one time."

Lillie nodded at the other eleven ladies, who all smiled and collectively stood up. Curiously, they all began heading towards the well-travelled trail onto the mountain behind them. Rachel watched them as Lillie and Jerry remained seated. As soon as the ladies had disappeared onto the trail, Jesus stood up.

"Today, you'll begin learning something very important about my kingdom," the Lord said. "And after you're finished, you and I will take a nice stroll together and have a little chat. How does that sound, Rachel?"

"That sounds wonderful, Lord. Thank you for such a lovely day, today. I never thought that dying could be so wonderful."

Jesus smiled and nodded. He stepped towards them, heading in the direction of the forest trail that Jerry and Rachel had emerged from. Lillie then departed as Jesus stopped to hug His newest citizen of Heaven once again, before departing Himself.

"Enjoy yourself as you climb the mountain, Rachel," Jesus said, gently holding her shoulders in His hands. "I'll see you again very soon."

"I can't wait," Rachel said, almost breathless.

As Jerry and Rachel watched Jesus disappear into the forest trail, Jerry said, "Now you know the truth of *1 Chronicles 16:11 ... Look to the Lord and his strength; seek his face always.*"

"I sure do."

Jerry and Rachel stared at the mountain for several minutes, taking in its majesty.

"Come," the angel finally said. "Let's begin our journey up the mountain of truth. I'll be with you throughout the program today, guiding you along."

"That's great, Jerry."

They both headed towards the trail.

"It seems that so many worldly temptations kept me from experiencing the fullness of the Lord," Rachel said. "Although I'm overjoyed to be here in Heaven, I would have been able to do so much more with my life if I had embraced these things when I was younger."

"Yes, we've only heard that about a gazillion times over the years," Jerry joked. "I like to respond to that with *1 Corinthians 10:13 ... No temptation has overtaken you except what is common to mankind. And God is faithful; he will not let you be tempted beyond what you can bear. But when you are tempted, he will also provide a way out so that you can endure it.*"

"I see. So what will I learn on the mountain today?"

"You'll learn the basic differences between the world and God. You'll also learn that Satan's attacks on mankind fall into three basic categories: the lust of the flesh, the lust of the eyes, and the pride of life. All of these categories are temptations, but God can help you overcome them if you let Him."

"It sounds like we have a busy day ahead of us," Rachel said.

"We certainly do," Jerry said, as they slowly entered the mountain trail. "We certainly do."

.

PART 2

TWELVE APPOINTMENTS

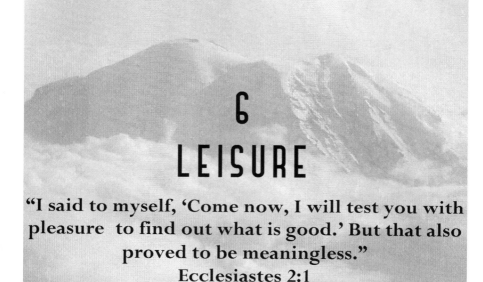

6
LEISURE

"I said to myself, 'Come now, I will test you with pleasure to find out what is good.' But that also proved to be meaningless."
Ecclesiastes 2:1

Rachel and Jerry strolled along the slightly inclined, curvy trail as they began their initial ascent towards the top of the mountain. Beset on both sides of the path was a thick forest that served as a calming gateway; similar to the path that led them from the forest lodge to the banquet table at the bottom of the mountain.

"So here's how this whole thing works," Jerry began. "As we transition from location to location, we'll chat and I'll usually give you some passages that relate to the upcoming visit with each hostess; although sometimes, I'll wait until we arrive to do so."

"Why do you do it that way?"

"To mix it up for you, of course."

Rachel chuckled. "Suits me just fine."

"Okay, so when we visit each of the ladies, they'll share their story with you, and then we'll move on to the next. By the time we're near the top of the mountain, you'll have a much sharper understanding of Jesus Christ and how Satan opposes all people in the world with sin, temptations, and idols. Are you with me?"

"Oh, yes. That sounds wonderful."

"Okay, then. Before we meet with Lillie, here are my opening comments. The first verse is from *1 John 4:19* ... *We love because he first loved us.*"

"I've heard that a few times this past week. I think it's definitely starting to make sense. Please—go on."

"Next, we have *Jonah 2:8* ... *Those who cling to worthless idols turn away from God's love for them.*"

"Honestly, I'm starting to see that now. So what do you think my biggest idol—?"

"Now, now, now," Jerry cautioned. "Let's not get ahead of ourselves. We need to stick to the plan."

Rachel grinned. "Of course."

"The third verse for this lesson is *Haggai 1:5* ... *Now this is what the Lord Almighty says: "Give careful thought to your ways."*"

"I was so blinded by my own goals; I never stopped to think about what God may have wanted for my life."

"Welcome to the human race," Jerry said, gently nudging Rachel. She laughed and they continued chatting about this and that as they continued along the trail.

"So here we are at our first stop—Lillie's place," Jerry said, after walking for a short while.

As they rounded the bend, a lovely home on a lake came into clear view. The rustic log cabin blended into the forest like it was a natural part of it. A thin stream of smoke steadily billowed out of the chimney as a beautifully bright blue lake adjacent to the home gracefully framed the area in a type of warm embrace.

They walked downward towards the charming log structure.

After knocking on the sturdy wooden door, the short blonde-haired Lillie opened it. Beaming, she said, "Welcome Rachel! Welcome Jerry! Long time, no see, huh?!?!?"

Rachel hugged Lillie as they entered.

"I can't wait to get started," Rachel said. "I have no idea what to expect today."

"Then I'll try to not disappoint you," Lillie said, leading the others towards her living room. "Can I get either of you anything?"

"No thanks," Rachel said. "Not just yet. I had some coffee at the forest lodge a little while ago."

"Yes, you sure did," Lillie said, smiling. "I remember the day I arrived, also. I was so surprised at how all of my senses exploded at every sight, sound, smell, touch, and taste in Heaven."

"Oh, I agree" Rachel said. "But I'm also surprised at how common things are in Heaven. I mean, sometimes I see something spiritually mind-blowing like meeting Jesus Christ or this stunningly beautiful mountain. Other times, I see a regular-looking living room with a view of a lake behind this lovely cabin. It's just surprising to me how some things in Heaven blow my senses away; but at the same time, everything else here seems to be so familiar and ... well ... regular."

"That's because of the unique nature of Jesus Christ," Jerry added. "You see, Jesus is both fully man and fully God. Doesn't it make sense that Heaven would be replete with things both common to man and common to God?"

Rachel shrugged. "I suppose that makes sense."

"Give it some more time," the angel said. "You'll see what I mean."

"So let me set the stage for you," Lillie continued. "This is the first of twelve stops on the mountain for you today. And trust me, a ton of thought has gone into how this whole thing is laid out. To enhance your learning experience, our angelic friend Jerry, here, has organized and sequenced these visits according to the three types of temptations shown several times in the Bible. Take it away, Jerry."

"Very well," Jerry said. "We set this program up with one thing in mind—women who are veterans of Heaven teaching newly arrived women some important spiritual lessons with the help of an experienced angel. By the way, that's me."

"Sounds great," Rachel said.

"Anyway, since all of you in this program are ladies, let me read you a passage about another historical lady named Eve. Her story will help you understand exactly how this program is being presented. It's in *Genesis 3:6* ... *When the woman saw that the fruit of the tree was good for food and pleasing to the eye, and also desirable for gaining wisdom, she took some and ate it. She also gave some to her husband, who was with her, and he ate it.*"

"Coincidentally," Lillie said. "Or perhaps not, those are the three temptations also shown in *Luke 4:1-13.*"

"What does that mean?" said Rachel.

"These were the temptations of Christ by Satan in the wilderness."

"Oh. I'm afraid I'm not very familiar with that."

"It's like this," Jerry said. "One of the most under-rated attributes of the Bible is its amazing consistency. In this case, there are three common temptations of mankind that are spoken of from the very beginning of the Bible in *Genesis 3:6*; they're further explained in the recounting of Jesus being tempted by Satan in the wilderness in *Luke 4:1-13*; and they're also mentioned towards the end of the Bible in *1 John 2:16*. If you're keeping score, that's three different writers, spread across many centuries, with one common message."

Rachel nodded. "So you're saying that God gave us a consistent biblical message about the temptations in our life?"

"Absolutely," said Jerry. "Now, then. Within these categories of temptations, the first four visits today will concentrate on the category of *lust of the flesh*. In the passages I just gave you, they tell us the next category of temptations are the *lust of the eyes*. And finally, the third set is *the pride of life*. But that's not all. Strictly as an example in each of our lessons, we've arranged the twelve ladies to present you with the false idol which they indulged in before coming to know Jesus Christ as their savior. Please understand, these idols merely serve to accentuate the biblical teaching about temptations. Our walk up the mountain today is designed to demonstrate this essential biblical truth to you."

Rachel looked quizzical. "I think I understand, but I'm not sure."

"Oh, it's pretty easy once we get started," said Lillie. "You'll see that the stories from the twelve of us are good examples that back up the biblical narrative about temptations and the resulting sin when they're indulged."

Rachel nodded. "So you're saying that false idols are related to types of temptations?"

"In a manner of speaking, yes," Jerry said. "False idols actually arise out of temptations and are sinful. I suppose you might say that idols are a type of fruit of temptations."

"Oh, okay."

"Anyway, please understand this. The temptations in those verses are what are truly important because they're the direct Word of God. The twelve examples today have been arranged so that we can illustrate some real examples of how idols can arise out of temptations. You see, idols are one of Satan's most consistent weapons against all people down on Earth, so it's important to understand them. Are you with me?"

"I am," said Rachel. "So how does all of this fit in with the topic of real love?"

"That's exactly what I asked when I first arrived," said Lillie. "But you'll soon see that Satan uses different kinds of idols for different generations—all in an effort to prevent people from experiencing real love."

"I see."

"However, the one thing that unites all idols is that they're essentially lesser things that we should either avoid, or should use properly—according to the Bible."

"Okay," Rachel said. "I think I'm with you. So getting back to some of my recent discussions regarding idols, they're basically shadows that block the real love of God, right?"

"That's exactly right," Jerry said. "Idols are the result of unrepented sin and indulged temptations. They're designed by the Evil One to block the glory of God from shining in your life."

"I understand."

"And one more thing, before we get rolling," Lillie said. "These first four idols—examples of *lusts of the flesh*—basically have two attributes they're founded on, in varying degrees. These attributes are *hedonism* and *fear*."

"What specifically do you mean by that?" said Rachel.

Lillie shook her head, "As you learn what the first four of us have to say about these lusts of the flesh, you'll see that one of the foundations of these idols is the self-seeking sin of hedonistic pleasure. This is often accompanied by a condemning fear that you're serving yourself and not God. In other words, these lusts of the flesh are largely manifested in the ways of self pleasure and the fear that one's flesh will not be fulfilled or satisfied. They're all about self-focus."

Rachel nodded. "It almost sounds like the first four of you ladies were engaged in idols that served as a type of pacifier—no offense."

"Exactly," Lillie agreed. "These idols are the self-focused fear that the flesh will not be satisfied—and they most certainly exclude God. The reason someone's not satisfied with God is because that would essentially dethrone them as having the autonomy of being their own god. The end result is that something tangibly simple has been wrongly elevated and has taken the place of the real God in the temptations of the lust of the flesh."

"I'm with you," said Rachel. "So how and when do we get started?"

"Actually, we already have," Lillie said, grinning. "So I'll lead us off today with my sinful idol of leisure."

"Leisure?" said Rachel. "That's not quite what I was expecting."

"Oh, I'll make some sense of it for you," said Lillie. "I promise."

"I'm sure you will."

"The first thing I'd like to say is that it's a terrible lie that God is somehow boring and doesn't enjoy fun and happiness. To illustrate my point, I'd like to share with you what King David did in *2 Samuel 6:14 … Wearing a linen ephod, David was dancing before the Lord with all his might.*"

"That's so neat," Rachel said. "I've never heard of such a thing."

"It sure is," Lillie agreed. "But fun and happiness must be balanced with the truth that God is in charge of His universe and His will is of paramount importance. Unfortunately, far too many people get caught up in pursuing leisure activities as a self happiness quest instead of following God's will."

"In order to understand this," Rachel said. "I'm going to need some solid examples."

Jerry sat back and allowed the ladies continue with their dialogue.

"Let's start with some of the idols I filled my soul with," Lillie said. "For example, my family and I had a house on a lake and we spent *soooo* much of our leisure time on the water. Oh, we had a big boat, jet skis, fishing equipment … the whole shebang. And honestly, our house on Earth was much bigger than this wonderful cabin I now live in."

"Hmmm," Rachel murmured. "That doesn't sound so sinful."

"If my leisure time had been balanced with work and duty to God, then it wouldn't have been sinful at all. Please remember, many of the idols we'll discuss today aren't necessarily sinful—that is, unless they're used improperly or to excess. You see, God wants us to have a balance between work and leisure. It's only when we elevate leisure activities above our duty to serve the Lord and others—that's when leisure activities approach idolatry."

"I suppose that makes sense. What else can you tell me?"

"Another thing I did was to make the childhood activities of my children a huge idol."

"Childhood activities?"

"Yes. You know, like various sports, ballet for my daughter, musical lessons for my two sons … things like that. I had our social agenda so jam-packed with activities, we had very little time to enjoy ourselves as a family. And we had zero time to worship and serve Jesus Christ."

"I see. So are you saying you stayed so busy, it became an idol in your life? I can see how this may be a little bit sinful, but not that much, really."

Lillie shook her head. "In order for this concept to make more sense, let me dig a little bit deeper for you. My story is that I grew up in a lower, middle class family. Although we never missed a meal, my parents struggled with their finances and my siblings and I never had much money to do the things other kids were doing. As a result, when I became an adult and married a man who had a good job, I was bent on giving my kids the things I never had. Unfortunately, it became an obsession."

Rachel nodded. "I never had any children, so please help me understand exactly how you felt."

"Basically, I spent most of my adult life trying to lick the wounds of what I felt like I didn't receive as a child. The problem is, I had a false image of what success in life really is."

"In what way? What do you mean by success?"

"I felt that success was providing for my children what I never had when I was growing up. But that was a lie. True success in life is to lead your children in the ways of the Lord; regardless of how many material things you have. I actually thought my success in life was based on how many things I gave my children."

"Really?"

"Oh, yes. I felt as though I could only be proud of my life when my children were able to engage in activities I never could because of the lack of money when I was growing up."

Rachel nodded. "Although it's been a bit of a whirlwind since I arrived in Heaven a little while ago, everything I'm seeing has a different perspective. Just last week, you would have never convinced me that what you're calling an idol was sinful. But now, since I've been washed in the blood of Christ, I'm obviously seeing things much differently."

Lillie smiled. "As did I. Actually, I passed from Earth only a few months ago—not long after I surrendered my life to Christ. So when the Holy Spirit entered my heart, my perspective changed immediately. And when I left the sinful domain on Earth and arrived here, I saw just how right I was to have repented of my idol of leisure."

"As I look back on it, although I lived for seventy-five years, it passed by pretty darned quickly."

"I only lived into my sixties, but I ended up losing my husband to divorce several years ago. Unfortunately, all of my children are still mired in the world as adults—just like I taught them to be. And that, my friend, is why a woman must be determined to use her strength to serve God, not leisure activities or other idols."

"Do you feel regret about what you neglected to do when you were still alive?"

Lillie shrugged. "Perhaps a little, but it's not the same as regret down on Earth."

"What do you mean?"

"I realize you're new here, but you must remember that one cannot feel sadness in Heaven. Having said that, however, I do pray every day for my ex-husband and children that they'll repent of their worldly ways and trust alone in Jesus Christ for their salvation."

"That's wonderful."

Lillie nodded. "Now that I'm here with God forever, I want the same thing for everyone. In fact, although I don't feel an earthly type of sadness, I do feel a type of regret that my focus on Earth wasn't more on God's kingdom until near the end of my life. In other words, I wish I had been a better disciple."

"That sounds a lot like my situation," Rachel said. "I suppose that's why God chose for me to hear your story today."

"Indeed," Lillie agreed. "That's the way this program works. Listen, my lesson today centers on our natural instincts to make gods out of the activities that please us. This includes all of the material things we unwittingly hoist up as idols and essentially worship. Some other examples of this would be techno gadgets and new technology, cars, boats, musical instruments, video games, sporting events, fishing, golf … you get the picture. Just about every possession or activity you have or engage in can become an idol if you're not careful."

Rachel nodded. "Now that I'm thinking about it, I used to hang out with some bohemian types who were very artsy. I wonder if—?"

"Yes, artistic expression can also devolve into idolatry," Jerry quickly added. "It all depends on how balanced the artist is with their work. It also depends on who or what is being glorified by their artwork."

"That's interesting," Rachel said. "So about these artsy friends of mine, you're saying that some of them may have made an idol out of their natural artistic talents?"

Jerry nodded. "In all cases, when someone has a natural or learned talent, they must learn to glorify and worship God through it. Those who merely indulge themselves with their talents—be it sports, art, music, or otherwise—are actually worshipping themselves. It's as if God isn't in the picture at all."

"I see," said Rachel. "So what about things like ... say ... gambling. How does that work?"

"Oh, I did lots of that also," Lillie said. "My husband and I would often roll into a casino and blow lots of his hard-earned money. I suppose some people can use it as entertainment in a controlled way, but most people who gamble are placing their hope in hitting a financial jackpot. We both are now well aware the real jackpot in life is walking into Heaven."

"I understand—"

"In other words, gambling does nothing but provide false hope. I wish I'd never have spent a single penny in those casinos."

"I suppose gambling has been around for awhile," Rachel said. "But that's one thing I never really enjoyed."

"Ahhh," said Jerry. "But you were focused on a different kind of idol which you wrongly felt gave you hope. You focused on the false hope that becoming the wife of Blaine would have given you everything you always wanted in life."

"That's true," Rachel said. "And that turned out to be a big fat lie."

"Although idols have somewhat changed over the years," Lillie said. "They all serve the same sinful purpose—to divert your attention away from Jesus Christ. If there's one thing I've learned since arriving in Heaven earlier this year, it's that the simple things in life are the most valuable. If I could only go back and live a simple life serving the Lord, my life on Earth would have been so much better. I actually had the power of God right there at my fingertips. But unfortunately, I allowed the false image of overcoming my austere childhood blind me to the reality that life on Earth is very short and always ends the same—with every person either finding God through Jesus Christ or not."

Rachel shrugged. "I can now see I also had the freedom to choose a simple life honoring God, but my idolatry kept my attention on other things—lesser things."

Jerry quickly added, "Now is a good time to add something that speaks to the full power of God. It's *2 Timothy 1:7 ... For the Spirit God gave us does not make us timid, but gives us power, love and self-discipline.*"

"Self-discipline is what we both lacked," Lillie said to Rachel. "We both had blinders on and our focus was on temporary things that failed to honor and serve the Lord. Once you have the Holy Spirit in your heart, you have the true power and discipline to resist the world's sinful idols. Without God, the natural inclination for everyone is to cling to the world. This is humanism in its most basic essence."

"So what now?" Rachel said. "Now that you're in Heaven, are you finally balanced in your leisure activities?"

"Of course," Lillie said. "You may not understand this right now, but you'll soon see that every single thing we do today in Heaven is building for eternity. The Bible teaches us there will one day be new heavens and a new earth. Until then, we're all preparing for the triumphant return of Jesus to Earth to finish the prophecy and usher in the eternal state of the world."

"That's wonderful," Rachel said.

Lillie smiled widely. "So to wrap up this first lesson, everyone should keep a balance between serving God and enjoying their life on Earth. Trust me, once you've surrendered your heart to Christ, you'll be enjoying His kingdom forever. And a forever of enjoyment is pretty incredible."

"Is that because God's kingdom has no end?"

"That's correct," Jerry added. "But I'm afraid it's time for us to move on. We have a schedule to keep."

"Sounds good to me," Rachel said. "I can't wait to see what's next."

"One more thing, before you go," Lillie said. "Please remember that the temptation to indulge in an over-abundance of leisure activities is nothing but a selfish desire to focus on you. I'm afraid that in God's world, there's just no room for that. After all, God isn't a cosmic Santa Claus—He's God."

"Very well put," Jerry said, standing up.

The ladies joined him.

"I'll see you again soon," Lillie said to Rachel as they hugged goodbye.

"I sure hope so," Rachel said. "I thank you for your time today."

"It was all my pleasure," Lillie said. "Enjoy the rest of your trip up the mountain."

7
HUNGER

"Their destiny is destruction, their god is their stomach, and their glory is in their shame. Their mind is set on earthly things."
Philippians 3:19

As Rachel and Jerry exited the lake area and headed around several winding curves in the forest trail, the thick tree cover slowly began to thin out. Within a short distance, the terrain shifted from forest to pastoral, and ultimately led them towards a charming village, which was comfortably nestled in a small valley. Everything within sight was bright and smelled clean and pure. They chatted about the splendor of Heaven until they wandered onto a primary road through the center of the small town.

"So who're we seeing next?" said Rachel. "It looks like we're arriving somewhere significant on this journey."

"The next hostess on our agenda is my good friend Olivia. By the way, Olivia is also a redhead, just like you."

"I think I like her already!"

Jerry chuckled. "Trust me—you will."

"So where is Olivia? Is she somewhere here on Main Street?"

"As a matter of fact, she is. Take a look straight ahead."

At the end of the short thoroughfare through town stood a tall-but-narrow Victorian-style house that was painted a sky blue throughout its four levels. Up and down the street were several interesting shops. Various people milled about at a relaxed pace, but it was clear that this house was the centerpiece of the village.

"Wow—what a pretty house," Rachel said. "I can't wait to hear Olivia's story."

"And she has a good one, for sure," Jerry said, waving to a few of the shopkeepers on the street.

They all recognized Jerry and waved back.

By the time they arrived at the front of Olivia's house, Rachel could hardly restrain her excitement.

"Let's go on up," she said. "The interior must be beautiful."

"Be my guest," Jerry said, pointing the way up the stairs.

When they arrived on the porch, Rachel eagerly knocked on the ornately decorated front door, which sported faded stained glass and light-colored wood.

Answering the door was a thin woman with red hair tied up neatly in a bun. Although she was somewhat petite in stature, she had a great strength about her.

"C'mon in here, Rachel," she said with a slightly raspy voice. "I'm Olivia."

"It's nice to meet you," Rachel said, joining hands with their hostess. "Although I haven't had much time to think about it, I'm glad to see I'm not the only redhead in Heaven."

"Oh, don't be silly," Olivia said, showing them the way to the densely decorated living room. "Heaven and Earth are certainly different, but they're not *that* different."

Olivia's house appeared as part apothecary, part library, and part hippie-pad from the seventies. She continued, "While it's true that many things in Heaven are far beyond what any of us could have possibly imagined, they're also very similar to Earth—only perfected."

"So far, besides meeting Jesus Christ, that's the thing about Heaven I love the most. While I'm totally blown away at the brightness and holy perfection, I'm also very comfortable with everything I see. It may seem odd, but it's as if I'm home for the very first time."

Olivia smiled. "Yep, that's how it works, dear."

"So—?"

"Before we get started," Olivia interrupted. "Can I get either of you anything?"

"Actually," Jerry said. "I wouldn't mind some of that lovely herbal tea you're so famous for."

"That sounds good to me also," Rachel added.

"Oh, I figured as much," Olivia said, matter of factly. "Here, let me pour you both a cup."

Olivia reached over to the table on her right and started pouring her slightly sweet nectar into three white tea cups, which sat squarely on floral-splashed saucers.

"So Jerry," she said. "While I'm getting our tea ready, would you mind starting us off in your traditional way?"

Rachel looked quickly at the angel. "Hey, we didn't do any verses on the way over here."

Jerry chuckled. "We sure didn't. I wanted to keep you guessing throughout our journey today."

Olivia fell into a robust laugh. "You have to watch these angel-types, Rachel. They take their job of serving God *very* seriously."

"Oh, I noticed," Rachel said. "I first met Jerry … well … it had to be over six decades ago down on Earth in my home town. If you ask me, that's pretty dedicated."

"All right now, ladies," Jerry said. "Let's go ahead and get started. Rachel—before we delve into Olivia's story, I'll set the stage with this key verse: *Psalm 107:9 … for he satisfies the thirsty and fills the hungry with good things.*"

"That's interesting," Rachel said. "But what does that have to do with our topic for this visit?"

As Olivia handed the cups of tea to the others, she said, "The idol I struggled with before my salvation was hunger."

Rachel's eyebrows furrowed. "Hunger?"

"Yep, that's what my problem was. Jerry, please go ahead and finish before I tell Rachel my story."

Jerry nodded. "Here we go. *1 John 5:21 says … Dear children, keep yourselves from idols.* The next one is *1 John 4:18 … There is no fear in love. But perfect love drives out fear, because fear has to do with punishment. The one who fears is not made perfect in love.* And lastly, *Ephesians 5:18 … Do not get drunk on wine, which leads to debauchery. Instead, be filled with the Spirit.*"

"Well, that was certainly a mouthful," said Rachel.

Olivia nodded. "And that, my dear, was my problem."

"What do you mean?"

"A mouthful. You see, my idol was hunger, but the engine that drove my hunger was gluttony. Unfortunately, my gluttony manifested itself in various and evolving ways during my life. The problem was that it could never have even possibly satisfied my soul."

"So how were you a glutton?"

Olivia sighed. "Oh, it started out innocently, all right. In those passages Jerry just cited, you can see another biblical warning against idols, and that there is no fear in love; real love, that is. But the kicker is that I tried to fill myself with worldly things instead of the Holy Spirit. Well, I did that until near the end of my life when I repented of this terrible sin. Anyway, all of us have a hunger that can only be filled by God. He actually created us that way. But instead of reaching out to the Lord, my lust of the flesh was a gluttonous desire to fill my soul—and my body—with harmful things that only served to destroy me."

"What specifically do you mean by gluttony?" said Rachel. "Were you overweight or something?"

Olivia nodded. "Oh, sure. I went through a fat phase all right. But that wasn't enough. My lustful gluttony didn't stop at mere overeating. It actually went far beyond just being overweight."

"Hmmm," Rachel mumbled. "In what way? I don't quite understand what you mean by gluttony."

"Let me first tell you something that theologian John Calvin was quoted as saying: *'mankind's nature is a perpetual factory of idols.'* Not only is that true, but my testimony is that the nature of my hunger idol was a perpetual factory of wrongful consumables. In other words, throughout most of my life, I constantly fed the furnace of my sinful hunger with harmful things."

"Well, like what?"

"Like I said, it started out as overeating when I was a kid. Once I got into high school, it was both food and cigarettes. Ultimately, social pressure and vanity pushed me into losing weight, but then other harmful things took their place. After the cigarettes and food, it was smoking weed and drinking beer. After that, it got much, much worse."

"It sure sounds like it. Please, go on."

Olivia shook her head. "As I reflect back, it seems absolutely crazy. Anyway, because smoking pot and getting drunk on beer became inadequate to satisfy my hunger, I then branched out into hard drugs and hard liquor. The end result was ... How shall I say this? ... Nearly lethal. Both physically and spiritually."

"I'm so sorry to hear this," Rachel said. "You must've—"

"Oh, don't be, dear. Jesus was merciful and later sent one of my many former boyfriends to me who actually had been born again. He soon led me to Christ. After that, there's never been a single iota of a second that I'm not grateful for what the Lord has done for me—especially taking the punishment for my selfish sins."

"So is your former boyfriend here in Heaven?"

"Of course. Travis runs that little café down on Main Street. You actually passed it on the way to my house. Let me tell you something. His chocolate chip cookies are absolutely out of this world. Before you leave town, you simply must try one … or maybe two."

"How neat."

"Isn't it, though? Travis and I had no idea when we were living in sin together that we'd both end up overcoming the world and living near each other here in paradise with Jesus."

"That's a wonderful story," Rachel said. "So getting back to your hunger. Do you feel your gluttony for various things wrongly tried to fill your soul with the hope and satisfaction that only Jesus can fill?"

Olivia smiled widely. "You bet. My lust for drugs and everything else was like clinging to various types of false hope. Like I indicated a minute ago, all humans are born with some kind of hunger—a lust of the flesh. The only antidote is to fill one's self with the spirit of God."

"Why do you think God designed us this way?"

Jerry quickly added, "God designed humans to be hungry for fellowship with Him in every way. However, Jesus doesn't force someone to love Him."

"I'm not sure—?"

"Before sin entered the world, Adam and Eve were fulfilled with the Lord in a perfect paradise. But right after sin entered the scene, God cursed mankind as a punishment. What remains is that every single person can only be fulfilled in Him. Everything else is a temptation that can be turned into an idol. That is, if you let it."

"Look at it this way," Olivia said. "When I was filling my body and soul with an overabundance of food, alcohol, drugs, cigarettes, and everything else you can imagine from the world, it was like putting tomato soup into my car's gas tank instead of gasoline. No matter how much you may want your car to run on something else, it's only designed to run on the proper fuel. The same thing applies to your life. If you fill your spiritual gas tank with something besides God, your car just won't run right. In fact, down on Earth, you would've destroyed your car if you had put soup in it … am I right?"

Rachel nodded slowly. "Yes, you sure are. That makes sense."

"Please don't forget," Jerry said. "Most idols are laced with prideful attempts at control, which only gives temporary gratification at best. False pleasures like that aren't really pleasures at all—they're just a slow form of suicide."

"I'm afraid the angel has that right," Olivia said. "Every time I got drunk or shot poison into my veins, I was taking another step towards physical death. Worse yet, but my physical death was also bringing about my spiritual death. And that, my friend, is Satan's primary goal of using the false idol of hunger against people."

"The more one focuses on themself," Jerry said. "The more they move away from the Lord. It's just that simple."

"I see," Rachel said. "So … like other idols … your hunger blocked the glory of God's real version of love, right?"

"Indeed," Olivia said, nodding. "You know what's cool, though?"

"What's that?"

"After I finally surrendered my life to Christ, I got involved with recovery groups and told them my story. I really wanted to warn others about the dangerous idol of hunger. There's no doubt in my mind that people who struggle with the various forms of hunger are only searching for God, but they often just don't know it."

"That makes sense to me."

"Listen," Olivia continued. "Regardless of how someone falls into the idolization of the various forms of hunger, God expects people to sacrifice those sins by resisting them. Remember, God gave His only Son as a sacrifice for us. I think by now you realize that real love cannot be found, unless—"

"Unless there's sacrificial, agape love," Rachel interrupted. "Yes, I've figured that out already."

Olivia chuckled. "I'm glad Jerry's doing his job properly."

Rachel smiled. "Oh, yes. And there were others who also taught me that, just before I passed away."

"Speaking of that, I passed from Earth way back in the seventies; about a year after I surrendered my life to Jesus. Although I wish I had served God longer while I was down there, the Lord has often assured me that the time I did serve Him, He was very proud of me for that. Isn't that awesome?"

"It sure is," Rachel agreed.

Olivia nodded. "The one thing I always stressed to those who I spoke to about my hunger was that getting in touch with a 'higher power' doesn't do squat. Only getting in touch with Jesus Christ matters, because there's no higher power in the universe than Him. Know what I mean?"

"I sure do. Honestly, when you first mentioned gluttony, I only envisioned that hunger would entail overeating and being overweight. I didn't realize that drugs, alcohol, and tobacco could also be things people hungered for."

Olivia's brow furrowed with concern. "Yeah, Satan is pretty tricky about that ... as well as everything else."

"So tell me something," Rachel began, looking over at Jerry. "What's the story behind people falling into the hunger trap? I mean, I never struggled with it too much, but I've had lots of friends who did. Since you're an angel and all, what can you tell me about Satan using this weapon against people?"

Jerry shrugged. "It's really a rather simple strategy in Satan's playbook against God's image-bearing creations. Like we spoke with Lillie about earlier, fear is the origin of many idols—particularly those of the temptations of the lust of the flesh. It works as a kind of mathematical formula: fear of something causes anxiety, which then causes stress, which then creates a hunger for sanctuary and to be filled with something. Unfortunately, one cannot find fulfillment with anything other than the Spirit of God."

"Hmmm," Rachel mumbled. "Do you have any passages to back that up? You're actually causing me to expect an answer from the Bible when I ask you questions."

Olivia laughed as Jerry nodded. "I sure do," the angel said. "Let's start with *Acts 13:52 ... And the disciples were filled with joy and with the Holy Spirit.*"

"I'm with you. Please go on."

"The next two are about Jesus. The first one is *Luke 1:41 ... When Elizabeth heard Mary's greeting, the baby leaped in her womb, and Elizabeth was filled with the Holy Spirit.* The other one is *Luke 4:1 ... Jesus, full of the Holy Spirit, left the Jordan and was led by the Spirit into the wilderness.*"

"I'm starting to see a recurring theme," Rachel said. "I actually felt the Holy Spirit descend on me right before I died. It was really kind of incredible—like nothing I had ever felt before."

"That's the way it's supposed to be," Jerry said. "So let me tell you an interesting story about hunger from ... you guessed it ... the Bible."

"I know this one," Olivia said, taking a sip of her tea.

Jerry continued, "In *Genesis 25:29-34*, we see the story of the twins, Jacob and Esau. In this passage, Esau was so hungry, he ended up giving away his birthright as the elder brother for a mere bowl of stew. In the end, the younger brother Jacob ended up being named Israel and fathered the twelve tribes of Israel's history. That's not a small thing in God's plan."

"That's shocking," Rachel said. "How could Esau have done that?"

"It's not that surprising to me," Olivia said. "When you're focused on yourself to that degree, it's easy to forget the fact that this is God's world and God's will is what's really important. Many people who I've known over the years just callously gave away their life to a bottle, a bong, a needle, or a box of Twinkies. I only wish that I could've found my faith earlier than I did. Perhaps I could've helped them."

"When you were finally able to stop focusing on yourself," Jerry said. "God's truth was able to penetrate your soul. And that, ladies, is the key to overcoming the world. One can scarcely hear the Lord's holy voice with hunger's selfishness making such a racket in their life. To overcome the lust of hunger, one must turn their gaze away from themself and look towards God. Hunger is a perpetual factory of gluttony in many different forms, but none of them are good for you. Only the Spirit of God filling you can satisfy your hunger."

Olivia nodded. "When I finally sacrificed my self-focus, I was clearly able to see the glory of God. Love without the sacrifice of your devotion to self is like trying to eat a hamburger down on Earth without the burger patty. Once you remove the burger, it's not really a burger—is it?"

"Ahhh," Rachel said. "So you're saying that the meat of real love is in the sacrifice of our self-focus. And your hunger was nothing but that—an unhealthy obsession with self."

Olivia chuckled. "That's a good way of putting it. Of course, here in Heaven, we don't actually have burgers like down on Earth—they're actually far better up here."

"That's right," Jerry said. "There's no death in Heaven, so our food can't possibly involve the death of an animal. But no worries, this will make more sense to you, Rachel, as we make our way up the mountain."

"Speaking of food," Olivia said. "Before you leave town, you absolutely *must* go have one of Travis's cookies at his café over yonder."

She pointed out the bay window, down the street.

"I think he's expecting you guys to come say hello," she continued.

Rachel grinned. "How can we turn down an offer like that? Jerry, what do you think—?"

"No worries," the angel said. "That's certainly a part of the program today. Let's head on over there now."

Everyone stood up and said their goodbyes. As Rachel and Jerry left Olivia's house, they could smell the lovely aroma of freshly baked cookies wafting up the street, seemingly like an olfactory invitation. They leisurely moved towards the heavenly bouquet.

8
BEAUTY

**"Charm is deceptive, and beauty is fleeting;
but a woman who fears the Lord is to be
praised."
Proverbs 31:30**

Rachel and Jerry emerged from Travis's café after enjoying the most scrumptious chocolate chip cookies in the entire universe. As the euphoria over this simple pleasure carried them forward, they wandered towards Olivia's house and turned right, back towards the well defined trail up the mountain. Olivia waved at them from the bay window in her living room as they left town. They smiled and waved back.

Rachel looked behind them as they entered the trail. She could see clearly how the pathway into town led right up to Olivia's house. It was as if the entire village was designed for her home to be the featured destination. Rachel instinctively knew this was Olivia's mission in Heaven.

"So where are we headed next?" she said, turning towards Jerry.

"Our next visit is with Veronica. She isn't far from here."

"And what's the topic of our next lesson?"

Jerry shot Rachel a mysterious glance. "I'd actually like to see if you can figure it out, my friend."

"Ah-ha. So we're going to have a little fun during our trip up the mountain, huh?"

"Sure, why not?"

"Okay, Jerry. Why don't you give me some passages and I'll see if I can figure out Veronica's idol. How about that?"

Jerry nodded approvingly. "I was hoping you'd start to get out in front of our topics today. Not all of my students catch on as quickly as you have."

Rachel chuckled. "So how're you going to lead us off?"

"I'll start you off with *Ecclesiastes 3:11 … He has made everything beautiful in its time. He has also set eternity in the human heart; yet no one can fathom what God has done from beginning to end.*"

"Hmmm. That's not really enough info to figure out anything. However, it's pretty neat that God set eternity in the human heart."

"He sure did. That was written by King Solomon from the Old Testament. Solomon was incredibly wise."

"I look forward to learning more about him."

"By the time we reach the top of the mountain, you certainly will."

"That's wonderful."

"Anyway, the next verse gets a little closer to our lesson with Veronica: *Isaiah 53:2 … He grew up before him like a tender shoot, and like a root out of dry ground. He had no beauty or majesty to attract us to him, nothing in his appearance that we should desire him.*"

"That's interesting," Rachel said. "Who is the writer speaking of?"
"None other than Jesus Himself," Jerry said. "Isaiah was giving a prophecy about the coming Messiah—Jesus Christ."

"But I found Jesus to be incredibly beautiful when we first met earlier today—"

"That's because the difference between earthly beauty and heavenly beauty are focused on different things. A little while ago, you saw the fully glorified Jesus who created this place and will return to Earth one day to execute His judgment on the world. The prophet Isaiah was speaking of the Lord's lack of physical beauty from the strictly humanistic, earthly perspective. Once again, the world's take on something is directly opposite of God's perspective."

"Okay, so please give me one more verse so I can give you my prediction."

"This next passage of what will be several verses for this lesson is in *1 Peter 3:3-4 … Your beauty should not come from outward adornment, such as elaborate hairstyles and the wearing of gold jewelry or fine clothes. Rather, it should be that of your inner self, the unfading beauty of a gentle and quiet spirit, which is of great worth in God's sight."*

"Okay, I think I'm starting to see a pattern here."

Jerry nodded. "I employ this technique in most of my teaching programs. My astute students always pick up on this and see that I'm using the Word of God to demonstrate just how important it is in teaching folks these lessons, which are obviously centered on God's kingdom."

"I think it's wonderful. But I also think I've figured out Veronica's idol. You've made it pretty apparent that it has something to do with physical beauty."

"Bingo, Rachel. That is correct."

Jerry and Rachel continued along the trail. Gradually, the tree cover began to form a quasi-tunnel of green once again. The sound of chirping birds and animals scurrying throughout the wooded area on both sides of them was very comforting. Since they were in Heaven, there was nothing in this place that could possibly harm them in any way. After all, this was the home of Jesus Christ.

As they rounded another curve on their ascent, a steep cliff face opened up in front of them. Out beyond the cliff to the right was an immense valley of lush green forests and an incredible brightness above, which was beyond compare. On the left-hand side of the trail was the steep side of the mountain, which framed the pathway they were on.

They continued along the trail on their left until a house carved into the stone face appeared. The ornately appointed building reminded Rachel of the Lost City of Petra, only it was smaller and livelier.

They headed towards it.

Once Rachel and Jerry arrived at the front of the house, they veered towards the entrance on their left. The twosome stopped right in front of the structure, which was carved into several shades of marble. Above the large wooden double-doors was an inscription in stone: *Psalm 73:26 ... My flesh and my heart may fail, but God is the strength of my heart and my portion forever.*

"That's neat," Rachel said. "A Psalm over the doorway."

"Every home should have one," Jerry said. "Especially that Psalm."

"Amen."

They headed inside.

The light in the foyer was muted and peaceful, and the harmonious sounds of gentle, running water could be heard in all directions. The ambiance was almost mesmerizing. From the left, a voice gently said to them, "I'm glad Jerry remembered he never has to knock on my door. Angels and guests are always welcome here."

"You must be Veronica," Rachel said, turning towards the voice.

Veronica nodded. "I am."

Rachel gazed at her hostess and was amazed at how beautiful she was. Standing before her was the loveliest Hispanic woman she had ever seen. Her flowing black hair and piercing dark eyes accented her smooth bronze skin.

"It's so nice to meet you," Rachel said, as Veronica embraced her. "I can't wait to hear your story."

"It's nice to meet you also."

Veronica smiled and then locked arms with both Rachel and Jerry, guiding them towards an open atrium area, beyond the foyer.

"You absolutely must try some of my delicious hot cocoa," Veronica said. "I use a few secret spices to make its flavor beyond your imagination."

"That sounds great," Jerry said, taking a seat in a lush garden area in the atrium. A small hole in the stone above created a type of spotlight into the area. "But let's wait just a minute—we just had some cookies at Travis's café."

"Ah, Travis," Veronica said. "He gives out his blessings to so many of the mountain's sojourners. But that's fine. I want you to get the most out of your visit today, Rachel."

Rachel grinned. "I must say; you're so beautiful, Veronica. I think I have an idea, but what are you going to teach me today?"

"I would like to begin by sharing with you two things that stood out to me when I entered Heaven earlier this year. The first one is *Leviticus 19:4 … Do not turn to idols or make metal gods for yourselves. I am the Lord your God…* I'm afraid my idol was my own personal beauty and all of the accompanying narcissism that went along with it. The other thing is in the book of *1 John 4:16 … And so we know and rely on the love God has for us. God is love. Whoever lives in love lives in God, and God in them.*"

"I see," said Rachel. "So you feel that you made an idol out of your own personal appearance, and that blocked the real love of God?"

"That's correct, but it was much worse than that. Since I was born with physical beauty, I felt like that somehow entitled me to live a perfect life where everything went my way."

"Oh, I know what that feels like, all right. I was so bent on having my life go exactly how I laid it out in my mind, nothing else would do. My lack of humility was astounding."

Veronica smiled. "Perhaps you'll have a chance to share your story with others on this mountain one day."

Rachel was quiet for a moment, deep in thought.

"Although I only passed away a few hours ago," she said. "The thought of serving God really hasn't sunk in yet."

"It didn't for me either," Veronica said. "I died just a short time after finally surrendering my life to Christ. When I arrived here, I was later asked by Jesus to share my story in this lovely home. Who knows what He will ask you to do after you reach the top of the mountain? Whatever it is, it will be wonderful."

"That's very interesting. So tell me, how did you die down on Earth? Were you young, or older?"

"I was still in my late twenties when I passed away."

"Wow."

"At the absolute pinnacle of my career, I contracted pancreatic cancer and died a few months after that. Unfortunately, it took something radical like that horrible disease to knock me off of my self-made throne. It was only then that I was able to see what the real world around me was like."

"What do you mean by that?"

"The year before I passed away, I was commanding as much as a seven-figure fee for modeling sessions. But instead of being grateful for what God gave me, I abused my soul by engaging in many forms of vanity due to my physical beauty. Deep down, I actually felt like I was the queen of the world and no one else mattered."

"Or god of your own false world," Jerry added. "Rachel—do you remember Veronica? She was pretty famous."

"I'm afraid not," Rachel said. "I was much older than she, and didn't pay much attention to modern trends and whatnot."

Veronica nodded. "Being famous down on Earth for all the wrong reasons isn't anything to be proud of—or anything that lasts. With what I now know, I wish so much that I could go back and use my God-given blessings for Christ's kingdom, not my own."

"Do you have an example of that? What would you like to have done?"

"Of course. Think about how much money I made by just posing in front of a camera or walking down a catwalk. Never once did I consider doing something for God—or for my neighbor. The only thing I could think of back then was how to build my earthly kingdom. I somehow thought I was invincible and would live forever. Fortunately, when I was very ill and my body was being ravaged by the cancer, I had an old boyfriend from high school present the Gospel to me. It was only after I had been dethroned by my disease that I was able to see the real kingdom of God, which is the only one that lasts forever."

"Your life sounds so sad," said Rachel.

"In the end, it was far from sad. God gave me enough time to ensure that my estate would serve Him on Earth, even from my grave."

"Once Veronica surrendered her life to Christ," Jerry said. "Our good friend Mick paid her a little visit. It was just a couple of weeks before Veronica passed away, but it was after she had surrendered her heart to Jesus."

"So what did Mick and you discuss?" said Rachel.

Veronica smiled. "Getting an earthly visit from a holy angel was quite a shocking event. During my modeling and fashion career, I was surrounded by false angels everywhere around me. But Mick showed me how I could serve God's kingdom by how my estate was distributed after I passed."

"Were you surprised to get a visit from a holy angel?"

"Not really. Since I had seen so many demon-types during my career, meeting a real angel of God fit even my own twisted and selfish worldview."

"That sounds very interesting—"

Jerry shook his head. "Ladies, we're not delving into the world of the demonic during our visit on the mountain today. Spiritual warfare is on Rachel's agenda for another day. As Veronica knows, that program is quite lengthy and intense."

"Hmmm," Rachel mumbled. "I suppose I've still got a lot left to learn, huh?"

Jerry nodded. "Since God chose for you to leave Earth before you learned much about Him, we have several programs for you to go through during these special orientation sessions here in Heaven."

Veronica laughed. "Don't worry, Rachel. You'll enjoy every minute of them. And since Jerry wants me to stay on topic, I'll now read you a couple of important verses."

"That sounds good," said Rachel.

"The next one is from the most romantic book of the Bible. It's in *Song of Songs 4:7 ...You are altogether beautiful, my darling; there is no flaw in you.*"

"That's in the Bible? It sounds like it's in a love letter or something."

Jerry quickly added, "Although the Bible is much more of survival guide than a love letter, there are enough parts of it to remind people how important the topic of love is in God's world. The Lord understands beauty and love far better than anyone else since He's the one who invented them."

"Very true," Veronica said. "After I started into my biblical studies upon moving into this house here in Heaven, I found something which reminded me of what happened before I died. It's in *2 Corinthians 4:16 ... Therefore we do not lose heart. Though outwardly we are wasting away, yet inwardly we are being renewed day by day.*"

Rachel nodded. "Oh, I can attest to that. I was also quite the looker back in my day. But over the years, I became more-and-more panicked at how much my youthful looks were fading. In fact, as my body began to slowly deteriorate, my self-esteem also faded along with it. I suppose you could say, if someone depends on beauty for their self-worth, they're destined to be severely disappointed."

"Amen to that," Veronica said. "That is, they're disappointed unless they end up arriving in Heaven like we both did. For those who become followers of Jesus Christ, the blessings of His promises are that our sufferings are only temporary."

"I have to admit," Rachel began. "In a failed effort to maintain my youthful appearance, I had a few cosmetic surgeries performed throughout the years. Now that I'm in Heaven, I definitely wish I hadn't done them."

Veronica shrugged. "I had some done also, even at my young age. Not only that, but I was absolutely obsessed with physical fitness. I spent no less than three hours every day working out, all in a vain effort to keep every ounce of fat off of my body. As I approached my late twenties, it became harder and harder to do."

"Now that we're being honest, I spent a huge amount of money on trying to keep up with the latest fashion trends. I'm sure in your former line of work, you probably had quite the wardrobe also."

Veronica chuckled. "To say the least."

"Why do you think we both were obsessed with our own beauty?"

"Oh, that's easy. As I see it, the reason breaks down into two primary areas. Number one, we didn't understand our true beauty in Jesus Christ. Sadly, I think we both fell into the trap of trying to conform to the world's false image of what a woman is."

"I can definitely see that."

"Number two ... and this is a tough one ... our vanity was indelibly tied into a hierarchy of sorts. To be blunt, we both felt like we were better than others due to our physical appearance. And that, my friend, is one of the most egregious sins in the universe."

"How so? I mean, I know it's bad and all. But why is it one of the worst?"

Veronica shook her head. "Let me have Jerry recite to you the reason why. Jerry—can you help?"

"Certainly, ladies. Becoming obsessed with your own beauty and feeling that you're better than others because of it was a big reason why Satan was cast out of Heaven. This is very dangerous business, indeed. We see this in Ezekiel 28:17 ... *Your heart became proud on account of your beauty, and you corrupted your wisdom because of your splendor. So I threw you to the earth; I made a spectacle of you before kings.*"

"Wow," said Rachel. "That's powerful, indeed."

"Obsession with one's own beauty is self-worship in the mold of Satan," Veronica said. "And too much focus on fashion is its evil twin sister."

"You must remember," Jerry said. "That Satan typically uses temptations and false idols against people in combination. We'll get into this a little deeper as we ascend the mountain, but the end result is that these lusts of the flesh all point towards a type of prideful entitlement to nurture what one can mistakenly feel are their personal needs."

"Yes," Veronica said. "During my self-centered lifestyle, I actually needed Jesus Christ more than anything else. Ironically, I neglected the one ingredient in my life I couldn't live without—Him."

"Oh, I don't know," Rachel said. "In my generation, it was common for women to be made to feel inferior to men. I always felt like I had to use my beauty to level the playing field. Back then, I thought it was a necessary evil."

"You're definitely onto something with that," Jerry said. "But I'm afraid you're also missing something."

"What do you mean?"

"All of that nonsense about God being a chauvinist, or that Christianity is misogynistic, is a lie straight from the pit of Hell. Let me demonstrate that with one simple verse: *Genesis 1:27 ... So God created mankind in his own image, in the image of God he created them; male and female he created them.*"

"That's funny," Rachel said. "I've always heard that God favored men over women."

"And thus, the lie," Veronica added. "God actually designed women to not only be equal human beings, but also to capitalize on our strengths in becoming a righteous companion to men. Let's face it, men desperately need us. Have you ever wondered why that is?"

"Yes, actually I have."

"The reason is simple. God designed us to use our tremendous strength to build men up. It's only when sinful men follow Satan's lies that we see them trying to dominate women. Far too often, men are merely little boys in bigger bodies. The way I see it, God designed men to need our support. And for someone to give support to others, they must have tremendous strength in order to do so."

Rachel nodded. "I've never considered that."

"That's because you're just now learning the Bible," Jerry said. "But no worries—we have a lot more in store for you."

"Good. I can't wait."

"Ladies, I hate to say this," Jerry said. "But Rachel and I need to head on out to our next appointment."

Rachel didn't want to leave. She was enjoying herself.

"The days of no stress are finally here for you," Veronica said, sensing Rachel's feelings. "Very soon, you'll get accustomed to not having to rush around to accomplish things. You see, since you're a brand new citizen, you're still accustomed to feeling the pain of goodbyes. And believe me, I cannot wait until our next visit. But you must remember that earthly timetables do not matter up here. I will undoubtedly see you again very soon, Rachel. And on that day, we will celebrate our Savior in this perfect place."

"Thanks so much for that," Rachel said. "I'll definitely have to come back for some of your hot cocoa."

Veronica smiled. "Indeed. Let me show you to the trail where your next appointment awaits. Please … join me…."

Veronica stood up and escorted Rachel and Jerry to her front door. Once outside, the three of them looked out over the magnificent valley together.

After a few moments, Rachel said, "I think it's amazing that God gave you such a beautiful vista to enjoy."

Veronica nodded. "Our Father gave me my true beauty in His Son Jesus Christ. Because of that, I now can enjoy the wonders of His Paradise."

"That whole concept is just starting to sink in with me," Rachel said. "And I can't think of anything better than that."

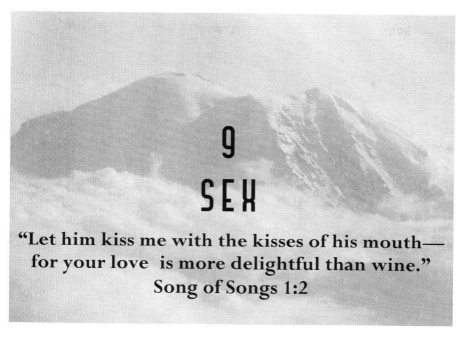

9
SEX

**"Let him kiss me with the kisses of his mouth—
for your love is more delightful than wine."
Song of Songs 1:2**

After spending some time viewing the beautiful vista in front of Veronica's home, Rachel and Jerry followed the trail downwards, along the other side of the mountain. The rock face towered over them on the left, while the thickly forested valley to their right continued to dazzle with its lush accouterments. The trail was much narrower on this side of the mountain, but it was distinct, solid, and comfortable.

After a few minutes, Rachel noted, "This is some pretty rugged terrain. I like how there's so much to look at on this part of the trail."

Jerry nodded. "It's definitely rugged, but isn't it wonderful?"

"It sure is. But I'm definitely glad we're here in Heaven. This would seem pretty dangerous down on Earth—perhaps for only the most intrepid explorers."

"There's no doubt about that. But hey, that's kind of the point."

"What is?"

"During this journey, God is showing you some of the vast differences between Heaven and Earth. While you've certainly been enjoying some of the things which are similar to being down on Earth—like drinking tea and eating cookies—you may have been overlooking some of the obvious differences that are imbued in Heaven's experience."

"Let's see. Is an example that there's no chance I can be hurt in any way by walking along the side of this mountain?"

"That's correct," Jerry said. "But there's something else you're missing."

"What's that, exactly?"

"It's also the symbolism of our next idol."

"Oh—?"

"We're now moving into perhaps the most dangerous and prevalent idol among the twelve that are being demonstrated to you today. By the time we're finished with Eva—our next hostess—you'll have a powerful idea of what these first four idols are all about ... as well as the other ones following it."

"So how is this part of the trail symbolic?"

"Our next idol casts the widest and most dangerous shadow in eclipsing the human heart. It actually prevents God's real love from penetrating one's soul because it's so personal and entrenched in each person's psyche. Actually, its tendrils snake themselves throughout the entire human soul and it's very difficult to root them out."

"Well—?"

"Here's the symbolism. Although you can't be hurt by walking on the side of this mountain today, many humans on Earth have had our next idol corrupt them with its humanistic propensity all the way to eternal separation from God. In other words, it's like they fell off of their mountain of life, all the way down to Hell. This is obviously an extremely dangerous idol."

"Wow, that's pretty serious. So I suppose we're hitting a crescendo with the lust of the flesh idols?"

"We are," Jerry said, nodding. "And every other temptation. Do you have any idea what's next?"

"No, no, no," Rachel said. "You have to first give me a clue before I'll offer a guess."

Jerry chuckled. "Have it your way. I'll lead you off with a powerful verse from *Colossians 3:5* ... *Put to death, therefore, whatever belongs to your earthly nature: sexual immorality, impurity, lust, evil desires and greed, which is idolatry.*"

"Yeah, I thought so."

"You thought what, exactly?"

"Sex is the next idol."

Jerry nodded slowly. "It sure is...."

As they reached the bottom of this rugged part of the trail, it abruptly turned right and headed through some trees on a generally flat terrain. They continued ahead.

Rachel sighed. "Okay, this one's going to be quite convicting. It's not like I was super promiscuous or anything, but I did commit adultery with Blaine countless times. Of course, I really regret that now. I think I should've paid more attention to the Ten Commandments."

"I understand. Listen, just beyond these trees is Eva's place. Why don't we wait until we arrive before digging into any of these important details ... okay?"

"Of course," Rachel said. "But can I get the other verses from you before we get there?"

"Let's give it a try. Since you're now stealing my thunder due to being such a fine student, I'll have to step-up my game by watching what I give you before each lesson. I don't want to make it too easy for you."

Rachel smiled. "I'm not trying to make your job more difficult, Jerry. I promise."

"No worries," Jerry said. "So the next one is *1 Peter 4:3 ... For you have spent enough time in the past doing what pagans choose to do—living in debauchery, lust, drunkenness, orgies, carousing and detestable idolatry.*"

"That verse hits dead center on this next topic."

"It sure does. Hey—there's Eva's place...."

As they exited the forest, a beautiful red barn suddenly appeared on their right. Surrounding the barn as far as the eye could see were fields of thick green grass. Around the perimeter of the fields was a continuous white fence, which sported three horizontal wooden beams in between each fence post.

"This place looks like Vermont," Rachel declared.

"Perhaps Vermont on steroids," Jerry said, grinning. "And before you ask—no, the fence serves no real purpose up here other than to look familiar ... and perhaps add to the aesthetics."

Rachel laughed. "Yeah, I suppose that's because animals can't get lost up here, huh?"

"Now you're catching on."

Rachel and Jerry continued until they arrived at a driveway on their right, which led directly into the immense barn. When they reached the barn's huge sliding door, Jerry knocked a few times, paused, and then slid the door open.

"Get on in here!" Eva said, rushing up to Rachel and Jerry. "I've been eagerly waiting for y'all to arrive."

Eva had medium-length brown hair, and in general, girl-next-door features. She spoke with a slight southern accent and had a great excitement about her.

She grabbed Rachel and hugged her tightly.

"Welcome to my place," Eva said. "I have so much I want to share with you."

"And I, as well," said Rachel.

"Good. Listen, before—"

"And who is this?" Rachel interrupted.

A golden retriever suddenly arrived at her side, tail wagging into overdrive.

"This is Sasha," Eva said.

Rachel held Sasha's face in her hands, petting her. "What a pretty doggie you are."

Eva giggled. "Of all the things on Earth I'm glad I left behind, I'm soooo thrilled that God gave me my beloved dog to live with forever. Sasha has always held such a huge part of my heart in her little paws. In fact, I think our pets on Earth are wonderful repositories for our love and memories—which carry forth into Heaven, and ultimately on the new Earth."

"That's so sweet."

"Did you have any pets, Rachel?"

"No, unfortunately not. But I do love animals."

"Good. You'll probably find a few you can befriend up here. God's creatures are actually all over the place. When I arrived in Heaven a couple of years ago, I was surprised at how many animals were here."

Jerry shook his head. "Of all of Satan's lies, I believe I detest that one more than any of the others."

"What do you mean?" said Rachel.

"The thought that God would discard His animals to oblivion is absolutely preposterous. Quite to the contrary, the Lord has a real affinity for His beloved beasts. He actually created them for all of you to enjoy."

"I guess I never gave it much thought," Rachel said. "As you know, I didn't remain on Earth very long after I gave my life to Christ."

TOP OF THE MOUNTAIN

"Most of us on the mountain fall into that category," Eva said. "I died back in 2005, just a few months after I overcame my addiction to sex and surrendered my life to Christ."

"Well now," Jerry said. "It looks like we're off and running.""We sure are," Eva said. "But let's go have a seat before we dig into my story."

Eva showed them to a nice seating area that had a square coffee table in the middle of a large, square sectional. There were some obvious resting quarters not far away, towards the back of the barn, and several smaller animals milling about. Rachel sensed that the animals somehow knew to give them some distance because they had some important things to discuss. She marveled at this subtle difference between Earth and Heaven as the reality of her forever home continued to settle into her soul.

"So Jerry," Rachel began. "We only covered a couple of verses on the way over here. Do you have any more for me? Isn't that how this thing works?"

Jerry nodded. "Of course I have some more. Actually, Eva and I have several little goodies in store for you."

Rachel giggled. "These lessons are as sweet as those cookies back at Travis's café."

Jerry nodded. "So the next passage covers all manner of sexual sin. It's *1 Corinthians 6:9-10 … Or do you not know that wrongdoers will not inherit the kingdom of God? Do not be deceived: Neither the sexually immoral nor idolaters nor adulterers nor men who have sex with men nor thieves nor the greedy nor drunkards nor slanderers nor swindlers will inherit the kingdom of God.*"

"The teaching in that passage is what I ignored for most of my life," Eva said. "I used to feel like any and all sexual relations were quite natural, so I engaged in just about every sexual sin you can imagine."

"That's no surprise," Jerry said. "In accordance with virtually all humanistic beliefs, doing anything you desire sexually is the natural paradigm. So it shouldn't be surprising that prior to following Christ, one feels they should be able to do whatever they want to do; sexually speaking or otherwise."

Rachel nodded. "I suppose it's undeniable that sexual sin is a direct rebellion of God's commands."

111

"Oh, trust me," Eva said. "It is. As I reflect on my life, I've come to realize that ironically, improper erotic passion actually cheated me from experiencing real love instead of enhancing my joy."

"How so?"

"Sex must be used according to God's prescription, or pain and suffering will certainly ensue at some point. Of the four basic types of love you're learning about, passionate love—or *eros* love—is not real love if it's only used in a physical way."

"What exactly do you mean by that?" said Rachel.

"It's … like this…." Eva said slowly. "When I engaged in sexual activity outside of marriage to my husband, I was only feeding the furnace of my flesh. And trust me, there's no other temptation, idol, or sin that comes close to the powerful feelings involved in sexual attraction. In my opinion, sexual sin is, by far, Satan's most common strategy against mankind."

"I can see that. But what do you mean by the assertion that eros love isn't real love? I'm not following you on that part."

"What I was driving at was that eros love is *incomplete* if it's only intended as a physical act. God designed sex to be enjoyed within a man-woman marriage because it's a spiritual act also. Essentially, if you step outside of God's command for sex within a biblical marriage, that type of love, lust, or activity is only based on feelings, which inevitably fade. In other words, mere sexual attraction is incomplete without other forms of love *plus* the commitment of a man-woman marriage being a part of the mix. That's how God designed sex. Outside of His way, you're asking for trouble."

"I'm still not with you on this yet," Rachel admitted. "The feelings I experienced with sexual attraction were quite powerful. And to be perfectly honest, sometimes I only wanted the physical end of the equation."

"Yes, but that's the humanistic, sinful way of looking at it," Eva said. "Let me lead you through a few things that'll help you better understand what I'm saying. In *1 John 4:17* we see this … *This is how love is made complete among us so that we will have confidence on the day of judgment: In this world we are like Jesus.*"

"Ahhh, so you're saying that real love models Jesus. And modeling Jesus involves following God's prescription for sex. Is that right?"

Eva's eyebrows raised and she glanced at Jerry, nodding. "Rachel is moving along quite nicely in our program."

"She sure is," Jerry agreed. "Let me also add this one to what you just said: *John 14:31 ... but he comes so that the world may learn that I love the Father and do exactly what my Father has commanded me. 'Come now; let us leave.'*"

"Soooo," Rachel began. "I assume you cited that verse because you're saying we must follow God's commands, right?"

"That's right," Eva said. "But please hear me on this. For most of my life, I mistook love for lust. Every single time I did that—and trust me, it was often—the lust ultimately faded and there was nothing left in the mix to keep the relationship from failing. The result was constant frustration and gut-wrenching heartbreak."

Jerry held up his hands. "Now's a good time for me to point out something about sex and marriage that's been true since God created mankind. The reason I say this is because followers of Jesus Christ revere the marriage between one man and one woman to a level that non-believers largely cannot understand."

"What is it they can't understand?" said Rachel.

The angel leaned in. "They can't understand that marriage—according to biblical teachings—incorporates all four types of love that we've discussed. In no other human-to-human relationship is there this kind of powerful, compound love. You might say that biblical marriage is a wonderful hybrid of all four types of love."

Rachel shook her head. "But don't Christians have the same basic divorce rate as non-Christians?"

"Probably so," Jerry said. "But that's not the point."

"Then what is?"

"The point I'm trying to make is that regardless of how many people stray from God's commands on the covenant for sex and marriage, the truth remains that the right way to do it is for a couple to put God first, and then to love each other in all four ways. And yes, I said *all four ways.*"

"Once again," Eva said. "Those four ways are passionate love, family love, friendship love, and sacrificial love. Since all people are both physical and spiritual beings, God made us to be in balance according to His ways. It's when we step outside of that balance that we begin to spiritually destroy ourselves—oftentimes unaware."

"Another important thing you need to remember," Jerry said. "Is that the idol of sex is the least disguisable of all sins."

"Why is that?" said Rachel.

"Because sex cannot be mistaken for philanthropy or anything altruistic like some of the other temptations. At its core, sex is a basic, powerful human instinct and it must be tamed and brought into submission into God's ways. If this fails to happen, it will overtake you and drag you towards its headmaster, the religion of humanism."

Rachel's eyes furrowed. "Did you just say the *religion* of humanism?"

"I did," said Jerry. "Humanism wrongly elevates human thoughts and desires over God, which is the ultimate deal buster in God's kingdom. When you elevate anyone or anything over God, it violates the first commandment to have no other gods before the real one."

"And—?"

"And—nothing. At its basic core, the term 'religion' is a set of beliefs adhered to by a group of people. Since Scripture tells us that all people are born sinful, the natural, humanistic default tendency when one is born is to believe whatever humanism says about all things— especially sex."

"Let me add this," Eva said. "These last two verses helped me quite a bit when I finally committed my life to Christ—"

"That's great," Rachel interrupted. "But can you first tell me where you're from? I've been curious about it during our discussion. I find it interesting that you're stationed here in this wonderful barn."

"Oh, sure. I'm originally from the southeast U.S. Unfortunately, when I was young, all I wanted to do was to escape the small Georgia town I grew up in. After attending college in Atlanta, I went to live in Manhattan and whooped it up for many years. I ultimately met my husband there, and we stayed in New York until the day I hit rock bottom and had my moment of clarity about God."

She paused for a moment.

"Please—go on," Rachel encouraged.

"I woke up one day after one of mine and my husband's sex parties at our downtown apartment … and … well … I looked around at everything. Suddenly, God hit my soul with the futility of it all. You see, pursuing sexual freedom is actually the ultimate road to misery. As with all of the lusts of the flesh, trying to find the ecstasy of God in false idols is terribly frustrating and very much depressing."

"I see," said Rachel. "So what happened next?"

"After my so-called moment of clarity, I reached out to some Christian friends of mine. They ultimately led me to surrender my life to Jesus. Of course, this didn't go over well with my worldly husband, so we divorced when I refused to continue with all of our sexual shenanigans."

"Wow. So you left your husband over your relationship with Jesus?"

"No," Eva said, shaking her head. "Not exactly. Since I refused to continue living our life of debauchery, my husband gave me an ultimatum to continue with our allegedly great life together—or else. Of course, I flatly refused. After that, he gave me a nice settlement to just go away. My ex-husband was pretty wealthy and it was he who actually divorced me. Right after that, I moved to northwest Vermont and bought a farm."

"That's so interesting," Rachel said. "So your last home on Earth was similar to your new home in Heaven, huh?"

Eva nodded. "It seems God planned it that way, for sure."

"Listen, Rachel," Jerry added. "If you'll notice thus far, all of our visits have been strategic in that every sister's house is related to their life on Earth somehow. This is no coincidence."

"Hmmm," Rachel mumbled. "Let's see … Lillie lived on a lake; Olivia lived in a Victorian house, similar to San Francisco; Veronica lived in a unique house that accentuates God's beauty; and now Eva lives in a pastoral setting."

"I live in a pastoral setting because it's similar to what I grew up living in," Eva said. "All throughout school, I hated my lovely home town and sought after the world for fulfillment. I now understand that God actually made me for a place like this. It was only after I discovered the world had nothing to offer me that I learned to appreciate the value of a quiet, peaceful life on a farm."

Rachel smiled. "This whole experience is simply wonderful. I wonder what God has in store for me after I reach the top of the mountain?"

Jerry shook his head. "Let's not get ahead of ourselves. Eva dear, can you please give us those two verses you mentioned earlier?"

"I sure can. Listen, Rachel. We must always remember that our lives are incredibly valuable to God. We learn in *1 Corinthians 6:20 …you were bought at a price. Therefore honor God with your bodies.*"

"Well, that certainly fits in with your testimony," Rachel said. "It's funny how none of us intended to conform to the world—we just ended up doing so."

"You're right about that," Eva said. "And that leads me to this powerful verse: *2 Chronicles 12:14 ... He did evil because he had not set his heart on seeking the Lord.*"

"All humans are lost if they don't follow the Lord," Jerry said. "It's hard enough for a Christian to obey God's commands and resist the flesh as it is. When you remove God from the equation in someone's life, it's impossible to find real love because the flesh constantly gets in the way."

"There's no doubt about that," Eva said. "Even after I repented of my sins, the temptation to fall back into sexual sin was always there. However, I continually overcame it with the strength of the Holy Spirit. *Matthew 26:41* says ... *The spirit is willing, but the flesh is weak.*"

"That makes sense to me," said Rachel.

"I have one more thing to share with you," said Eva. "This is a subject I just cannot stress strongly enough. This last thing tortured me and steered my soul right into the dead end of sexual selfishness. Do you have any idea what it is?"

"Honestly, no."

"It's pornography," Eva said sadly. "What so many people celebrate as 'natural' is perhaps Satan's greatest victory in the modern world of the internet. Trust me when I tell you, there's absolutely nothing spiritually valuable in viewing pornography. And from what Jerry tells me, it's nothing new in this world. The trap of the obsession with sex has been around for as long as sin has existed."

"Pornography, huh?" Rachel mused. "I was never a big fan of it, but I can certainly see how it would divert someone's focus on God and place it on something ... well ... of the flesh."

"That's it," Jerry said. "There's absolutely zero eternal value in pornography. It's as destructive a force against God as there is."

"There's actually zero value at all in pornography," Eva said. "All it did to me was to make me focus on my idol much more acutely. With every single day I'm getting to enjoy here in Paradise, I'm aware that without finding God, I'd be separated from Him forever. That, my friend, is what Hell is. Trust me, no one wants to be separated from the Lord."

Rachel shivered. "I'm overjoyed that Jesus took the punishment for my sins. I really don't deserve His grace, but I sure am grateful for it."

Jerry nodded, approvingly. "God's grace goes far beyond what anyone of us—angel or human—can possibly understand."

"And with that," Eva said. "Let me show you the way back to the trail. You have another important appointment waiting for you...."

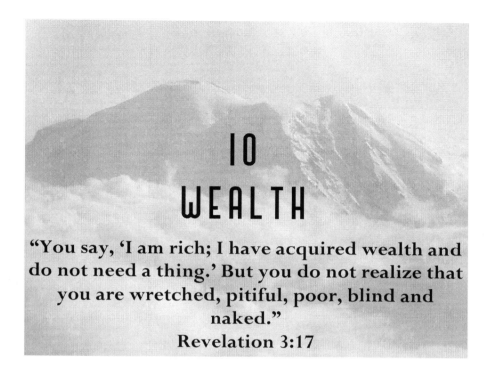

10
WEALTH

"You say, 'I am rich; I have acquired wealth and do not need a thing.' But you do not realize that you are wretched, pitiful, poor, blind and naked."
Revelation 3:17

Rachel, Jerry, and Eva said their good-byes at the end of the driveway as the angel and his student entered the mountain trail once again. Rachel felt her head spinning after examining the temptations of the lust of the flesh, but she looked forward to her next visit with an enthusiasm and hope that can only come from living in Paradise.

"Okay young lady," Jerry said. "It's time we move into the next set of four temptations with the lust of the eyes. Are you ready to get started?"

"You bet," Rachel said. "So who's next on our agenda?"

"Next, we have Irene. Here, this way…."

Jerry led Rachel through some trees as they climbed upwards once again. The trail ultimately led through a flat plateau that looked like a sparse highway in the Southwest. The light was muted on this part of the trail, and as they walked, their surroundings appeared as a back road in New Mexico during early evening.

They did a recap of each of the first four lessons as they chatted and walked along at a comfortable pace. After a while, they saw a beautiful cottage on their right. The impressive layout of Irene's home, which was located in the center of several smaller buildings and placed around a lush vegetable garden, was a veritable tableau.

"So what do you have to whet my whistle before we get to Irene's?" said Rachel. "Let's see if you can stump me."

"That'll be hard to do with this next idol, but let's try. The first one is *1 Corinthians 10:14 ... Therefore, my dear friends, flee from idolatry.*"

"Oh, c'mon. That's not much info."

"True, but it does show you how much idolatry is warned against in the Bible—in both the New Testament as well as the Old."

"I'll have to admit, that part has been a bit of a surprise to me. I've often thought of idols as only being in the Old Testament."

"Get used to the surprises. We're not even half-way done."

"This is a wonderful journey. I almost don't want it to end."

"Good deal. Now this next one hits a little closer: *1 Samuel 2:7 ... The Lord sends poverty and wealth; he humbles and he exalts.*"

"Hmmm ... It's starting to take shape. Go ahead and give me the last one."

"This one will surely give it away. It's in *Ecclesiastes 5:10 ... Whoever loves money never has enough; whoever loves wealth is never satisfied with their income. This too is meaningless.*"

"Ahhh, I thought so," said Rachel. "It appears that we're going to delve into the subject of wealth or money."

"Both. They actually go hand-in hand, wouldn't you say?"

"For the most part, yes. Not everyone has wealth, but most everyone strives for it."

When they arrived at the entry to Irene's place, they could see her pulling some vegetables out of the ground in her garden. Irene saw her guests and waved them over as she wiped herself off. When Rachel and Jerry reached her, Irene held her arms out to each of her guests, who gladly took her hands.

"I'm so happy you could make it," Irene said.

The cottage owner had grayish hair tied up neatly in a bun, but also youthful looks. She was short and thin in stature and carried a warm sense in her soul.

"And we're delighted to see you," said Rachel.

Irene nodded once. "I've never enjoyed gardening as much as I love it here in Heaven," she said. "In fact, before I arrived here a few weeks ago, I never worked a single day in my previously privileged life."

"Oh—? Can you tell me more about that?"

"I can. But first, let's go sit down. I have much to share with you."

Irene led Rachel and Jerry into a covered veranda that had a stone fire pit sitting squarely in the middle of it. A gentle fire crackled away as the three of them took seats on a round bench area surrounding the fire.

"So what did you mean by your previously privileged life?" Rachel said. "Can I assume you were wealthy?"

"Oh yes," said Irene. "As they often say down on Earth, I was born with a silver spoon in my mouth. In fact, my life was completely enviable to most people. I was born rich, I married a rich man, and like I said, I never actually had a job throughout my fifty seven years on Earth."

"And that was the problem," Jerry said. "Irene was so accustomed to using her wealth as a type of false storm shelter; she failed to see the value of work until she had left the fallen world and arrived here."

Irene shrugged. "Jerry's right. In fact, while I was in the hospital after my third surgery to remove some cancerous tumors, that lovely angel named Mick came to see me. At first, I thought he was some kind of weirdo hippie or something. But thankfully, he shared the Gospel with me. It didn't take long for it to penetrate my worldly cocoon and I was able to see my wicked ways of depending on something as fleeting and as flimsy as money. Unfortunately, my wealth was my de facto god."

"That reminds me," Jerry began. "A good teaching on this can be found in *Acts 8:20 … Peter answered: 'May your money perish with you, because you thought you could buy the gift of God with money!'*"

"That was me all right," Irene agreed. "I somehow made a god out of my wealth. I actually felt like I could control the world around me with it. The ironic fact is that I felt like my money was a type of shield that could protect me from harm. It was as if only poor people could get terminal diseases. Anyway, that whole illusion came crashing down when the cancer came-a-calling."

"That's what these next four idols are all about," said Jerry. "The lusts of the eye centers on to whom and/or what you worship. It's about allegiance, covetousness, ambition, and above all else, control."

"What do you mean by control?" said Rachel. "In the lust of the flesh, hedonism and fear were the foundational girders of that group. In the lust of the eyes, are you saying that it's centered on control?"

"Essentially, yes," Jerry agreed. "The key to these idols is this: where is your allegiance? To whom or what are you placing your desire to worship? What do you covet?"

"I learned something very important just before I arrived here," Irene said. "It's in *Zephaniah 1:18 … Neither their silver nor their gold will be able to save them on the day of the Lord's wrath.' In the fire of his jealousy the whole earth will be consumed, or he will make a sudden end of all who live on the earth.*"

Rachel whistled and said, "Wow. That sounds serious."

"Placing your trust in anyone or anything but the Lord *is* serious," Irene said. "God loves us enough to allow us to have the freedom to choose. However, there are both positive and negative ramifications to our choices. You see, God's holy jealousy is righteous, and only He deserves our allegiance."

"That makes sense."

"Yes, but think about it for a moment. Imagine how angry you'd rightfully be if you created people who used your blessings of money and other things as a way of actually rejecting you? It's like saying: *Hey God, thanks for the cash, but you can get out of my face now.* How would you feel about that?"

Rachel shook her head. "I wouldn't be very pleased, that's for sure."

"And that's what these lusts of the eyes are centered on. Used properly, they can often be tremendous blessings. But used selfishly and to the exclusion of the Lord, they're incredibly harmful. Remember, real love cannot be achieved without God's involvement."

"I'd like to add a few things we taught Irene when she first arrived," Jerry said. "The right way to use your wealth—if you're so blessed with it—is found in *Proverbs 3:9 … Honor the Lord with your wealth, with the firstfruits of all your crops.* In addition, we learn something very important in *1 Timothy 6:9 … Those who want to get rich fall into temptation and a trap and into many foolish and harmful desires that plunge people into ruin and destruction.*"

"I see," said Rachel. "But what about those who aren't destined to be wealthy on Earth?"

"The first thing I have to say about that," Irene said. "Is that poverty should never be glorified. Instead, every person should be good stewards of whatever God gives us on Earth. Of course, in

Heaven, we have the most important inheritance a child of God can have—eternal life."

"It basically gets down to this," Jerry said. "You can't allow your wealth to replace God. To back that up, we have *Matthew 6:24 ... No one can serve two masters. Either you will hate the one and love the other, or you will be devoted to the one and despise the other. You cannot serve both God and money."*

"It sounds like the Bible warns people about money quite often," Rachel said. "Y'all have been hitting me with this one-two punch since we arrived."

"That's true," Jerry said. "Jesus actually talked more about money than just about anything else."

"Humph," Rachel snorted. "Now that surprises me."

"Oh, it's not for the reasons you're thinking," Irene said. "It's because Jesus knows the human heart and He knows how easily money can become an idol. It's not that He needs anyone's money—it's much bigger than that. The Lord knows that humans have the tendency to use money to give them a false sense of control in their life and He just won't stand for that."

"Well ... I suppose that makes sense. It seems like the fear of losing control is a fear most humans have in some form or another."

"Please remember this," Irene continued. "Materialism—like accumulating lots of wealth for yourself—is one of the hallmarks of humanism."

"It bears noting once again," Jerry said. "That Satan often uses more than one idol against each person to tempt them. For example, those who value humanism often display worldly traits in unison."

"Like what?" said Rachel.

"Like striving for an abundance of wealth for yourself, complete sexual freedom, obsession with leisure activities or pursuits, etc. It's all about each person and what *they* desire."

"Oh, I'm sure the rest of the idols we're examining today are part of this equation also. In fact, I'd be surprised if Satan didn't tailor his attacks on people based on several concurrent temptations."

"You don't know how right you are," said Jerry. "In the spiritual war down on Earth, an army of demons study humans and often devise a personal recipe of temptations to entice people to reject or focus on something or someone other than God. When this happens, the results evolve into a garden of idols in their life. As you know, these sinful things block the real love of God. As we continue to ascend the mountain, you'll see exactly what I mean."

"That was pretty eloquent for an angel," Rachel joked.

Jerry laughed. "I'm glad to help."

They were all quiet for a moment.

"In all seriousness," Irene said. "When anyone elevates something like my idol of wealth above God, we essentially place our dependence on it—whether we realize it or not. The reason why is that the sinful human tendency is to recoil at not being in total control of our life. People hate the lack of control because it dethrones us as god of our own world. That, my friend, is the essence of the ongoing struggle between God and mankind—control."

"Everyone has a type of Jesus in their life," Jerry said. "To some like Irene, it was her wealth. Like we discussed with the previous ladies, they all had other types of a false Jesus they came to depend on. So the real question for every single person is this—*who's your Jesus?*"

Rachel shook her head. "I'm not following you on that."

The angel now had a serious expression on his face. "Only Jesus Christ can save someone. *That's what I mean.* When someone pledges their allegiance to someone or something besides the Lord, they're placing their eternal fate on something that cannot carry them over the chasm of death into eternal life. This is an enormous mistake."

"The difficult part about my dependence on wealth," Irene said. "Is that I just couldn't picture my life without the comfort of a high-society lifestyle. When you think about it, that's as absurd as it is self-absorbed when you consider how many people in the world don't even know where their next meal is coming from."

"I can definitely see that," Rachel said. "So is it fair to say that how much wealth someone acquires is completely in God's hands?"

"That and everything else," said Jerry. "Let's go ahead and talk about the extreme biblical story of Job. I think this will help lend some perspective to our discussion."

Rachel nodded. "Even though my biblical knowledge when I died wasn't very strong, I do remember the story of Job. In fact, I'll have to admit, I even used to—"

"Let me guess," Jerry interrupted. "Your previously humanistic position was to ask why God was so cruel to allow Job to suffer like that. Am I right?"

Rachel shrugged. "You read my mind."

"Not exactly," Jerry said, shaking his head. "I merely recognize one of Satan's favorite attacks on the Bible. It's nothing new, my dear."

"No one should expect to be tested like Job was," Irene added. "If someone can simply comprehend the fact that God is God and not some divine sugar daddy, and that whatever happens according to His will is His business, then someone can come to understand the Lord. One of the things I learned in studying the book of Job is that God doesn't answer to any of us. I also know that He's always working behind the scenes for the good of His kingdom."

"In the extreme example of Job," Jerry said. "He never lost faith throughout his horrible tribulations. Yes, Job was disheartened and his own friends let him down, but his relationship with God is one for the ages. Like Irene said, Job's story is a dire example, so others shouldn't expect to experience such horrible things in their life."

Rachel chuckled. "That's good to hear."

"Think of it this way. Job's position has already been filled in biblical history. Suggesting that someone else might also suffer like that is extremely unlikely."

Rachel was quiet for a few moments.

"Now that I'm thinking about it," she said. "If wealth is so valuable and enviable, then how come so many people who win the lottery end up losing all of it—and sometimes more?"

"Good point," Jerry said. "In the lives of most lottery winners, the sudden influx of a huge amount of wealth turns out to not be the type of Jesus they thought it would be when they discovered the winning ticket."

"Yes, but it doesn't happen that way for everyone," Irene said. "Some people are wise and use their money properly. In fact, I often still think about how much I'd like to go back to Earth and use my wealth to God's glory, not my own. I can assure you, things would be vastly different."

Jerry nodded. "That's the lament virtually all people have when they've squandered their time on Earth to serve God. Trust me, it's a common story up here. The key for all people while they're still on Earth is to begin storing their spiritual treasures in Heaven. When someone does that, they won't have to look back when they get here and wish they had used their time and resources for God instead of themself."

"That's where faith comes in," Irene said. "Faith in Christ is more important than any temporary riches down on Earth."

"I see," Rachel said. "So if you could say one thing to your friends on Earth, what would it be?"

Irene grinned. "I've actually thought about that many, many times. I'd say this: *1 Timothy 6:17 ... Command those who are rich in this present world not to be arrogant nor to put their hope in wealth, which is so uncertain, but to put their hope in God, who richly provides us with everything for our enjoyment.*"

"Oooo, that's a good one."

"You know, when I think of the many outlandish spending sprees I used to go on, I can't help but to wonder what good I could have done with that money if I hadn't been so greedy. Unfortunately, this wisdom came to me at the end of my life when it was mostly too late."

"Join the club," Jerry mused. "There's nothing new under the sun."

"What do you mean by that?" said Rachel.

"Do you remember what I said earlier about learning more about King Solomon as we climbed the mountain?"

"I do."

"Well, now's the time to continue that process. To that end, let me say that King Solomon was reputed to be the wisest man who ever lived—besides Jesus Christ, of course. He was also the richest. Yet, when we examine the book of Ecclesiastes, which he wrote towards the end of his life, we see a man who saw nothing but futility in his earthly ways."

"Didn't you give me a passage from Ecclesiastes on the way here?"

"I did. Let me repeat it: *Ecclesiastes 5:10 ... Whoever loves money never has enough; whoever loves wealth is never satisfied with their income. This too is meaningless.*"

"Now I see why you used that verse," said Rachel.

Irene nodded. "It really hits you between the eyes."

"And one other thing about Solomon," Jerry said. "He was rich, wise, and had hundreds of wives and concubines. He also had tremendous power and could do most anything he wanted to. But when you see the wisdom from the book of Ecclesiastes, Solomon realized that money, sex, wisdom, and power were nothing when compared to the holiness of God. Trust me when I tell you this. When you examine most of our lessons today, you'll see that the man,

Solomon, who had it all from the worldly perspective, thought it was all futile apart from the Lord."

"I'll be sure to keep that in mind," said Rachel. "So Irene, do you have any other pearls of wisdom for me today?"

"I do," Irene said. "The idol of wealth dulled my sense of the divine and created a chasm that prevented me from finding the real love of God for most of my life. However, I've been forgiven for my sins—and that's why I'm here. I just cannot tell you enough times how important it is that people who are blessed with wealth should use it for eternal things, not just temporary pleasures. As I look back on my life on Earth, it came and went so quickly, I can hardly believe it. The older one gets, the closer they get to leaving Earth and entering their forever home. How you use your money matters because it demonstrates where your heart is."

"I understand," Rachel said. "In a strangely divine way, I feel like I'm the luckiest woman in the world because I was fortunate enough to have surrendered my life to Jesus Christ just before I passed away. Thank God for the angel Mick who came and visited me."

Irene grinned. "Like I said earlier, I had a similar, blessed experience with Mick. Although it was pretty incredible, very few people are blessed to receive a visit from an angel like we both did."

"Oh, we-angels are all over the place," Jerry said. "But most of us operate from the spiritual realm. You ladies just got lucky to encounter an angel like Mick in-person before you entered Heaven."

Rachel grinned. "Don't forget that you and I also saw each other several times when I was growing up, Jerry. As I look back on it now, that's pretty neat to think about."

"You're so right," the angel agreed. "It was my honor."

Irene stood up. "Anyway, as a veteran of Heaven, I'm here to say that people should concentrate on Jesus Christ instead of their selfish goals to attain wealth. Money can only provide temporary pleasure at best. At worst, it'll certainly dull one's sense of the divine."

"I'm onboard with that," Rachel said.

"Very well," Jerry said, also standing up. "Rachel, we need to head to our next appointment."

11
POWER

"But Gideon told them, 'I will not rule over you, nor will my son rule over you. The Lord will rule over you.'"
Judges 8:23

As Rachel and Jerry left Irene's cottage behind and continued climbing the mountain, the trail gradually returned to a more enclosed appearance as the flat plateau gave way to heavy forest once again. The dense green trees towered above as a shroud of light fog gradually descended upon them. The fog was cool and slightly moist on Rachel's skin; providing an interesting sense of serenity.

"So who do we have next on our agenda?" she said.

"Next up is Martha. To set the stage for her testimony, I'll start you off with *1 John 4:20 ... Whoever claims to love God yet hates a brother or sister is a liar. For whoever does not love their brother and sister, whom they have seen, cannot love God, whom they have not seen.*"

"I notice you often quote from the book of 1 John 4."

"I'm pleased you're seeing that pattern, dear. There's lots of good information about love in that chapter."

Rachel chuckled. "Can we call this journey, *everything you wanted to know about love and idols?*"

"I wouldn't argue with that. All joking aside, however, it's pretty serious how idols arise out of temptations. As you've noticed, that's precisely what our walk of discovery is centered on."

"You've certainly made that abundantly clear many, many times today. Anyway, can I assume you're going to give me an idol-related passage next?"

"Why do you say that?"

"Because the first one was obviously about love."

"Very good," Jerry said, nodding. "The idol passage is this: *Isaiah 46:5 ... With whom will you compare me or count me equal? To whom will you liken me that we may be compared?*"

"I'm not sure I'm following you on that one."

"Oh, c'mon Rachel. This is about God being compared to idols."She was quiet for a moment. "Can you repeat that?"

Jerry did so.

"Okay, I see that now. But in order to figure out Martha's idol, I'll need that third passage to give me a stronger hint."

"Okay, here ya go ... *2 Kings 19:26 ... Their people, drained of power, are dismayed and put to shame. They are like plants in the field, like tender green shoots, like grass sprouting on the roof, scorched before it grows up.*"

Rachel shook her head. "I think you've stumped me on this one."

"It's rather simple," the angel said. "Martha's story is about her obsession with power."

"Power?"

"That's it. You see, the problem with having power over people is that it often masquerades as altruism. That's certainly the case in the story of my good friend Martha—"

"Is that her place?" Rachel interrupted, pointing to her right.

"As a matter of fact, it is," Jerry said. "Let's head that way."

The trail jogged right as the fog began to thin out. There, directly in front of them, was a beautiful white house. An elongated rectangular garden fronted the ornate home, while plush flower beds dotted its perimeter.

They exited the trail.

As Rachel and Jerry neared the house, a beautiful African-American woman stood up from one of the several white rocking chairs adorning the front porch. She waved them over. Martha smiled broadly and was obviously very excited to receiver her visitors.

When they arrived at the bottom of the stairs to the porch, Martha warmly met them and embraced Rachel as if she had known her all of her life.

"Welcome to my home," Martha said, excitedly. "I've been eagerly waiting for you to arrive, Rachel."

"Thanks for having us," Rachel said.

Martha glanced over at Jerry. "Can I get y'all some lemonade?"

Jerry turned towards Rachel. "Trust me. You don't want to miss out on Martha's magnificent lemonade."

"Sounds good," Rachel said.

Martha hooked her arms into both Rachel and Jerry, leading them up the stairs. She then said, "Now this may sound strange, but I sure wish I had stuck with selling lemonade to earn my living when I was down on Earth. Instead, I chose the wicked inferno of politics. Unfortunately, I spent most of my adult life toiling in that dark arena. I believe I would've been much more focused on the Lord if I had avoided politics and just sold some refreshing lemonade. Instead, my aspirations for power became my obsession."

They all sat down on three rockers in a semi-circle.

"That's a powerful statement," Rachel said. "Are you saying the whole political scene is bad?"

Martha shook her head. "Not necessarily. The problem with politics is that it's one of Satan's most cherished playgrounds. Actually, all of your visits today are areas where Satan has an enormous amount of influence with his lies, deceit, and treachery."

"Can you explain that further?"

"Sure," Martha said. "Let's use my example. I believe that many of the people—perhaps even most of those who enter the political arena have good intentions to help others. The problem is that money always wins in the end. You see, politics and money are bedfellows which fit together like peas in a pod. Actually, this may surprise you, but Irene and I were very good friends down on Earth. We also both entered Heaven about the same time, not long ago."

"Wow, that's interesting," Rachel said. "I never considered the possibility that any of you ladies might have known each other before."

Jerry quickly added, "We actually have several surprises in store for you in the near future, Rachel. Please be patient." She grinned. "It'll be hard to top what I've already seen and heard."

"So what happened to me," Martha continued. "Is that I entered the battlefield of politics with some pretty lofty goals and a ton of ambition. The problem was that I wasn't grounded enough in my faith to take on the enormous demonic army which is firmly entrenched in the world of politics. I was so naïve; I thought my altruistic intentions could carry me into battle and would help me to win."

"What exactly did you want to win?" said Rachel.

"I had my sights set on becoming the first female President of the United States."

"Wow," said Rachel, whistling. "That's a pretty lofty goal. In my later years, I didn't pay much attention to politics, so I'm afraid I don't know who you were. I hope you're not offended."

"That's okay, honey. I didn't know who I was either. I understand you were much older than I when you died, right?"

"I was seventy-five," Rachel said. "How old were you?"

Martha shook her head. "I was only forty-two. I died in a car accident in Washington DC."

"I see. Were you a member of Congress or something?"

"I was a U.S. Senator from a state up in the northeast."

"So how did you find your way to Jesus Christ?"

Martha shrugged. "Oh, I attended church for my entire life," she said. "I even used to sing in the choir. The problem was that to me, church was more of a social event than a spiritual encounter. Don't get me wrong—I believed in God and all. And I certainly felt holy when I went to church and did churchy things. But deep inside, the god I worshipped was me; along with my humongous ambition."

"I see. It doesn't sound like your life was headed in the right direction—towards Heaven. So what changed? Something must've happened to change your life."

An angel suddenly appeared from the front door with a tray of lemonade. He quietly brought the tray over and handed a glass to each of them before departing.

Martha nodded. "Something did change, but please bear with me and I'll get to that in a moment."

"That'll work."

"After years of determination in school that I was going to escape my poor upbringing, I went to college and ended up with a Master's degree in political science. Since my minor was in speech, I was well-prepared to run for office. It seems that I was quite the orator back in the day, and I was very convincing when I spoke. Anyway, it started with the state house of representatives, and soon thereafter turned into the U.S. House. After my predecessor in the U.S. Senate retired, I switched over and won my senatorial election in a landslide. With all of those achievements, I thought I was the most powerful woman in the world—with nothing to stop me from making history by one day taking the White House."

"That's interesting."

"Fortunately for me, however, when I was home on break from Washington, I ran into a little old lady from my original home district. It was then that everything changed in my life."

"What exactly caused everything to change?"

"A wonderful lady named Agnes ran into me at a church luncheon and took me aside to give me some unsolicited advice. That encounter ended up becoming an earthquake in my previous spiritual life. Every false idea I had about Jesus Christ suddenly crumbled to the ground."

"So what happened? What did she say to you?"

"She simply hit me with an incredible verse. Which, by the way, she recited from memory. She said it had been her life's focus since meeting a nice bald gentleman when she was a young girl. Since Agnes was in her eighties, I listened to her very closely. I figured she had some wisdom which could be valuable."

Rachel shrugged. "So what was the verse?"

"It's *Philippians 2:3 ... Do nothing out of selfish ambition or vain conceit. Rather, in humility value others above yourselves.*"

"Ahhh, I see. Tell me something. Why do you think it hit you that hard?"

Martha looked intently at Rachel and said, "God's word cut right through my pride like a hot knife slicing through butter. From the very heart of God and from the mouth of this little old lady came the sword that sliced my heart into pieces and convicted me that I was trying to attain power for my own ego, not God's glory. And certainly not for my constituents."

"Wow. That's very powerful. I suppose the 'selfish ambition' part is what hit you the hardest?"

Martha nodded. "It did. Sadly, it made me realize I was valuing myself above others. I also realized that I wanted more and more power so I could feed the furnace of my own covetous ego. My selfish intentions were masked by the big fat lie that I was in office to help others."

They were quiet for a few moments before Rachel said, "I suppose whoever that 'bald man' was in Agnes's past ended up helping you later on in your life. How neat is that?"

Martha smiled widely. "It's pretty incredible. Actually, that bald man who spoke to Agnes is also your guide today—our angel friend, Jerry."

Rachel's mouth dropped open as she looked at Jerry. "Really???"

Jerry shrugged. "Ladies, please consider *Psalm 91:11 … For he will command his angels concerning you to guard you in all your ways*. It shouldn't be a surprise that I've been looking after the both of you for many decades now."

They were quiet as everyone took a sip of their lemonade.

"Getting back to what that passage in Philippians did to convict my heart," Martha said. "I could see that my ambition was the fuel for the engine of my lust for power. Without realizing it, after I was elected to my first public office, I started manipulating people in order to get what I wanted; not what was good for them or my district. In other words, people became pawns in my little game of politics. It's most unfortunate that what started out as good intentions to *serve* the people, turned into my selfish ambition to *control* the people. In truth, that's what my political career evolved into. I think most politicians unwittingly follow that same, wrongful script that Satan entraps them with."

Rachel nodded. "So you're saying that your political career was corrupted by the sin of your ambition for power?"

"Yes, dear. But there's more. As I blindly moved ahead in my political career—without regard to God and the Bible—I ended up acquiring some terrible habits along the way."

"Such as—?"

"Such as the illusion of self-sufficiency, the attitude of superiority, and the pride of ability."

Rachel shook her head. "Whoa—let's take those one at a time. Can you first elaborate on the illusion of self-sufficiency?"

"Certainly. The problem with the idol of power is that the idea of gaining it for the good of others is almost always a lie. In fact, once you've started down the trail of lusting for power, it's actually very much like being sucked into a cult."

"In what way?"

"In the beginning, those who fall victim to cults are often given false information about what the cult actually stands for. It's usually much later on when you fall deeper into their trap that you figure out their nefarious intentions. By the time you discover you've been snookered by lies, you're in too deep and have a difficult time finding your way out. That's what happened in my case. My political donors essentially put me in office. Once I was settled in, they came-a-calling for what they wanted. I should have known that powerful people who don't love God always expect a quid-pro-quo when doing something for you, or when they give you lots of money."

"Okay, so how does that fit in with self-sufficiency?"

Martha shook her head. "By the time I realized I was no longer in control of my political life, it was too late. You see, I got into politics in an effort to save the world. During the process, I felt like that would ensure I'd never be poor again. So instead of depending on the Lord for my provision, I wanted to amass my own riches so I would never want for anything ever again. Unfortunately, Satan uses this tactic on poor folks all the time."

"I see. So your sin started with the desire to not have to depend on God, right?"

"Basically, that's right. Instead of depending on God, I wanted to depend completely on myself. Like I said, self-sufficiency is nothing but an illusion."

Rachel nodded. "Okay, I can see that now. So what about the next one—the attitude of superiority?"

"Oh, this one is straight-up narcissism, sweetie. Ironically, I used to be a pretty humble person. But as I saw my name in lights and had so many people telling me how wonderful I was, all of that praise slowly began to sink in and I started believing my own press."

"So you stopped valuing others above yourself, just like the Philippians passage warns against?"

"You've got it," Martha said. "It was only a couple of months after Agnes took me aside that I died in the car accident. Before Agnes, I was comfortable and lived in a bubble of my own ego. After that, my soul was convicted by my sin and every day was a spiritual battle between me not wanting to let go of my worldly life, and the Holy Spirit penetrating my heart. Fortunately, God ultimately got through to me."

"That's an incredible testimony," Rachel said. "So what about the third item—the pride of ability?"

"Let me read you something to answer that. It's *John 5:30 ... By myself I can do nothing; I judge only as I hear, and my judgment is just, for I seek not to please myself but him who sent me....*"

"Please—go on."

Martha smiled. "I can do nothing apart from Jesus Christ. He gave me the life and the talents I have. Who was I to think I could just discard Him and become—"

"Let me guess," Rachel interrupted. "And become the god of your own world—in complete control, above others, and filled with pride. Am I right?"

"You are indeed, dear."

"I think it bears noting," Jerry added. "That one's goal in life shouldn't be to try to save the world, which is hopelessly lost. Instead, you should spend your time telling others about the only safe exit door on Earth, which is Jesus Christ. It's a natural human instinct to set up a perfect world, which is what people in power often endeavor to do. But as it stands now, this world belongs to Satan and is filled with sin. One day, the current Earth will be put away and radically changed when Jesus Christ returns."

Rachel nodded. "So you're saying that striving to attain power is wrong?"

"For the most part, yes," Jerry said. "It breaks down like this … trying to attain power is almost always a ruse for someone trying to feed their ego. So instead of pursuing worldly power, Christians are called to spread the Gospel."

"So what's the bottom line?" said Rachel.

"Instead of pursuing power, followers of Christ should instead use their *influence* as the fuel for their efforts, not power."

"And how does one attain influence?" said Rachel.

Jerry looked at both ladies intently. "Righteous influence is attained by loving your neighbor, studying the Bible, and praying fervently every day. When you do this, your focus moves away from your own selfish desires and moves into being a proper son or daughter of the Most High God."

"If I knew back then what I know now," Martha said. "I would have used my influence to help bring others here to Heaven. Instead, I tried to use my power to make history and control a broken world. That's what the bottom line in my story is."

Rachel grinned. "I just realized something very interesting."

"Oh, what's that?" said Martha.

"You ended up living in a white house here in Heaven. Although it's not the white house you were striving for when you were down on Earth, I'm sure this one is far better."

Martha laughed heartily. "You bet it is! I'm glad you've come so far in such a short time, Rachel."

"Thanks."

"Listen, dear," Martha continued. "Although I never made it to the White House on Earth, another wise person once did. His name was Abraham Lincoln. He's quoted as once saying, 'nearly all men can stand adversity, but if you want to test a man's character, give him power.'"

Rachel nodded. "That's right on the money, so to speak."

Martha laughed. "It sure is."

"I'd like to add something," Jerry said. "Earthly kingdoms and kings come and go. Only Jesus Christ is forever. Unfortunately, the Bible is full of individuals who came into power and felt invincible. Ultimately, as it is with all worldly endeavors, their power waned and they faded into either history or obscurity."

"I believe Jerry gave you a verse from 2 Kings on the way here," Martha said to Rachel. "Do you remember it?"

"I do."

"In that passage, Isaiah prophesied the fall of Sennacherib—the king of Assyria. At the time, Sennacherib felt like nothing could take him down. But the Lord knew better."

"That's interesting," Rachel said. "I'm sure that throughout history, many kings felt like they would reign forever."

"How true," Martha said. "But since we serve the King of kings, our situation is different."

"How so?"

"When it gets down to it, those who don't serve God and only serve themself are actually turning their backs on righteousness. To prove my point, I give you *Amos 5:7* ... *There are those who turn justice into bitterness and cast righteousness to the ground.*"

Rachel was quiet for a moment. "In thinking about all of this, isn't it also true that politics are played in more than just public office? Isn't it true that this kind of lust for power exists in the corporate world as well?"

Martha chuckled. "You're right about that, sweetie. The lust for power actually exists in all kinds of places—the workplace, volunteer organizations, little league sports, and even homeowners associations. Anywhere you have people, you have the sinful human propensity to desire gaining control or power over others. I'm afraid it's just the way of the fallen world."

"Yes, but things are different up here in Heaven," Rachel said. "And I'm sure glad of that."

"I am too," Martha said, taking a relaxed sip of her lemonade. "I am too...."

12
FAME

**"For they will take nothing with them when they die,
their splendor will not descend with them."
Psalm 49:17**

Martha escorted her guests back to the trail by way of her lovely garden. During their stroll, Rachel paused several times to take in the incredible aroma of the exotic flowers, which exploded with the amazing colors, vibrancy, and bouquet of their Creator's magnificent handiwork.

As they reached the trail, Martha said, "I hope you enjoy your visit with Mary. For what it's worth, I think you're coming along very well, Rachel."

"Thanks so much," Rachel said. "I'm sure we'll have a great time."

Jerry and Rachel waved, then turned and continued their march up the mountain.

The wooded area on the trail returned to being the norm, but the fog had lifted in this particular section. Glorious beams of light now pierced their way down to the forest floor, like spotlights on a stage.

After a few minutes, Rachel said, "We just said goodbye to Martha, and now we're about to visit a sister named Mary. Wasn't there a Martha and Mary in the Bible?"

Jerry chuckled. "There sure was. That's just another one of God's wonderful attributes people rarely think about."

"Oh—what's that?"

"God has an incredible sense of humor. Hey, without the Lord, humor wouldn't exist at all. Have you ever considered that?"

"Hmmm … I suppose you're right."

"Soooo," Jerry said. "Before we get to Mary's place, I'm going to switch things up and attempt to stump you again. Are you ready?"

"I am."

"Okay, the first one is *Habakkuk 2:4* … '*See, the enemy is puffed up; his desires are not upright—but the righteous person will live by his faithfulness.*"

"I have no clue. Keep going."

"Will do. The next one is *Obadiah 1:3* … *The pride of your heart has deceived you, you who live in the clefts of the rocks and make your home on the heights, you who say to yourself, 'Who can bring me down to the ground?*"

Rachel shrugged. "What—nothing specific on love or idols?" "The lesson's not over yet."

"Oh, okay. So we're talking about being puffed up and the pride of the human heart. I still don't have enough information to make a guess about our next topic."

Jerry nodded. "Okay, let's try this one: *Esther 1:7* … *Wine was served in goblets of gold, each one different from the other, and the royal wine was abundant, in keeping with the king's liberality.*"

Rachel chuckled. "Although I think the passages are wonderful, it seems you've now stumped me again."

"Now, now, now," Jerry said. "I'll admit, this one is pretty difficult to figure out; given the clues thus far. But let's see if I can lead you to the answer."

Rachel grabbed Jerry's arm. "It's your show, Jerry. As long as I never have to face sin or death ever again, everything's fine with me."

"Oh, I can assure you of that. You'll never have to live in a world with evil ever again. That's for sure. God has promised it."

"That's fantastic."

"Okay, then. In the verses just cited, we're seeing some imbedded clues. In the first passage, the key words are that the person's desires were not upright or righteous and they were puffed up. Let's start with that. Then, we see that pride has deceived people who think God can't bring them down a notch after they've raised themselves up in their own eyes. After that, we see the result of a desire for a lavish lifestyle…."

"Hmmm," Rachel mumbled. "Given that we've already talked about wealth … and since we're talking about something within the lust of the eyes ... did Mary's idol have something to do with her wanting to be royalty or famous ... or something like that?"

"That's it! Mary's idol was her desire for fame."

"Wow—that was a lucky guess."

Jerry chuckled. "As far as I can tell, luck still counts on the scoreboard."

Rachel looked quizzical for a moment. "Wait a minute. How do you angels know so much about humanity and our culture down on Earth? I've been wondering about that all day."

"That's merely our job, my dear. We can't serve humans if we don't study and understand them, can we?"

"Oh ... I suppose not."

"Don't forget now," Jerry said. "The enemy also makes a habit out of studying humans. While it's the job of holy angels to serve and protect the sons and daughters of God, I'm afraid Satan's demonic army is charged with doing just the opposite."

"That must be why there's so many temptations. It seems that demons are good at cooking up special recipes to corrupt God's children. I can definitely see how this happened in my own life. You know, my eyes are now opening to the fact that several of these idols have been used in combination against both me and the other ladies."

"Indeed. As we make our way to the top of the mountain, you'll see more and more how this simple-but-evil gameplan has been utilized against humanity for a long time now."

As Rachel and Jerry rounded a turn to their left, a broad opening in the trees appeared. There, right in the middle of an open space on the forest's floor, was a large picnic table with a beautiful lady sitting comfortably on one side of it.

Mary had long black hair and a warm smile, which she sported gleefully as she waved them over.

"Greetings Rachel," Mary said, also nodding at Jerry as they arrived. "Please join me and have a seat."

"Will do," Rachel said, reaching across the table to take hands their newest hostess. "Thanks for taking the time to visit with me today."

"The pleasure's all mine," said Mary.

"Let me lead us off," Jerry began. "By saying that Rachel actually figured out your idol before we arrived."

"Really?" said Mary, surprised. "As the clues get harder, not many of our visitors can figure out these things. You must be a natural at this."

"Oh, I don't know about that," said Rachel. "But I'm definitely seeing the result of my lack of focus on Christ and how dangerous it was during my life on Earth. If I could go back, I feel like I'd be pretty good at serving the Lord ... instead of myself."

"Of course, we on the mountain all feel that way, my friend. The key for anyone still down on Earth is to serve God while they still can."

"Soooo," Jerry added. "Since I gave Rachel her initial three verses, would you mind, Mary, providing the love and idols renderings?"

"You betcha," said Mary. "The first one is *Isaiah 44:9 ... All who make idols are nothing, and the things they treasure are worthless. Those who would speak up for them are blind; they are ignorant, to their own shame.*"

"That was me for sure," Rachel said.

"And I, also," Mary said. "The next one is from—"

"Let me guess," Rachel interrupted. "It's from 1 John 4."

"It sure is—very good. Here goes: *1 John 4:7 ... Dear friends, let us love one another, for love comes from God. Everyone who loves has been born of God and knows God.*"

"Okay," Rachel said. "So what can you tell me about the perils of fame, Mary? What's your story?"

"My testimony is simple. When I was a little girl, my parents felt that since I was attractive and loved the theater, I should consider becoming an actress. And that's exactly what I did. Unfortunately, they didn't provide me with enough spiritual grounding along my journey, so I wasn't prepared to withstand all of the pitfalls of fame."

"Well, this is starting off very interestingly. I also had parents who often told me I should move to Hollywood and become a famous actress."

"Oh, there's nothing wrong with acting per se, Rachel. But if someone's going to venture into one of Satan's beloved playgrounds, they must be prepared for the ensuing spiritual battles. If someone is unprepared for this kind of warfare, they'll be absolutely consumed by it. Trust me, I was nowhere near ready for the spiritual buzz saw I ran into due to my choice of career."

"Can you explain further? I find this very interesting."

Mary shook her head. "Just like all idols, I thought that becoming famous would somehow become my salvation in life. Do you remember any of the songs about fame that have filled the airwaves over the years?"

"I sure do."

"So many songs and movies seem to say the same thing. They point you towards the glory of attaining fame and stardom so that your name can live forever. Some even seem to indicate that attaining fame will somehow help you make it to heaven. I'm sorry, but that's just not true."

"No, it sure isn't."

"Listen, my story isn't about condemning anything in particular. It's about demonstrating just how incongruent the love of fame is with the reality of Heaven and trusting alone in Jesus Christ as your Savior. There are many things in the world of entertainment that glorify human fame. I disagree with all of them."

"I see. So when did you die?"

"I died of a drug overdose last year when I was only thirty-seven years old."

"A drug overdose? Really?"

"Unfortunately, yes. Every single idol you've seen thus far was involved in the temptation-laden formula against me—plus some of the ones you haven't seen yet. It's like Satan dropped all of these temptations into his evil crock pot and simmered them for many years. The end result was that the hole in my soul was so huge, the drug overdose was inevitable. Mine is a sad, but all-too-familiar story." Rachel nodded. "It seems that the lust for fame is as intoxicating as anything else I've seen today—perhaps even more."

"And that's the problem," Mary said. "Every one of these temptations that become idols have special qualities that corrupt people. In the case of fame, it's the overpowering lust for your name and accomplishments to live forever. In truth, wanting your name to be up in lights is almost always a way to replace the Holy Spirit in your life."

"What do you mean by that? How can fame replace God?"

"It's easy. That's actually what every idol attempts to do—replace God's righteous place in your heart and in your life."

"Wait a minute," Rachel said. "I can see where these idols were a spiritual minefield, for sure. But you're claiming that your lust for fame was actually an attempt to replace God in your life?"

"Of course. All idols do that. My self-focus was so intense; the god who took over the throne in my life was *me*."

"It bears noting," Jerry added. "That Satan doesn't need for you to believe in him to defeat you. All he needs is for you to not reach out to Jesus Christ for forgiveness of your sins. In the case of people who lust for fame, who would even imagine they need forgiveness for anything at all? If you think of yourself as the god of your own world, you'll never even consider the fact that you might need to be forgiven for anything. From that humanistic perspective, God is actually subservient to you."

"To Jerry's point," said Mary. "Even the tiniest notion that I was a sinner in need of a savior was not only ridiculous, it was extremely offensive to my formerly prideful mindset."

"So what changed your heart?" said Rachel.

"One day, my father came to see me at my house in Hollywood. After all of my years of living under the shadow of the kingdom of idols, I'm fortunate that my dad found his way to the Cross and repented of his sins to become a follower of Jesus Christ. By then, my mom had already passed away. At that point, dad was very lonely and some friends gave him the Gospel message. It was just that simple— but it changed everything for him ... and fortunately, for me also."

Rachel nodded. "So what happened when your dad came to see you and told you about Jesus?"

"At first, I'm sad to say, I almost threw him out of my house. But things calmed down after that and we spent some quality time together. As we shared things with each other that week, my pride gradually began to erode. Although I really can't explain it, something was just different during that time dad and I spent together."

"Why do you think that is?"

"It's probably because he was a good listener and didn't jump down my throat for all of the foolish things I said and did. After he left, my conscience started objecting to my worldly lifestyle based on the seeds he had planted."

"So what changed things for you? I mean, didn't you say you died of a drug overdose?"

"I did," Mary said, nodding. "The mistake I made was that after I hit a spiritual rock bottom soon after dad's visit, I called him in Texas and he led me to confess my sins and repent of them—over the phone, of all things. Fortunately, he didn't wait and my heart changed in that very moment. However, I didn't move as quickly to remove the unsavory elements from my life, so it ended in tragedy."

"Unsavory elements? What—do you mean your partying friends?"

"Yes. Even though my heart had changed and I knew I was a sinner who couldn't live without Christ in my life, I failed to make the immediate changes in my lifestyle. These changes were absolutely necessary to remove the temptations of my former way of living. Looking back on it, I was a fool because my faith was new and I didn't understand how Satan attacks people with his spiritual weaponry."

"I see," said Rachel. "So let me ask you a question. Overall, do you think your move to Hollywood was a mistake? I mean, you achieved a decent level of fame and all, but do you think the culture there had something significant to do with your overall downfall?"

"Of course it did. Like I said, when I first moved out there, I was woefully unprepared to live in such a humanistic cesspool of ungodly narcissism. It was even worse when I turned to Christ. That change clashed greatly with the humanistic culture in the area."

"Those are some pretty strong words."

"I'm sorry, but it's the truth," Mary said. "No matter how much those who chase after fame don't want to hear this, human fame ends at the grave. Period. End of story. Human fame never lasts, and it certainly won't get you into Heaven."

"It bears noting," Jerry added. "That choosing the profession of acting—spiritually speaking—is virtually the same as other entertainment professions when it comes to the pitfalls of fame."

"For example—?" said Rachel.

"Well, professional sports for one," said Jerry. "Another one is the music industry. No matter what your talent is, the lust of the eyes to either become famous, win awards, and/or collect accolades from other people is an enormous temptation so many people desire."

"It's true," Mary said. "I was more concerned with the effects of my reputation and gaining admirers than I was to live an honorable life. I'm sad to say, I was so obsessed with gaining fame, I never married."

"That's probably better than what I did," said Rachel. "I actually married the wrong fella several times. I almost wonder if I should've avoided— "

"Oh, I disagree," Mary said. "At least you tried to achieve a proper relationship when you married; your bad choices for men notwithstanding. My problem was that I was searching for the perfect man who would fit into my neat little mold that would help my reputation and notoriety. As you can imagine, my quest for the right husband always ended in severe disappointment."

"It almost sounds like you were looking for a robot—not a husband."

Mary laughed heartily. "Indeed! The foolish image I had in my head of what I expected in a husband was a monumental disaster of epic proportions."

"Let me add this," Jerry said. "We see what God wants for His people in *1 Thessalonians 4:11 … and to make it your ambition to lead a quiet life: You should mind your own business and work with your hands, just as we told you.*"

"Ahhh," said Mary. "A simple life where I loved and served God is what my life on Earth should have been centered on. Instead, I lusted for reputation and fame. All I got for my efforts was a bunch of phony friends and utter sadness. I should've lived my whole life as my dad advised me to do, just before I died."

"Is your father still alive?" said Rachel.

"Yes, he's still down on Earth. I can't wait for the day he comes walking into Heaven so I can tell him how sorry I was for not ridding myself of my worldly lifestyle and phony friends. I can't imagine the pain he's gone through with having to bury a child."

"That's an overbearing pain for any parent," said Jerry.

They were quiet for a moment.

"Now that we're talking about leaving someone behind," Rachel said. "I'm pretty sure the man I should've married—Harvey—is probably heartbroken at my passing. In fact, I doubt he even knows I repented of my sins and made it to Heaven."

"Hang on a minute," Jerry said. "We'll discuss that subject in-depth after a little while. We still have our agenda to finish today, so let's stay focused."

Rachel grinned. "Of course, Jerry. I'm very grateful for all of this. It's been an amazing journey up the mountain so far."

Mary nodded. "To wrap things up, I'd like to share something with you, Rachel. While lusting for human fame is certainly misguided and ultimately painful, sometimes certain people can achieve the right kind of fame by obeying God and by serving Him."

"That's interesting," Rachel said. "Do you have an example?"

"Of course. Let's look at the example of Joshua in the Old Testament. In particular, I often think of *Joshua 6:27 ... So the Lord was with Joshua, and his fame spread throughout the land.*"

"Oh, I see. You're saying that loyal servants of God can achieve the right kind of fame, right?"

"Not exactly," Mary said. "I'm saying that pursuing fame is always wrong. Instead, pursuing Christ is the only worthy thing to do. In the end, if you serve God and obey Him, you just may achieve a proper type of fame in God's eternal kingdom—if He so deems."

"How does that work?"

"From the humanistic perspective, if you try to achieve fame, you're probably only doing it for yourself and your ego. On the other hand, if your focus is on serving God, you just may achieve the right kind of fame in God's forever kingdom, which is much different than what is currently going on down on the fallen Earth."

"You know, that's something I find amazing," Rachel said. "When I turned to Jesus Christ, I became a daughter in God's forever kingdom. Since I now understand that everything on Earth will be gone one day, it makes sense to gear one's self towards the kingdom that will have no end."

"Amen," said Mary. "But I'm afraid our time is up. Here, let me show you the way towards your next appointment."

13
IMAGE

"In the same way, on the outside you appear to people as righteous but on the inside you are full of hypocrisy and wickedness."
Matthew 23:28

As Mary, Jerry, and Rachel stood up from the table, an effervescent aroma of pine settled into the clearing. A gentle breeze then entered the scene and led them back towards the trail, which Rachel and Jerry headed towards. Mary said her warm good-byes to the angel and his sojourner as the trail opened up before them once again, right behind the picnic table.

"That was a *great* visit," Rachel said to Jerry. "But I can't wait to see what subject will wrap up our lusts of the eyes temptations."

"I'll try to make this next one a little easier for you," Jerry said. "You've shown yourself to be a good student, so I'll lighten it up for you a bit. Without further adieu, let's start off with this: *Proverbs 29:25 ... Fear of man will prove to be a snare, but whoever trusts in the Lord is kept safe.*"

"Hmmm. Which part is more of a hint—the first or second part?"

"The first."

"Okay, gotcha. What's next?"

"Next we have the words of Jesus in *Matthew 11:19 ... The Son of Man came eating and drinking, and they say, 'Here is a glutton and a drunkard, a friend of tax collectors and sinners.' But wisdom is proved right by her deeds.*"

Rachel shook her head. "So far, this isn't getting any easier."

Jerry chuckled. "Okay, okay. The last one is a real slam dunk: *Colossians 1:15 … The Son is the image of the invisible God, the firstborn over all creation.*"

"Hmmm. While I think about this, who are we seeing next?"

"Our next hostess is Alice."

Rachel shrugged. "Okay, let me think about your clues before we arrive there."

"No problem. While you do that, check out this incredible vista…."

As they rounded a turn during their ascent, an astounding sight opened up on their right—an absolutely breathtaking ridge of snow-covered alpine trees, which framed a small valley below. Since this was such a unique panorama, Rachel knew this change signified something important about their next visit. This was confirmed when the trail started turning white with a beautiful blanket of snow. A light cloak of fluttering flurries began to descend as an overcast sky hovered overhead.

"Have you given our next subject any more thought?" said Jerry, breaking their peaceful silence.

"I have," Rachel said.

"Well—?"

"Your first two clues weren't quite enough. The third one gives me a good hint, but it's probably just a positive version of our next idol, because it talks about God. So if you don't mind, please provide me just a little more information."

"Sure thing. The first two verses had to do with appearance and perspective. The third one—"

"Okay, I've got it." Rachel interrupted. "I think Alice is going to teach me about someone's perception or public image."

"You've got it—image is our next topic."

"Very well. Hey, not to change the subject, but this snow is really pretty. Although it feels cool, I'm not cold at all. This is obviously different than my past experiences with the white stuff."

"Oh, I think it goes without saying that God adores certain things in His creation—especially snow. Some people on Earth mistakenly think of Heaven as somehow being less real than what you experience up here."

Rachel shook her head. "I'm seeing a reality in Heaven that's quite the opposite of conventional thinking. Heaven is much more intense than anything down on Earth—by far."

"Let's also not forget that Heaven is also a place of complete perfection," Jerry said. "All of the new citizens up here experience some level of awe when they first arrive here. In some cases, it's total astonishment."

"No doubt."

"Anyway, we're almost there."

Jerry led Rachel through a meticulously aligned row of short evergreen trees that had curiously pointed tops. When they arrived on the other side of the trees, a lovely park opened up on their left. Framing the back side of the park was the shear wall of the side of the mountain. Directly in front of them, standing in the shadow of the wall, was a centralized circular area with a blazing campfire in its center. Several pathways in the park led directly into the central area, where a beautiful woman with strawberry blonde hair in a pony-tail awaited them.

Alice waved them over.

"It's so nice to meet you Rachel," she said, embracing her visitor. Alice then gave Jerry's shoulder a gentle squeeze. "As usual Jerry, thanks for escorting our newest citizen here. I always enjoy sharing my story of victory over sin through Jesus Christ."

They all sat down.

"It's my pleasure," Jerry said. "So Rachel, I'll go ahead and lead us off before I give the floor over to Alice."

"Sounds good."

"The first thing as we finish up the subjects within the lusts of the eye is that if you'll remember, some of the defining characteristics of these idols is that they involve control and to whom you have allegiance. Now that we're about to move into the next phase, I'd like to whet your whistle with this one: *Psalm 20:7 ... Some trust in chariots and some in horses, but we trust in the name of the Lord our God."*

"That's interesting," said Rachel. "The word *trust* jumped out at me. Is that the point you're trying to make?"

"Essentially, yes," Alice said. "As you've progressed through Jerry's program, you've seen how these temptations and idols are used in combination with one another. As we discuss the idol of image, some of the aspects of it are actually shifting into the final phase of your journey."

Rachel shrugged. "What do you mean by that?"

"What you've heard thus far in this group has largely centered on control. The problem I had in building my selfish image was not only about control, but also in where and with whom I placed my trust. Of course, that was in me. It was always about me."

"Aren't all of these temptations and idols about filling our souls with substitutes for God?"

"They are," Alice admitted. "Let me go ahead and tell you my story. I think that'll help you understand."

"Okay. But first off, when did you die?"

"I died last year."

"And where did you live?"

"In a typical gated community in suburbia. My pride was so off the charts, I wouldn't settle for anything less than what I thought was perfection."

"Were you married?"

"But of course," said Alice. "To have the right image, it could be no other way."

"That makes sense."

"My husband was very successful and my three children were as perfect as I could make them be. Everything in my life was about how things looked to others."

"Okay, but how did you die?"

"I was killed in prison."

"In prison???" Rachel said, gasping. "Now *that's* a surprise."

Alice shook her head. "It shouldn't be. Let me explain. My husband was very successful in the investment business. My basic job in our family was to present him to the world as the perfect husband with the perfect family and the perfect life. Somehow, we both felt like this would promote his image and ultimately make us more money. Anyway, everything worked like a charm for many years until something entered my life and attempted to fill the huge hole in my heart. Unfortunately, that 'something' was the beginning of my undoing."

"Oh—what was that?"

"I started smoking crack cocaine."

"Really? So you had what many people would consider to be the perfect life in suburbia, but you turned to drugs?"

"I did. When I finally figured out that doing everything to maintain a certain false image in my life was actually wearing down my soul, I absolutely panicked. And since I didn't have Jesus Christ to fill that void, my hunger had to be satisfied in a worldly way. Unfortunately, that way was with drugs."

"Ahhh," Rachel exclaimed. "Now I see. Your image idol was so imbedded in your soul, you used another idol—hunger—to fill the void caused by the pressure and the stress. And thus, a lethal concoction was born."

"That's an interesting way of putting it," Jerry added.

"Unfortunately, that's how Satan works," Alice said. "The doctor of lies wrote a sinful prescription for me and I unwittingly filled it."

Rachel shook her head. "So how did you end up in prison?"

"It started off innocently enough. I needed to hide my drug use from my husband, so I took a part-time job with a local charitible organization— "

"Why did you need to hide it from your husband?"

"Oh, he wouldn't have tolerated the image of a lowly crack smoker for his wife. Unfortunately, my image idol was actually an unspoken-but-evil partnership with my former husband. And speaking of him, I understand he's now remarried and is doing the same thing to his new wife."

"Wow," said Rachel. "So what about your prison stint?"

"Oh yeah," said Alice. "After awhile, my part time income wasn't enough to cover my burgeoning drug use, so I began to siphon money away from the organization I worked for. After about two years, they found me out and I ended up going to prison for embezzlement."

"I see. So was prison rough?"

"It was as close to rock bottom as I could have possibly imagined back then. However, something wonderful actually happened in that year of living in prison Hell."

"Oh—what was that?"

"One of the ladies in my cell block began to read the Bible to me. After a few months of that, my pride was knocked against the ropes and the Holy Spirit penetrated my sinful heart."

Rachel whistled. "Wow. So it took going to prison for you to repent of your sins and surrender your life to Christ?"

"That's right. During my trial, my humiliation was so intense; I almost killed myself several times. To someone who worshipped their image like I used to do, nothing is as bad as incarceration. Nothing."

"I see. It sounds to me like greed somehow played a part in your downfall. Am I wrong?"

"No, you're absolutely right," said Alice. "Actually, greed is an underlying sin in most of the idols you'll discuss today. But within the lust of the eyes, greed plays a particularly prominent role."

Rachel thought about this for a moment. She considered wealth, power, fame, and image, and saw that Alice was right.

"So what do you think fueled your obsession with image?" she said.

Alice shook her head. "It started out with the seemingly simple pride of my reputation. As I was growing up, I became enamored with what other people thought about me and my family. Since my parents weren't wealthy, I decided I wasn't going to have anyone look down their nose at me when I had my own family."

"I'd like to add something," Jerry began. "There's a great passage for this: *Romans 1:25 ... They exchanged the truth about God for a lie, and worshiped and served created things rather than the Creator—who is forever praised. Amen.*"

"Yes, indeed," Alice said. "I worshipped a false image of the American Dream and ignored God's calling for a righteous life. By doing so, I ended up worshipping created things, not God. Of course, I now understand that moving away from God's way of doing things is always a road to disaster. For example, let's take a look at what the prophet said in *Jeremiah 2:5 ... This is what the Lord says: 'What fault did your ancestors find in me, that they strayed so far from me? They followed worthless idols and became worthless themselves.*"

"That's interesting," Rachel said. "So your image idol started out with a certain pride in reputation and advanced beyond that?"

"It did," Alice said. "After that nonsense simmered in my soul for awhile, my overbearing desire to appear successful took over. Success was the next natural step in my sinful downfall."

"Ahhh, I see. The foundation of your obsession with image started out with a desire for a perfect reputation from the world's perspective. It then evolved into the desire to appear very successful."

"That's correct. Back then, there was no way I'd tolerate any blemishes in my life. Ironically, because I was so obsessed with not allowing anything to tarnish our perfect life, it turned out to be an incredibly lousy way to raise my children."

"How so?"

Alice shook her head. "I couldn't allow an imperfection of any kind to invade the foolish little false bubble we lived in. For example, one of my daughters had a slight learning disability. But instead of dealing with it like a compassionate adult, I blamed the teachers and the school. I was in denial about her special needs because I was so focused on not appearing to be flawed in any way. I actually thought things like that only happened to trashy people."

"Wow. So tell me something, Alice. Was there something beyond the pride of reputation and appearance of success that drove you into your obsession with image?"

"There sure was. Above all of it, I longed for the appearance of total control. I'm afraid I bought into the lie that one's life must be free of tribulations or it's totally worthless. Or even worse, it's cursed. Although I'm not going to delve into anything you'll discuss during your next visit, I guarded and protected my family's appearance to the outside world with a seething passion. I wanted my family to appear to be rich, successful, and totally devoid of any flaws."

Rachel nodded. "Why do you think that is? I mean, what do you think drove you to have such an unhealthy focus on your family's image?"

"It was all about a twisted type of hierarchy," said Alice. "I simply wanted to appear to be better than anyone else. Everything in my life was a competition, and I often used gossip as a weapon. Regretfully, I used gossip as a way to distance myself from the other ladies in my circle, who also were obsessed with image."

"I think it's a good time to add something," Jerry said. "We see this little nugget in *1 John 4:21 … And he has given us this command: Anyone who loves God must also love their brother and sister.*"

"And that's exactly what I neglected to do," said Alice. "I desired to align myself with the way of the world and pledged my allegiance to Satan's false narrative about what a successful life looked like. Thankfully, my little stint in prison eliminated that nonsense."

"So in summary," Rachel began. "You tried to appear perfect and without any kind of flaw. Is that right?"

"Absolutely," said Alice. "And that's the problem with the temptation to worship a false image of what real love and success in life is. In essence, I feel like I was pursuing a type of godship over others with my obsession with image. To make my point, let me read you something interesting from Solomon in *Ecclesiastes 7:20 ... Indeed, there is no one on earth who is righteous, no one who does what is right and never sins.*"

Rachel nodded. "All of us were sinners."

"In the end," Jerry added. "Everyone has a choice to make—they can care about what God thinks, or they can care about what the world thinks. In the case of the world, it's really a trap of Satan to lead you away from God and towards the opinions of other flawed people. It's just another subtle form of humanism."

"I see," said Rachel. "As it relates to being around flawed people, didn't Jesus hang out with sinners during His ministry down on Earth?"

"Not exactly," Jerry said. "I know that people love to say that, but that's not the whole story."

Rachel's eyes narrowed. "What do you mean?"

"It's simple. Jesus *engaged* all people—especially sinners. However, it's not like He hung out in bars and partied with them. He cared enough to take the punishment for mankind's sins, but God absolutely never endorses sin. Never."

Rachel nodded. "That makes sense to me."

"The point I'm trying to make," Jerry said. "Is that Jesus eschewed His society's norms for public image and took His message to all people. The same thing applies to all followers of Christ. No one should worry about their image as it relates to what the world thinks. The only thing that matters is for everyone to obey the will of God."

"Amen," said Alice. "As we begin to wrap things up, the problem with the idols within the lusts of the eye is that an attempt to gain control of your life without God is a downward spiral towards trusting alone in yourself. Believe me, that's no way to live a victorious spiritual life."

"I see," said Rachel. "It seems you worshipped a false image of success over what Jesus actually wanted for your life. In that way, you chose the idol of image and made it your god. Am I off base with that?"

"Not at all," Alice agreed. "To finish up my story, some evil women in a rival group in prison hated the fact that I turned to Christ and joined the group of Christian women in my cell block. Sometimes, people become pawns in prison, as in life. Anyway, these women decided to make an example of me and attacked me in the shower one day. The injuries I sustained ultimately caused me to die in the prison infirmary."

"That sounds awful," Rachel said.

"It was and it wasn't. Since a person only has to die once, I've now found the total happiness I was seeking down on Earth. It's ironic that being sent away from the wicked life and false image I created was my true path to salvation and happiness. Through my prison sentence, I discovered what real love is through Jesus Christ. This is a love that will last forever, not the lie I used to live."

"That's wonderful," said Rachel. "And yes, it's ironic indeed."

Alice nodded. "Nowadays, I'm thrilled to be able to serve God in a way I never wanted to when I was down on Earth."

"I'm getting that a lot from the ladies today. It's been a common theme."

Alice chuckled. "If you like common themes, just wait until you see what's next on your agenda."

14
FAMILY

"If you belong to Christ, then you are Abraham's seed, and heirs according to the promise"
Galatians 3:29

After enjoying the crackling fire and some idle chit-chat with Alice, Rachel and Jerry made their way back onto the trail from the snow-laden park to resume their ascent. As they did so, the snow gradually gave way to the forest once again.

"Okay, Rachel," Jerry said. "Now that we're entering our final four visits today, we're going to change things up a bit."

"How, exactly?"

"Let me first set the table. If you'll remember, the first four visits centered on the lust of the flesh temptations. Those were followed by the next four, which were the lust of the eyes. Now that those are complete, the third set of temptations will demonstrate some of the idols from the pride of life. Are you with me?"

Rachel grinned. "You bet I am."

"Okay, then. In an effort to keep you attuned to what God would like you to learn and experience today, our final setting for the four visits are all located adjacent to each other in a lovely town center in a village not far from here. There, you'll meet with our final four ladies and hear their stories."

"Really? It almost sounds like you're trying to somehow keep me off-balance."

Jerry chuckled. "In a manner of speaking, I am."

After trekking through the forest trail for awhile, Rachel noticed several animals on the outskirts of the village up ahead. She thoroughly enjoyed the incredible bounty of God's creation as she noticed something completely unexpected—a lion was lying right next to a deer.

"I know I'm new to Heaven and all," she began. "But I never expected to see something like that."

Rachel pointed at the lion and his friend.

"Yes indeed," Jerry said. "God has these animals stationed here so that you and other visitors to the mountain can absorb the vast difference between the death-stained Earth and our perfection here in Heaven, where there is no death."

"That's fantastic. Does the lion have a name?"

"He does. His name is Charlie."

"Can we go over and see him?"

Jerry nodded. "Yes, but not until after our visits. After we're done ascending the mountain, you'll have all of eternity to enjoy the wonderful animal kingdom here in Heaven—and ultimately, on the new Earth."

"I'm still marveling at how familiar-yet-new everything in Heaven is," said Rachel. "The contrasts are stark; while the similarities to Earth are surprising and wonderful."

The angel nodded. "Yup."

As they continued forward, an incredibly inviting village opened up in front of them, on the left. Enclosing the back side of the village were several majestic brick-walled structures, some with ivy coverings and others contained small shops. Other buildings along the perimeter had window ledges with beautiful hanging plants and gardens on the ground, adjacent to the structures. Several people were milling about.

Rachel and Jerry entered the back side of the village square from the southeast portal. After walking through a bustling passageway, Rachel was astonished when the village square opened up in front of them.

Numerous trees blended into the designed landscape with a divine homogenization that could only come from the mind of the Lord. Some of the village's attributes were natural; while others were obviously hand crafted. Instinctively, Rachel knew that Heaven was imbued with this incredible mix of God's handiwork through both natural means and hand-crafted structures. These were all blessings for and by His beloved children.

Smack dab in the middle of the square were four lovely ladies. Rachel and Jerry headed towards them.

"Greetings from all of us in the pride of life group," an Asian lady said upon their arrival at the center of the town square. "My name is Nancy."

"Hello Nancy," Rachel said. She then turned towards the other three ladies. "I'm Rachel. It's nice to see all of you again," she said to them.

An African-American woman stepped forward and said, "Greetings, Rachel. I'm Ursula, and this is Erica and Linda."

Ursula motioned towards the others. Erica had short cropped grayish hair, and Linda appeared to have originally been from India. Rachel recognized all of them from their original meeting down at the bottom of the mountain.

"I'm actually going to lead us off today," said Nancy. "My idol was my family. The other ladies are also stationed in other parts of our village, and they all have a great story to tell."

Nancy pointed to three different spots within the framework of buildings at the western, northern, and eastern ends of the square. Every pathway from the buildings led into the center of the square, where they all now stood. This was similar in layout to the smaller snow park they just left in their visit with Alice.

"This place is remarkable," Rachel said.

"It sure is," Nancy said. "So let's get started. My place is right behind us, near where you entered the village."

She pointed towards a series of buildings that were adjacent to the southeast portal.

"After you, ladies," Jerry said. "We'll see the rest of you shortly."

The other ladies nodded and departed.

Rachel and Nancy chatted as they strolled towards the south end of the square. When they arrived at the main entrance to the row of buildings, they entered and walked up to the third floor. Jerry followed behind.

"Here we are," Nancy said, opening her door.

She led them to a comfortable living room which had a magnificent view of the town square outside.

Rachel chuckled. "I love how you don't need door locks here," she said. "That's one of those interesting differences between Heaven and the sometimes frightening reality of living down on Earth."

"Indeed," Nancy said. "Up here, there's no need for door locks—or police officers, firefighters, homeland security, or a military force. Everyone in Heaven has sought out and received forgiveness of their sins, so there's no need for any of that. This is the home of the Most High God, so none of the sinful attributes of living in mankind's fallen world—with all of its obvious shortcomings—is ever needed here. I guess you could say, we only have the good stuff in Heaven."

"Yes! I've noticed how so many things in Heaven are a lovely combination of God's creation and mankind's handiwork. It seems to be an obvious nod at God's beautiful design coupled with His fellowship with the citizens of Heaven."

"Up here, it's a totally fulfilling relationship between God and His children," Jerry added. "The natural symbiosis between the Creator and His creation has been restored here in Heaven. Ultimately it will be the same thing down on the New Earth."

"How exciting," Rachel said. "So Nancy ... you said your idol was your family. What can you tell me about that?"

"Off we go," Nancy said. "Since we're not focusing on the exercise of you trying to guess the subject of each of our testimonies, Jerry and I will hit you with some relevant verses to help explain my story. The first one is *Ephesians 3:14-15 ... For this reason I kneel before the Father, from whom every family in heaven and on earth derives its name.*"

"The only people in Heaven are those who love the Lord," Jerry said. "And that's the most important family anyone will ever have."

"What do you mean?" said Rachel. "Are you saying that my earthly family didn't mean anything?"

Jerry shook his head. "Not necessarily. Here, I think this will help: *Hebrews 4:12 says ... For the word of God is alive and active. Sharper than any double-edged sword, it penetrates even to dividing soul and spirit, joints and marrow; it judges the thoughts and attitudes of the heart.*"

"What does that mean?" said Rachel. "It sounds a bit harsh."

"It only sounds harsh from the human perspective," Nancy said. "From God's perspective, everything starts with the Word who became flesh—Jesus Christ, who is Immanuel, God among us. Essentially, the word of God separates the world from His kingdom and cuts right to the core of every single person and what they believe."

"I see," said Rachel. "It sounds like Jesus meant business when He came to Earth."

"You bet He did," Jerry said, nodding. "The uncomfortable truth from the human perspective about Jesus' ministry on Earth is found here, in *Matthew 10:37* ... '*Anyone who loves their father or mother more than me is not worthy of me; anyone who loves their son or daughter more than me is not worthy of me.*"

Rachel was quiet for a few moments. She then said, "So I had an earthly family that's now been replaced by an eternal family?"

"Sort of," Nancy said. "Your genetic family on Earth was physical. Your eternal family is spiritual. In other words, your family is now comprised of those who love God and gave their life to Jesus Christ before they died. Hopefully, those who are in your earthly family are *also* in your eternal, heavenly family. Unfortunately, however, that's not always the case."

"Exactly," said Jerry. "The point Nancy is making is that oftentimes, people are puffed up in pride over their *birth* family. The truth is, however, they should be more concerned about who is or who will be in their *rebirth* family—fellow believers in Christ."

"And that's why sharing the Gospel is so vitally important," Nancy said. "None of us can read a person's heart like God can—that's not our job. Instead, one must focus on sharing the Good News about Jesus; knowing that our real, eternal family will be revealed one day when you arrive in Heaven."

"Ahhh, I see," Rachel said. "So my physical ancestry isn't as important as my spiritual ancestry—so to speak...?"

"In an eternal sense, yes," said Nancy. "I often like to describe it this way ... *Hebrews 2:11* ... says ... *Both the one who makes people holy and those who are made holy are of the same family. So Jesus is not ashamed to call them brothers and sisters.*"

"That's wonderful," Rachel said. "I understand."

"So about my testimony," Nancy continued. "I was one of the rare female hedge fund managers before I died a couple of years ago. Back then, I felt like I had it all—a high paying job, a stay-at-home husband, and both a son and a daughter who excelled in school. To most, I was living an admirable life. But below the surface, my idol worship roiled like a struggling ship, trying to survive a hurricane at sea."

"That's interesting," said Rachel. "So you were the breadwinner for your family and your husband took care of your children?"

"That's correct. Of course, there's nothing wrong with a woman being strong and using her talents to earn a good living. However, that wasn't what drove me."

"Then what did?"

"My problem was that I didn't follow this: *Titus 2:4* says ... *Then they can urge the younger women to love their husbands and children.*"

"I'm not quite following you."

Nancy sighed. "I was driven by the fear that others would look down on me if I didn't excel to a degree that was nearly impossible to accomplish—and even harder to maintain. You see, my parents raised me in an eastern religion that focused on me and my objectives. Over the years—even though I escaped the fallacy that life was about me and not about God—the fear that I would not achieve the most perfect type of family and career possible tormented my soul. I lived in a bubble of overwhelming terror that others would look down on me for being a failure in some way ... especially regarding my family."

"Wait a minute," Rachel said. "This sounds a lot like Alice's testimony about image. Am I missing something?"

"Not at all," Nancy said. "The image idol is an enormous component of the family idol...."

"Please, go on."

"As you discussed with Alice and some of the others, the combination of temptations and the resulting idols are intertwined in subtle ways. That's basically what Satan tempted me with—the fear that any kind of failure in my family not being perfect would make me look like a loser. You can also add in the idols of leisure, beauty, wealth, and others you'll soon learn about. But that's not all. I was mostly driven by the pride of hierarchy in my soul."

"Hierarchy? This seems to be a common theme on the mountain."

"Oh, yes. I had to have the best of everything, including the perfect family, which I absolutely obsessed over. My mindset back then was that I had to have everything in my life appear to be superior to others."

"Hmmm," Rachel mumbled. "So you had both a hidden fear and a false sense of hierarchy that drove you to obsess about your family?"

"That's correct," Nancy said. "And that's precisely what the pride of life idols are all about. My own recipe for disaster started with fear and was intertwined with the temptation towards image. The end result was that I felt like I could trust in myself and my own efforts more than in God. In fact, I felt like I really didn't need God at all. That is, until I got breast cancer and later died as a result of it."

"I'd like to add something," Jerry said. "We see this in *Nahum 1:7 ... The Lord is good, a refuge in times of trouble. He cares for those who trust in him.*"

"That's certainly a great verse," Rachel said. "But what point are you trying to make?"

"Once again, your real family members are those who love God. You see, it wasn't Nancy's husband; her high-paying job; her children in private schools; her parents; her expensive downtown apartment; or anything else that gave her solace when she was dying of cancer. Only the vital hope of Christ gave her the desire to ask Jesus to carry her over the terrifying chasm of death into eternal life. Only Jesus has the ability to do that. This unique ability is what cuts to the core of life on Earth for everyone."

"I understand," Rachel said. "So getting back to the common elements within the pride of life temptations. You're saying that fear and a prideful desire for hierarchy over others produced a false sense of trust in yourself. Is that correct?"

"It is," Nancy said. "But there's more. All of those ingredients point towards someone putting God to the test. It was as if I elevated myself to god-like status and asked Him to serve me."

"Okay, I think I'm with you," Rachel said. "Tell me this. Did your husband do a good job of raising your children?"

Nancy smiled. "My husband is a good man. He tolerated my prideful leanings and ultimately showed me the way to Jesus."

"Really? So your husband led you to Christ?"

"He sure did. Of course, he tried to do this countless times, both while we dated and during the course of our marriage. It was only when I was about to die that I finally dropped my pride and listened to him."

Rachel shook her head. "The man I should've married actually did that for me, also. He helped to save my life and probably doesn't even know it."

"You'll have your chance to see Harvey again one day," Jerry added. "That's something the Lord has allowed me to share with you. Harvey's name is written in the Book of Life."

"To be honest, I married four other men who were absolute schmucks in the end," Rachel said sadly. "Fortunately, Harvey never gave up on our friendship."

"My husband always did his best to lead me towards Christ," Nancy said. "It gives me great comfort knowing he's still raising our children in the ways of the Lord. If the cancer hadn't struck me, I'd probably still be fighting with him over what was the best spiritual option for our kids."

"Tell me something, Nancy. What made your family such an idol? I mean, what did you do to make them such a big deal?"

"A wife's job, in part, is to help build her husband up to serve Jesus Christ. I ignored that calling by putting my children's accomplishments and activities up on a pedestal. I'm sad to say, I actually lived vicariously through my children. So instead of treating our marriage in a biblical way, my focus was on the world and what it thought about my children ... and ultimately, me."

"Do you have a specific example of that?"

"I do," Nancy said. "And this example is what makes the family idol so dangerous and distinct from the image idol. In fact, I believe this example is so rampant, many people can't even begin to recognize its deeply entrenched danger."

"This sounds interesting."

Nancy nodded. "When I was still in my sin, I was often quoted as saying, 'I live for my children.' Somehow, I felt like that was an altruistic notion. I now realize just how embarrassing it was."

"Yes, I've heard *many* women claim that."

"It really gets down to whether you value the world or the Bible," Jerry said. "We see this in *Galatians 1:10 ... Am I now trying to win the approval of human beings, or of God? Or am I trying to please people? If I were still trying to please people, I would not be a servant of Christ.*"

"That's the truth," Nancy said. "Although a lot of women down on Earth probably don't want to admit this, but their children are actually the center of their idol worship. This is not good in any way and must be turned away from. To make my point, here is the last verse we have for you, Rachel. It's in *1 Thessalonians 1:9 ... for they themselves report what kind of reception you gave us. They tell how you turned to God from idols to serve the living and true God*"

"So you're saying that to serve God, you must keep Him first? That makes sense to me."

"Yes," said Nancy. "That's it. It's very simple. And for those who indulge family idol worship like I did, they must be cautious about not elevating their family above God and His commands. This is always a recipe for disaster, which Satan obviously delights in."

"Well done," Jerry said. "To begin to close, let me say that many things in your life can become idol worship as it relates to family. One of the more subtle idols is when a couple spends an untold fortune on their wedding and almost zero effort on their actual marriage."

"Jerry is right," Nancy said. "My wedding cost as much as a small house—and it wasn't to honor God. It was to honor me. My eyes coveted a certain story line for our wedding, and that covetousness became the fuel for my pride and ego. It was downright narcissism."

They were all quiet for a few moments.

"I've been wondering about something," Rachel said slowly. "Jerry—what do you think my primary idol was?"

Jerry chuckled. "You're spiritual senses have grown a great deal in a short time, Rachel. Although you'll be receiving some more information on this a little bit later, the seeds of your idol began with your family, with a healthy dose of image. Unfortunately, you followed what you thought your parents expected of you—which was to chase after wealth, beauty, fame, and image with Blaine. Sadly, their false idol of what success in life looked like influenced you to overlook the real love in your life, who was Harvey."

This confirmation hit Rachel like a ton of bricks. She remained quiet; thinking.

"I wish I could go back and do it over again," Rachel said. "But I suppose mine and Nancy's actions are the result of—"

"They're the result of what the world looks like without Jesus," Jerry interrupted. "There's nothing more to it than that."

15
INTELLECT

"Woe to those who are wise in their own eyes and clever in their own sight."
Isaiah 5:21

After some lighthearted discussion, Nancy escorted Rachel and Jerry back to the town square. As they arrived, Rachel noticed that Ursula was already waiting for them on the marble bench surrounding the centralized fountain. An almost imperceptible mist from the fountain vaporized into the immediate area, covering the group with a gentle layer of refreshing comfort. Rachel felt absolutely wonderful.

"Hello again, Ursula," Rachel said, taking her new hostess by the hands before embracing her. "I can't wait to hear your story."

"Well, I've got a good one," Ursula said, standing up. "As usual, thanks Nancy," she continued. "I'll take good care of our new citizen."

"I know you will," Nancy said. "Oh, and Rachel, I'll be here to see you off after you finish your four visits to our village today."

"Great! See you then."

Ursula and Rachel turned towards the western series of buildings and headed that way. Once again, Jerry followed.

Once inside, the ambiance took on a different feel than the preponderance of living spaces in Nancy's building. Ursula's area actually looked very much like a college library.

"That's interesting," Rachel said. "I feel like I'm on the campus of a university."

Ursula smiled. "In a way, you are."

"I sure didn't expect that."

"In no way does learning cease at the grave, my friend. You'll be amazed at what you'll learn in Heaven; particularly during your first week."

"I love it."

"As did I. Anyway, please follow me…."

Ursula led Rachel and Jerry through a veritable maze of shelves and alcoves until reaching a lovely round table in an open area among the throngs of books. They all took a seat.

"Were you a professor or something?" Rachel asked Ursula.

"As a matter of fact, I was. You're pretty sharp, girl."

Rachel chuckled. "A lucky guess. So when did you arrive in Heaven?"

"Actually, it was just last week."

"Oh, so you're a newbie like me, huh?"

"I am. And like you, I also died in my later years."

"How did you pass?"

"My diabetes finally overtook me, so coming here and being released from the pain of my frail earthly body was very much a blessing."

"Ahhh, I see. Since you were older like me when you passed, you must've lived through the terrible 'back of the bus' days for African Americans. Am I right?"

"I sure did, honey. Those were some troubling days, indeed. But that's a story for another day. For today, I'd like to go ahead and get us started with an important concept for sharing my testimony with you. Now this one goes all the way back to the beginning of the Bible in *Genesis 3:5 … 'For God knows that when you eat from it your eyes will be opened, and you will be like God, knowing good and evil.'"*

Rachel shrugged. "So knowledge was your idol?"

"Not exactly. Knowledge was the object of my idol worship, just like all temptations are a type of starter-kit for sins which mature into idols. No, my idol was the desire for a superior intellect."

"Intellect?"

"Absolutely. You can see from that passage in Genesis that Eve was tempted by Satan with greater knowledge. This temptation quickly stoked the fire of her desire for a type of God-like intellect. Unfortunately, this prideful desire helped to ruin mankind's place in the garden; and soon thereafter, the entire universe."

"I see. So the temptation for superior knowledge—driven by the pride of life and your desire for hierarchy over others—evolved into your idol of intellect. Is that correct?"

"It sure is. Ironically, my pursuit of intellect actually prevented me from attaining something much more valuable than mere knowledge, which is wisdom."

"Really—wisdom?"

"Indeed. To make my point, here's something from *Proverbs 19:8* … *The one who gets wisdom loves life; the one who cherishes understanding will soon prosper.*"

"I'd like to add a wonderful thought from C.S. Lewis," Jerry said. "He's quoted as once saying, *Education without values, as useful as it is, seems rather to make man a more clever devil.*"

"Okay, okay," Rachel said. "Let's take those one at a time."

Ursula quickly added, "And while we're at it, I'd like to add another one. *Proverbs 1:7* says … *The fear of the Lord is the beginning of knowledge, but fools despise wisdom and instruction.*"

"I'm ready—let's do this," Rachel declared. "The passages in Proverbs seem to be saying that wisdom enhances your life and that there's no wisdom without the Lord. That makes perfect sense to me—"

"It's also a great commentary about what real love is," Jerry added.

"How so?" said Rachel.

"Like we've discussed many times today, there is no such thing as real love from the human perspective if you don't first love God. Think about it. The pursuit of knowledge outside of the Lord is always for prideful vanity—right?"

"It sure is," said Ursula. "When I arrived here last week, I learned this wonderful nugget: *James 3:15* says … *Such 'wisdom' does not come down from heaven but is earthly, unspiritual, demonic.*"

"Whoa," said Rachel. "Did you just say, *demonic?*"

"I sure did. In addition to that, our Savior showed the religious authorities of His day that godly wisdom is more important than mankind's wisdom in *John 7:15* … *The Jews there were amazed and asked, 'How did this man get such learning without having been taught?'*"

"Okay, okay. So how do you define the difference between knowledge and wisdom?"

Ursula grinned. "Knowledge is generally acquired through research, reasoning, and/or experience. On the other hand, wisdom is

171

the ability to determine how to actually *use* that knowledge. In the case of Christians, wisdom is used to glorify God, while secularists and others use knowledge without the benefit of God's wisdom. In a way, you might say that knowledge without wisdom is like a blind person driving a car at night, with the lights off, down the highway of their life."

"How poetic," Rachel said, chuckling. "No wonder you were a professor."

Ursula smiled.

"So let's see if I'm keeping up with you," Rachel continued. "From what you're saying, I'm inferring that knowledge can exist without wisdom. So let me ask you this. Can wisdom exist without knowledge?"

"Hang on now," Jerry said. "Knowledge and wisdom have had an oft-debated relationship throughout the ages. What's important for today is that from the Christian perspective, there can be no wisdom without the knowledge of the Lord. However, that's not all there is to it. Merely having *knowledge* of the Lord isn't nearly enough."

"What do you mean?" said Rachel. "I'm not following you on that."

"It's really rather simple," the angel said. "One can have all the knowledge in the world about Jesus, the Bible, and of God's commandments, etc. However, if you don't act on that knowledge by obeying God *and* loving your neighbor, you cannot have wisdom; at least, not from a biblical perspective. Wisdom is the fullness of God's commands."

"Okay, I see. So having knowledge without God and without obeying Him is just—"

"It's just useless," Ursula said. "Trust me when I tell you, I spent my whole career chasing after knowledge. The problem was that I had no wisdom to help me understand it."

"So what changed?"

Ursula sighed. "It was *I* who finally changed. The crux of my story is that my big sister finally got through to me. For all of her adult life, she's been nothing more than a housekeeping supervisor at a ritzy hotel in a big city. While I was pursuing higher education, she worked her tail off doing a job that most people snub their noses at. And to be completely honest, I used to think of myself as superior to her because of my education."

"Wow," said Rachel. "That's quite a confession."

"There's no darkness in Heaven, sweetie. The remnants of my pride completely melted away when I arrived here."

"I can see that."

"Anyway, for several decades, I thought of myself as being superior to not only my sister, but to anyone who didn't have a doctorate like I did. Actually, I had two."

"Very nice."

Ursula shrugged. "From the world's perspective, I felt like the accumulation of knowledge made me better than others. Back then, I only admired people who had better credentials than I did. In the end, I discovered that it was *I* who was the fool."

"This is a good time to add something important," Jerry said. "It's in *Romans 1:22* ... *Although they claimed to be wise, they became fools.*"

"That was me in a nutshell," Ursula said. "Just like some of the others, the unspoken sin in my quest for worldly knowledge was a desire for a greater sense of hierarchy over others. Fortunately for me, my sister had godly wisdom. There's no doubt in my mind that God's wisdom is far more valuable than a mere sense of intellectual superiority, which is nothing but prideful rubbish."

"Your sister must be an incredible person."

"She sure is. When my personal life hit rock bottom last year, I felt like I had fallen into a chasm of no return. Back then, I thought of God as a type of cosmic Santa Claus and I was totally unprepared for when my husband left me for a younger woman."

Rachel nodded. "So your sister shared the Gospel with you?"

"She did. When my spiritual eyes finally opened, I saw the futility of chasing after an idol like intellect, which basically attempts to leave God on the sidelines. You see, when tragedy strikes your life, if anyone clings to any kind of idol, they cannot expect that idol, yourself, or anyone else to help you out of the problem you're having."

"The answer seems obvious, but why do you think that is?"

"Because there's no real power outside of the Lord."

"I thought so. Do you have an example to make your point?"

"As a matter of fact, I do. It's in *Jeremiah 11:12* ... *The towns of Judah and the people of Jerusalem will go and cry out to the gods to whom they burn incense, but they will not help them at all when disaster strikes.*"

"I love how the Bible has so much wisdom. I sure wish I had treated it differently when I was down on Earth."

"Far too often," Jerry began. "Christians claim that the Bible is an instruction manual for life. However, I think that description is far too wimpy and incomplete. The truth is, the Bible is first and foremost, a *survival* guide. After you understand this critical concept, the 'instructions' in the Bible make far more sense. The result is wisdom."

"I'm with you on that," Ursula said. "I was all up into my own self-sufficiency until my health declined and my husband left me. When those disasters struck, my sister loved me enough to get on a train and come to see me with the only real remedy, which was Jesus Christ."

"So your sister had the wisdom that you lacked?" said Rachel. "The allegedly lowly housekeeper was able to provide true wisdom to the multi-degreed college professor?"

"That's exactly right. Isn't it ironic? I was on top of the world from the human perspective, with brains, degrees, tenure, and brilliant colleagues to influence me. But to God's kingdom, I was nothing but a little girl in Kindergarten—spiritually speaking, of course. Once I surrendered my life to Jesus Christ, everything changed for the short time I remained on Earth."

"It seems that all of the ladies on the mountain have that in common."

"What's that?"

"We didn't have much time to make an impact on others before we died and arrived here in Heaven. Do you think that's by God's design?"

Ursula shrugged. "Oh, I think so. Remember, I'm pretty new to Heaven also."

"Oh yeah, that's right."

"But this I do know, for sure. My ability to serve others in Heaven in this manner is a wonderful blessing. I mean, think about it. I'm spending time with a brand new citizen like you today, and I'm sharing how much Jesus did for me, even though I died down on Earth. How can anyone complain about that?"

Rachel chuckled. "Right you are."

"I have something to add before Ursula finishes her story," Jerry said. "This next verse demonstrates how having mere knowledge is often a product of pride and actually works against what real love is all about. It's in *1 Corinthians 8:1 ... Now about food sacrificed to idols: We know that 'We all possess knowledge.' But knowledge puffs up while love builds up.*"

"Amen," said Ursula. "So getting back to my career, I taught history for most of my tenure. Back when I was a know-it-all education snob, I bought into the lie that Natural Selection was the power behind life and that Christians who disagreed with it were of an inferior intelligence. In fact, many of my colleagues felt that anyone who believed in any of that ancient Christian nonsense was actually mentally ill and should be pitied. I can't say I went that far, but I was close enough to it to know what it looked like."

Rachel whistled. "Wow."

"Even though you and Jerry have talked about Solomon's mistakes during your adventure today, he was a very wise man. We see this interesting passage in *1 Kings 4:29 … God gave Solomon wisdom and very great insight, and a breadth of understanding as measureless as the sand on the seashore.*"

Rachel nodded. "Yes, but didn't Solomon waste—?"

"I agree," Jerry said. "Solomon didn't use his wisdom as he should have. But pay attention to the first part of that verse again. It starts with 'God gave Solomon wisdom.' That's the point which is so important. As we know, everything in the universe starts with the Lord. Because of His great love, God also gives humans a choice what to do with the gifts and abilities He bestows upon them. With those choices, a person can either use their abilities for themselves, or they can use them to glorify God."

"In my case," Ursula said. "Pride was the furnace I fed with my alleged intellectual gains. I so wish I would've used my gifts for Jesus instead of myself."

"Well … like you said … you're doing that now."

Ursula smiled. "Thank you, dear. Listen, I know you and Jerry have two more appointments, so I'll go ahead and finish my brief agenda with you."

"Sounds good."

"Even though history was my teaching focus, I spent a lot of time in academia, studying the natural sciences. I absolutely love science, as every single person in the world should. However, before my conversion to Christianity, science became my de facto religion. This unfortunate propensity is a common trap when people submit to the idol of intellect, which so easily can overtake your life with pride…."

"That's interesting. Please continue."

"Before I give you an example or two of the pitfalls of having science as your religion, I'd like to point out something you may not have considered before."

Rachel shrugged. "What's that?"

"Centuries ago, Satan used the religious establishment to persecute scientists and their discoveries. It was really silly, because there's nothing to be afraid of as it relates to the natural world. In fact, I believe the natural world absolutely screams the name of its Creator."

"I agree."

"The point I'm making is that back then, Satan used the religious establishment to persecute scientists. Are you with me?"

"I am."

"So for today, as it has been throughout history, the whole situation has done a complete one-eighty. This is most definitely the handiwork of Satan."

"How so?"

"In all of my experiences with the so-called intelligentsia, it's obvious they've now assumed the role of persecutor, while the people of faith in Christ are now the persecuted. In fact, these modern day naturalist persecutors show their hand when the focus of their attack is almost always Christians. Generally they don't bother people of other religions."

"What do you mean by that?"

Ursula sighed. "Satan's mission is to prevent people from finding their way to God, which is only through Jesus Christ. Therefore, any worldview without Jesus is pretty much okay as far as Satan is concerned. As a result, if you follow any religion or belief system that isn't true Christianity, Satan is quite happy with the results of his deception."

"That's interesting," said Rachel. "Now that I'm thinking about it, in the political world, it's Christianity that gets bashed all the time."

"That's right. People of other religions can say virtually anything they want, and it's deemed okay by my former secular colleagues. However, if Christianity offers an opinion, it's automatically denounced as being outdated and bigoted. You see, when a naturalist chooses to believe in a world without a creator, their de facto god of Natural Selection gets to make all the rules. This is an enormous spiritual pitfall. All of these lies are nothing but a covert effort to eliminate the real God from the equation."

"Yeah, that Natural Selection thing never made much sense to me."

"That's because Natural Selection is contrived and untrue. So is the so-called 'Mother Nature' or 'Mother Earth' that often accompanies this flawed worldview."

"Hmmm. My first reaction is that the use of the term Mother Nature seems pretty innocent—"

"Oh, I disagree," Ursula said. "The window dressing for the concept of Mother Nature may not seem all that bad. But underneath, it totally undermines our Father, who created all things. You have to be careful when examining some of Satan's subtle attacks on the truth found in the Bible."

Rachel considered this.

"Okay," she said. "I think I'm tracking with you. When I hear the term Mother Nature, I think of a goddess of the environment, etc. However, I can see that it's just a made up concept, just like Santa Claus and the Easter Bunny."

"That's the point," Jerry added. "The idol of intellect covers not only the many people on college campuses, but also the extreme environmentalists and the globalists. It only makes sense that a world without Jesus Christ still needs some kind of god to complete its barren worldview. And thus, the idol of intellect steps in with childish things like Natural Selection, Mother Nature, and the silly personification of the universe by claiming, 'the universe does this and that,' etc. These things are all humanistic in nature, and they're all lies. Essentially, pursuing intellect without God's wisdom is a path to nowhere. In the end, this world belongs to God, not mankind."

"I see," said Rachel. "So you're obviously saying that pursuing higher knowledge is not bad. It's only bad when you leave the Lord out of the equation."

"That's right, sweetie," Ursula said. "Being impressed with one's own intelligence provides an illusion of control that cannot be sustained when you measure it against the only One who was able to conquer the grave—who is Jesus Christ."

Rachel nodded. "Like you said, I imagine you saw a lot of this kind of sinful arrogance during your years of being a professor."

"There's no question about that. College campuses are full of what I consider to be the most arrogant form of humanism—one's own intelligence. But having survived that incredible sin of pride, I can tell you something without any hesitation whatsoever."

"What's that?"

Ursula smiled. "There's no one in the universe smarter than God. It doesn't matter if you have an IQ ten times greater than Einstein, you're still not really that smart when you consider the Creator of all things. You know, I've never seen anyone make something out of completely nothing. But God can—*and God did.*"

"He sure did."

"The power of the Lord is demonstrated very strongly by the complexity and incredible beauty of His creation. In fact, one has to look no further than the creation to make the logical assumption that God is far smarter than any of us."

Ursula then stood up.

"Come now," she said. "I believe it's already time for your next appointment."

16
CAREER

"So I hated life, because the work that is done under the sun was grievous to me. All of it is meaningless, a chasing after the wind."
Ecclesiastes 2:17

The pure and utter beauty outside the western set of buildings was headlined by the magnificent array of the village's bountiful flora. As Rachel took in the harmonious activity of the square, she noticed the faint aroma of lilac, with a splash of lavender. Everything looked, smelled, and felt unspeakably fresh as they made their way back to the fountain.

"Here we go," Ursula said, causing Rachel to fall out of her momentary daze. "Erica will take it from here."

"Thanks very much," Rachel said. "Will I see you at the end also?"

Ursula smiled widely. "Of course, dear."

Rachel felt a calming hand on her back. When she turned, Erica was standing there and moved in for a hug.

They embraced.

"This way," Erica said, her short-cropped grayish hair framing her beautiful smile. "Please join me."

Erica, Rachel, and Jerry moved towards the north end of the square.

When they arrived inside the understated brick building in the center, they walked up to the second floor and through a doorway.

After strolling through a short hallway, they entered a large rectangular room.

Rachel's immediate impression was that they had entered a company's board room. Although the room was faintly business-like, Rachel sensed that Erica's heavenly business was nothing like what she had likely dealt with down on Earth.

"Let me guess," Rachel said. "Your job was your idol?"

"That's a great guess," Erica said. "But it was actually a bit more than that. My idol is best described as my entire career."

"Close enough," Rachel chuckled. "I figured this topic had to be somewhere on the agenda today."

"Career is a very dangerous idol indeed. As you've earlier discussed with Jerry and some of the other sisters, the career idol is perhaps the one which is the most infused with numerous other idols to combine into a type of Frankenstein's monster of sin."

Rachel chuckled. "That's certainly an interesting way of putting it."

"As we dig in," Erica continued. "You'll see that not only was my career a veritable super-hybrid of idols, but that the underlying driving force was my desperate need to provide for my own godship."

Rachel's brow furrowed. "Your godship? This has come up a couple of times today, but—"

"Oh, yes. But first, let me give you an overview of my history.

"Sounds good."

"I grew up in a nice, middle-class neighborhood, and my parents were good people. Although we went to church most every week, our spiritual lives were not very strong—that is, below the surface. In fact, I'll have to admit, my father's obsession with his career was the example I ended up following for my own life. At first, that may sound like a good thing. But it ended up being a tragic pathway to my own ruin."

"How so?"

"After high school and college, I pursued a master's degree from an ivy league university. After that was behind me, I was off to the corporate world to do battle. Now this may seem like a normal rendering of the American Dream, but it was actually far from it."

"Why—?"

"Because I wasn't just driven to succeed to provide a good living for my family. No, I went *far* beyond that to the point where every single temptation and idol you've seen thus far today became stepping stones towards my ascension to a false throne of my own making."

Rachel's eyebrows rose. "Whoa—this is getting interesting. Can you elaborate?"

"You bet," Erica said, nodding. "The driving force behind the desire for my own godship was obviously my pride, and the vehicle to get me to where I wanted to be—which was like ascending to the top of my own mountain of life—was the substantial income I earned. I'm afraid I put everything I had in my soul into my work, and I steadily clawed my way to the top of the corporate world."

"I see," Rachel said. "So tell me more about your so-called super-hybrid of idols. What's that all about?"

"Oh, that part's simple. If you think about every single topic you've encountered on the mountain today, all of them have contributed in some way, shape, or form, to my career idol. This ended up happening in various and sometimes covert ways."

"Okay, okay. You've *got* to explain that part to me."

Erica chuckled. "Let's go through them, one-by-one. You started off today with the idols of Leisure, Hunger, Beauty, and Sex. Those examples were the temptations within the lusts of the flesh, and I engaged in every single one of them as I built my career."

"In what way? Did you turn to them instead of turning to God?"

"I did. When I started my career, I focused on myself with self-serving pursuits. Among them were doing whatever I wanted to do with my leisure time, indulging in drugs and excessive alcohol, an unhealthy focus on physical fitness and beauty, and sex with whomever I liked. However, that was only the foundation for my spiritual fall. As these lusts of the flesh took hold in my soul, my lust for Wealth, Power, Fame, and Image began to take form. If you think about it, in my case, the lusts of the flesh led right into the lusts of the eyes."

"Hmmm," Rachel mumbled. "That's very interesting. Although we've discussed how Satan uses temptations in combination, I never considered how they might be used as a type of domino effect."

"Well, in my case, that's exactly what they were—one led right into the other, to the other, and so on, and so on. Anyway, after several years of climbing the corporate ladder, I landed right in the middle of a personal Hell of my own making. It was very much like a prison. Unfortunately, I got exactly what I was striving for."

"I think now may be a good time for some Scripture," Jerry added. "That way, Erica can take a breath for a moment."

Erica chuckled. "Be my guest, Jerry."

"Okay," the angel continued. "Let's start off with some wisdom. We see this in *Proverbs 21:30 … There is no wisdom, no insight, no plan that can succeed against the Lord.*"

"That's the opposite of what I did," Erica said. "I was so bent on executing my own plan, I never considered what God may want for my life. In truth, I feel like I actually wrestled with the Lord all of those years."

Jerry nodded. "My reaction to that is in *Hosea 11:2 … But the more they were called, the more they went away from me. They sacrificed to the Baals and they burned incense to images.*"

Erica shook her head and looked at Rachel. "Baal was a false god or gods—or demons—from ancient times. They stood for essentially the same thing my false idol of career did—independence from the real God. And like Baal, although I didn't realize it at the time, I also demanded worship."

"Hang on a minute," Rachel said. "Jerry—are you saying the categories of idols we're discussing today are similar to some of the ancient idols from the Old Testament?"

Jerry nodded. "In a way, yes."

"But how?"

"You need to realize that demons are behind the worship of all idols. It'll be helpful for you to think of idols and temptations as weapons on Satan's utility belt of human destruction. In the case of Erica, a normal God-glorifying thing like a rewarding career was taken far beyond what God's plan was. God expects His children to treat their career in the proper light, not make an idol out of it."

"Jerry's right," Erica said. "A career should be something you do; not something that defines you. Or even worse—something that exalts you."

"Uh-huh," Rachel said. "So you're saying your career was like Baal worship in ancient days in that your efforts were a sacrifice for—"

"It was all for my own worship," Erica said. "I tried to convince people that my sacrifice of long hours was for my family, but that was nothing but false altruism. In truth, I really wanted everything for myself—success, money, notoriety, and every other sin you can think of. I wanted it all for me."

"So you weren't quite the queen of the world after all," Rachel said. "Trust me—I know how that feels."

"Anyone who rejects the Lord's way in favor of their own is engaging in idolatry and false worship," Jerry said. "We see this interesting passage in *1 Samuel 15:23 ... For rebellion is like the sin of divination, and arrogance like the evil of idolatry. Because you have rejected the word of the Lord, he has rejected you as king.*"

Erica nodded quickly. "In that passage, King Saul's evil was exposed. In a similar way, I chose my own evil will over the Lord."

"On the other hand," Jerry said. "Let's talk about real love. We see something interesting in *Colossians 3:14 ... And over all these virtues put on love, which binds them all together in perfect unity.*"

"We've covered that many, many times today," said Rachel.

"What's that?" said Jerry.

"That temptations, sin, and idolatry are things that actually prevent real love from happening in one's life."

"That's actually the point of ascending this mountain," Erica said.

"It all makes sense to me."

"Continuing with my story," Erica said. "The window dressing of the desire to build my career was the lie that I was working hard and building the American Dream. But underneath that cover, the pride of my self-will drove me to do treacherous things in the corporate world for career advancement and accomplishment. Somewhere along the way, I lost sight of my moral compass and found myself mired in the quicksand of Satan's playground of greed."

"What exactly do you mean?"

"The world of money without a proper focus on Jesus Christ is like the proverbial ship lost at sea. When you're playing around in one of Satan's strongholds like the world of business—without the North Star of Christ showing you the way—the fog of evil will descend upon you and envelope your ship. Ultimately, it will confuse you to the point where you're completely lost and have no choice but to chart your own course. That's what happened to me. By the time I reached the senior management level in my career, the line between legitimate profit and utter greed had pretty much disappeared. As a result, when questionable opportunities to generate revenue and profits became available, I had no real idea what was right and what was wrong. Therefore, I began to make terrible decisions, which in retrospect, were often quite greedy."

"Do you have an example of this?"

"Of course. Do you remember two years ago when Hurricane Katrina hit the Gulf Coast?"

"I do."

"One of our operating companies provided various supplies to the government for their relief efforts. Now at first, this may sound like we were doing a magnanimous thing. However, we boosted our prices to exorbitant levels and ended up gouging FEMA. We did this during a time when they were absolutely desperate to help those in need. As I look back, it was absolutely awful what we did. It was all in the name of profit."

"Really? I thought most companies that provided relief were praised for their efforts."

Erica shook her head. "Relief efforts at those exorbitant profits were not charitable at all. On the other hand, the volunteers and government employees who went over there and directly assisted the people in need are the real ones who should be praised—not the companies who profited so much from it all."

"So what are you saying?" said Rachel.

"I'm saying that Katrina was but one example of the opportunistic attitude I insisted on for my company. Essentially, we did not honor God with our greedy approach to business. The object of our worship every single day was our stock price. And trust me; we worshipped at its altar in every single company initiative we had. Since I was the CEO, I made sure the entire organization's focus was on shareholder value. Everything in the company cascaded down from this worldly approach."

"I see," said Rachel. "So how did you escape the convoluted career idol and make it to Heaven?"

"Jesus Christ provided the necessary grace from a unique and unexpected source for a wretched sinner like me to repent of my sins."

"Oh boy, do I know how that works—"

Erica burst out laughing. "Of course you do. You encountered the angel Mick. I'm just busting your chops."

They all chuckled.

"Before I tell you how my eyes were finally opened, let me share with you the single verse that initially moved me off of my wrongful path towards destruction, and on to the road towards Heaven. It's in

Ecclesiastes 4:4 … And I saw that all toil and all achievement spring from one person's envy of another. This too is meaningless, a chasing after the wind."

Rachel nodded. "Yeah, we've talked about Solomon quite a bit today. That's a great verse for what you've described as your career idol."

"So here's how my repentance all went down," Erica said, nodding. "Twice a day, I received my company mail from a nice young man in our mail room named Ned. Ned was very good at what he did, but he was also a special needs person. Although he functioned at a high level in carrying out his duties, he didn't have great social skills. Most of the people in our organization looked down on him for not being on their intelligence level."

Rachel's brow furrowed. "Really? That surprises me."

"Oh, people were nice to Ned to his face. But behind closed doors, they whispered snide jokes about him."

"That's sad. Really sad."

Erica grinned. "Oh, but wait! This story has a happy ending."

"I'm glad to hear that."

"So one Friday afternoon, I was enjoying a cup of coffee in my office when Ned knocked on the door. I asked him to come in and he politely handed me a certified piece of mail. As he turned to leave, I noticed his tee shirt, which was from a popular Christian musical group. It was casual dress that day, so most employees were wearing jeans and casual shirts. Anyway, I felt compelled to ask Ned some questions about his faith, knowing he would probably have some woefully inadequate answers. To me, this was a sneaky way to feel superior to him…."

"This is getting interesting," Rachel said. "Please, go on."

"After a few minutes of me asking Ned questions about Christianity, and him giving me beautifully simple-but-effective answers, I asked him to sit down and shut the door. It was then that everything changed in my life. After that hour-long chat with a special-needs mailroom clerk, my life turned on a dime."

"It almost sounds like Ned was some kind of angel," Rachel said, shooting a look over at Jerry.

Jerry held up his hands. "Not guilty, ladies. God uses angels like Mick and me in His kingdom all the time. However, He uses His children like Ned to shepherd the lost far more often."

Erica smiled. "Anyway, I thought Ned would be easy-pickings when it came to my previously deep-rooted objections to Christianity. However, it was he who made mincemeat out of my feeble attacks on his faith."

"Wait a minute," Rachel said. "Didn't you say you grew up in church?"

"I did. However, going to church in our family was all for show. There was no real conviction of sin in our home, so no real repentance took place. By the time I made CEO of a company decades later, there was virtually nothing left of my previously false Christian faith."

"I see. So what did Ned say to you?"

"It wasn't necessarily what he said. He also didn't use any kind of fancy or contrived technique. It was more about my sensing that his faith in Christ was the real deal, and it looked absolutely beautiful. Reflecting back on it, I feel that his lack of pretense and innocent, childlike love of Jesus caught me off guard. To be honest, if Ned wasn't along the intellectual level of say ... Forest Gump ... I would've probably entered the conversation with my intellectual shield on and my secular sword drawn. In the end, I walked into a spiritual battle with Ned and I was totally unprepared for it. His simple approach to understanding mankind's need for Jesus Christ absolutely crushed my lack of faith."

"I think what Erica is trying to say," Jerry said. "Is that on that fateful afternoon, she inadvertently wandered into the spiritual fortress of a common man's real faith. By the time Erica knew what was going on, the Holy Spirit had convicted her heart. You ladies shouldn't be surprised by this. There is no one wiser than the Lord."

Erica nodded. "After I peppered Ned with questions for a while, I thanked him and he left my office. That weekend, I lost a lot of sleep due to the deep conviction God was placing on my heart."

"That's interesting," said Rachel. "Was there anything in particular that Ned shared with you which led to your spiritual awakening?"

"Actually, there was. No matter how hard I tried, I had to face a daunting fact he kept going back to: *1 Corinthians 15:26 says ... The last enemy to be destroyed is death.*"

Rachel whistled. "Wow. How true is that? No matter what you said in objection, Ned kept coming back to that basic metaphysical truth, huh?"

"You've got it. The reality that everyone inevitably dies hit me hard in so many different ways. Since the false idol in my life was my career, the thought of me being gone one day and the company pushing ahead without me was absolutely devastating. I was nothing short of horrified at the thought of this."

"The faith you had in your idol was a proverbial house of cards," Jerry added. "In fact, when you measure the certainty of physical death against every single temptation, sin, or idol out there, everything will lose-out to the reality of death."

"How true," Erica said. "Anyway, a few weeks after my little chat with good ole Ned, I had several of my other Christian employees gather in my office at my request. It was there that one of our department managers—a man who was about four levels of management below me—led me to Christ. By the time he led me through a prayer of repentance, I was absolutely balling my eyes out. It was quite an emotional scene."

"So what happened after that?" said Rachel.

"A few months later, and after much reflection and prayer, I decided to retire and take a year off to figure out what to do with the rest of my life. By that time in my life, I had lots of time on my hands because my son was grown and married, and my husband and I had divorced."

"How sad."

"Not totally. The good news is that I had a humongous portfolio. I was actually able to leave the company and not have to worry about ever working again. It was a tremendous blessing."

"That's wonderful."

"So while I was enjoying my sabbatical, I tried to find the right balance between doing some charity work on the side, and some much-needed leisure activities. It was during that time that my doctors discovered a heart issue that was likely caused by the stress of so many difficult years in my working life. Anyway, I died of a heart attack a few months after that and ended up here in Paradise. The end."

Rachel chuckled. "That's quite a story, Erica."

Erica smiled and nodded. "The one thing I want to leave you with today, Rachel, is that if God is at the top of your mountain of life, you'll have far less stress to deal with. For me, personally, it was a huge relief when I relinquished the godship of my life because all of the pressure was off and I finally found peace."

"Sage words, Erica. Thanks for your time today."

"The pleasure's all mine. Hey, not to play spoiler or anything, but you're getting ready to finish up your final lesson, and it's probably going to be a bit of a surprise. Well, it was a surprise to me when I was sitting in your very seat. I expect it will be the same for you."

"I can't wait," Rachel said.

"Anyway, thanks for listening to my story."

"And I thank you, Erica. Your story was amazing."

17
RELIGION

"Those who consider themselves religious and yet do not keep a tight rein on their tongues deceive themselves, and their religion is worthless."
James 1:26

As Rachel, Jerry, and Erica arrived back at the fountain from the north end, a beautiful dark-haired, dark-eyed woman was already waiting for them.

"Greetings Linda," Erica said to her. "Are you ready to take Rachel through her final lesson today?"

Linda smiled. "I sure am. It's so nice to see you again Rachel," she said, turning towards her newest student.

"I suppose we're going that way," Rachel said, pointing towards the east end of the square. "That's the only direction left."

"Right you are," said Linda, gently placing her hand on Rachel's back and guiding her. "Thank you for also coming, Jerry."

"Of course, milady," the angel said, as they strolled towards the central structure on the east end.

Once they entered Linda's building, the ambiance took on an expressly cathedral feel. Although there were stained glass windows surrounding the main seating area beyond the stone-floored atrium, the general setting was more like a library than a church.

They all sat down on dark wooden framed chairs with red padding.

"The first thing I want to discuss," Linda began. "Is that I'm guessing you didn't notice the pattern regarding the twelve names of the ladies on the mountain today. Am I wrong? Did you somehow figure it out?"

Rachel thought for a moment. "No, you're not wrong. I have no idea what you're talking about."

Linda grinned. "Take the first letter of each of our names—in order—and see if you can figure out what I'm driving at."

Rachel thought about it for few moments as she recalled each lady's name, one by one. Suddenly, she blurted, "The order of your names spells out L-O-V-E-I-M-M-A-N-U-E-L."

"That's right!" said Linda. "And that's the key to your journey on the mountain today. You must know and love the one who carried the title of Immanuel—*God with us,* who is Jesus Christ. Very good."

"What a nice surprise."

"Love Immanuel is actually the name of the mountain we're on. If you'll notice, a name has never been previously used with the mountain since we first met, down at the bottom."

"How interesting—and you're right. The name of the mountain has not previously been disclosed. I've actually had that thought fluttering around the back of my mind all day."

Linda nodded. "And the theme of Love Immanuel Mountain is this: *John 14:15 ... 'If you love me, keep my commands.'*"

"That's so interesting. Jerry has been walking me through how sin, temptations, and idols block the love of God. But there it is; in just a few words."

"Absolutely. Humanity's entire problem with sin boils down to this one essential concept—either one repents and bows down to God and obeys Him, or one expects God to bow down and obey you."

Rachel smiled. "What a lovely way to open my closing lesson today. But I must admit; I have no idea what your topic of discussion is. It's not as apparent as most of the other ones are."

"The subject of my idol is one that's actually going to be greatly expanded upon in another class you'll be taking next week. For today, I'm merely going to do an overview for you."

"Why is that?"

"It's because this subject is far more substantial than the others, and it includes numerous sub-categories that necessitate much longer and deeper discussions. But no worries, you'll get a lot out of my brief overview. After that, we'll reconvene at the fountain with the other ladies for your graduation ceremony."

"Graduation ceremony?"

"Of course. This is Heaven. We love to celebrate."

Rachel grinned. "Great. So what was your idol? I'm very curious."

"Religion."

"Religion?"

Linda nodded. "Oh, yes. To launch our discussion properly, I have some references for you, starting with something that's crucial for everyone who's involved in Christian ministry. It's in *Psalm 127:1* … *Unless the Lord builds the house, the builders labor in vain. Unless the Lord watches over the city, the guards stand watch in vain.*"

"So what exactly do you mean by that?"

"Let's first start with my story."

"Good idea."

"What I have to say is rather simple. My family came to America from India, but we were already Christians when we arrived. After I graduated high school, I went to seminary and later became a pastor."

"That does sound simple."

Linda nodded. "My early Christian training was in a denomination that was works-based. This greatly diminished God's grace, which needs no human hands adding to it. Although it took a while, I ultimately found my way out of that religion and pastored a small non-denominational church inside a large city in the Midwest. Interestingly, our congregation was primarily from the area of the world where I was born. Although we didn't have a huge number of people in our church, the congregants were strong followers of Christ and were always eager to share their faith with others."

"That doesn't sound like most churches today."

"Oh, it wasn't. Unfortunately, many churches today are deceived into becoming quasi-spiritual country clubs. In these instances, they're really nothing more than places of hidden idol worship."

"What exactly do you mean by that?"

"If Christ isn't the focus of the church, then it's as humanistic as every other idol you've encountered today. You see, the modern idols of today generally influence people towards their self. That's unlike many of the ancient idols, which were often graven images and the like. People back then worshipped those demonic, graven images. Today, it's the same sin, but a different focus."

Rachel nodded. "It appears that Satan has amended his gameplan throughout the ages as it relates to idols."

"Indeed. But we must all remember this from *Micah 5:13 … I will destroy your idols and your sacred stones from among you; you will no longer bow down to the work of your hands.*"

"I see. So how exactly was religion your idol?"

"Before I saw the wisdom of turning from my works-based Christian views, my ministry itself became my idol. Well, that plus all of the other charity work I was involved in. For many of my early years of studying theology and being involved in church, I actually thought I had to do more good deeds than bad ones to atone for my sins. It was utterly exhausting."

"I'll bet," said Rachel.

"My attitude towards Jesus Christ was very similar to the ancient Pharisees, who Jesus rebuked during His ministry on Earth."

"How so?"

Linda shook her head. "I was constantly trying to add to God's commands. We're now under the New Covenant since the time of Jesus Christ's resurrection, so attempting to add to God's work is a sin. When you fall into the trap of adding rules to the simplicity of God's complete gift of grace, you've fallen into … you guessed it … idol worship."

"Why is that? I'm not sure I'm following you."

"When you feel the need to add to Christ's perfect sacrificial work on the Cross, you've basically exalted yourself above Him; even if you don't realize it."

"I'm still not sure—"

"Think about it. Does the suffering, torture, and death of Christ at Calvary need anything added to it to save you from your sins? Do your good works somehow complete what Jesus did—or was Jesus right when He said, *it is finished?*"

Rachel was quiet for a few moments.

"When Jesus was resurrected on the third day," Linda continued. "The punishment due all people for their sin and the miracle of Christ's resurrection showed mankind the way to Heaven—but only through God's grace. Without God's grace, we'd all remain in our sins—regardless of how many old ladies we've helped across the street during our lifetime. Always remember this: *1 Corinthians 15:17* says ... *And if Christ has not been raised, your faith is futile; you are still in your sins."*

"I'd like to add something," Jerry said. "It's in *Ezra 9:6* ... *and prayed: 'I am too ashamed and disgraced, my God, to lift up my face to you, because our sins are higher than our heads and our guilt has reached to the heavens."*

"There is no longer a reason to fear sin since Jesus paid the price," Linda said. "But one must repent of their sins and trust alone in Jesus to receive God's salvation and grace. It's just that simple."

Rachel shook her head. "But there are many world religions—and even some Christian ones—that have had additional 'prophets' come and attempt to add to what you describe as what Jesus did on the Cross. How do they explain something like that?"

"It doesn't matter how they try to explain it," Jerry said. "Satan influences people to amend the Word of God all the time to keep them from the Truth. The best way to think about it is just that—if someone is adding to Christ's work on the Cross, they're doing so to exalt themself."

Rachel was quiet for a few moments again. "So you're saying that the idol of religion comes into play when—"

"Oftentimes, it comes into play when you add-to or amend what God has ordained or revealed," said Linda. "On the one hand, many universalists believe that good and evil do not actually exist, and that God will bring everyone to Heaven...."

Jerry shuddered. "God certainly won't force anyone to come here. In addition, there must be punishment for sin or the Lord wouldn't be a just God."

Linda nodded. "On the other hand, many cults—both large and small—have tried to add to the work of Jesus on the Cross. Universalists don't require anything of God, and cults require falsehood beyond the Word of God. What I'm saying to you is this. As it relates to religion, there are many man-made idols out there. One must be careful, or it can become very confusing."

Rachel shrugged. "So what's the best way to be careful? It doesn't matter for me since I'm now in Heaven. But I'd like to know."

Linda smiled. "I'm glad you asked. The answer starts in *John 1:1* which says ... *In the beginning was the Word, and the Word was with God, and the Word was God."*

"Jesus is the Word of God," Jerry added. "Jesus is God."

"That's beautiful," said Rachel. "Simply beautiful. I look forward to digging deeper into this subject in that class you mentioned. I still have many questions."

"You'll love it," Linda said. "Okay, so I have just a couple more things for you before we head back to the fountain. The first thing is that I promised to get back to the passage mentioned earlier in *Psalm 127:1 … Unless the Lord builds the house, the builders labor in vain. Unless the Lord watches over the city, the guards stand watch in vain …* Do you remember that?"

"I sure do."

"This concept is very important for Christian ministries down on Earth. If the Lord isn't behind what they are doing, it's going to fail. The focus must always be on Jesus, not on false idols which distract people from the essential Gospel message that Jesus Christ is the only way to God."

"I see."

"Earlier in my career, I didn't realize that. It was when I fully embraced God's grace that the Lord granted me success in my ministry."

"Let me add," Jerry said. "That Linda's success wasn't necessarily stated in human terms—like the size of her congregation or weekly giving amounts. Her success was in spiritual maturity. When you look back on the subject of religion from Heaven's perspective, everything in church pales in comparison to this one, basic concept—did you do everything you can to make disciples during your life, or did you build a nice place to worship? Hopefully, it's both, but it should definitely be the former."

"Amen," Linda said. "Anyway, the last thing I wanted to cover with you today, Rachel, is probably going to hit home a little hard with you, so please be prepared."

"Oh—what's that?"

"Love itself is perhaps the biggest of all idols."

"Really—how so???"

"Think about it. I know you earlier discussed that your family was problematic in steering you towards idols. The downfall in your life was that you fixated on the incomplete version of love that humans define. You were also unaware of God's real version of love."

"Are you referring to agape love? If so, we've definitely covered that quite a bit today."

Linda nodded. "I am, but that's not all. Typically, when humans latch onto the expression that *God is love,* they're almost always referring to the concept of the proverbial cosmic Santa Claus that's been shared with you many times since the angel Mick came to see you recently."

"Yes. The idea that God is on-call to come drop presents on someone every time they want something is most definitely a lie."

"And so is the concept that *God is love* without God also being a judge of bad behavior and sin. Like Jerry mentioned a moment ago, a God who didn't judge sin wouldn't be a fair and just God at all. And for those who attempt to cherry pick God's love without also including the important element of God's judgment ... well ... they're committing the grandest sin of idolatry in that they're worshipping a contrived god; a false god; one that doesn't actually exist."

"I see," said Rachel. "So in the same way, you're saying that the idol which prevented me from truly knowing God was the human version of love, which is incomplete."

"That's it."

Rachel sighed. "I believed in a false god who was obligated to deliver me the perfect man in Blaine Billings, who was rich, handsome, intelligent, charming, and who would take care of me forever and ever. This was a false version of real love. It was all a lie."

Linda looked down for a moment, then back into Rachel's eyes. "Yes," she said. "That is correct."

Rachel started to speak, but then paused for a moment. She then said, "Somehow, I feel like I've now completed what I needed to learn on the mountain today. Is it time for graduation?"

Linda smiled broadly. "It sure is—congratulations. Are you ready to go and celebrate?"

"I sure am!"

Rachel and Linda embraced before the three of them headed back out of the building and towards the fountain. As they neared the center of the square, Rachel noticed that all of the ladies from her visit on the mountain today were now present once again; all smiling and waiting for her. She quickened her pace.

"I had no idea that *everyone* would crash my graduation party," she said to the group as they arrived. "What a nice surprise."

"Rachel, we have a word for you," Jerry said, moving into the center of the group of ladies. "This verse will make a lot of sense to you as we send you to your final part of today's journey. You only have one last thing to do, but none of us will be joining you for your real graduation party. Someone else will be handling that."

"Oh—who is that?"

"Jesus Christ."

"Oh, how wonderful," Rachel exclaimed, a surge of joy pulsing throughout her soul. "I suppose I'm going to have to get used to the fact that in Heaven, Jesus is not separated from me anymore."

Jerry nodded. "As simple as it sounds, that's correct."

"Listen, Rachel," Lillie said. "Since I led off your lessons today with our discussion of leisure, I'm the one honored to share with you this last passage. Now this word has been thought-out with great care and was chosen after great consideration. We all feel that you've learned quite a lot today, and we look forward to your fellowship for all of eternity."

"That's quite a build-up," Rachel said. "So what is this final word you have for me?"

"It's in *Deuteronomy 1:6 ... The Lord our God said to us at Horeb, 'You have stayed long enough at this mountain.'*"

Rachel laughed heartily. "So y'all are kicking me off of Love Immanuel Mountain, huh?"

Jerry took Rachel's arm as he led her towards the twelve ladies, who had now formed two rows for her to walk through.

"Jesus is waiting for you," the angel said. "If you follow this path through the northwest end of the village, it will take you above the clouds and to the top of the mountain. There, you will find your destiny."

"What do you mean by—?"

"Just go," Jerry said, releasing her hand. "Just follow the trail."

Rachel walked ahead, slowly at first. After a few moments, she turned back towards the others and waved. Everyone waved back. After turning back towards the trail, she felt fulfilled and excited.

This was the first time Rachel had been alone since passing from Earth earlier that day. She sensed that this moment was incredibly poignant and was the true purpose of why she had been brought to the mountain today. She felt a great sense of excitement and anticipation in her soul.

It was time to see her Savior again.

The pathway into the clouds was similar to the trail they used to ascend the mountain, but the forest was further to the sides of it. With each step she took, a gentle fog began to materialize. The fog was very light at first, but got heavier as the forest continued to peel further away from the trail. Soon, there was only the path in front of her and the brightest of piercing lights in its center.

She continued ahead, mesmerized.

When the light at the center of the path ahead became as sharp as anything Rachel had ever seen, the fog had become as thick as walking through an enormous puffy mattress. As she neared the end of the trail, her senses told her Jesus was near.

And she was right.

An ethereal passageway at the end of the path fully opened. As Rachel walked through it, the fog behind her seemed to suddenly disappear. When Rachel looked back at the doorway, she realized that the fog was actually a cloud.

She chuckled.

Rachel turned her gaze forward. Through the indescribable brightness above the clouds, Rachel saw Jesus Christ standing at the very tip-top of the mountain. He waved her over.

"Welcome, Rachel," Jesus said. "Did you enjoy your visits along the way up to see me today?"

"I did, my Lord. Thank you for teaching me so much about your ways. I have soooo enjoyed all of the sisters who shared their incredible stories with me."

"Good, my child. Were the lessons valuable to you?"

"Very much so. As you know, I was estranged from you for most of my life as I chased after idols instead of you. I hate to think about what would've happened if you hadn't sent the angel Mick to see me."

"You belong to me, Rachel. That is all you need to concern yourself with right now."

"Thank you, Lord."

"Please walk with me, back down the mountain. I promised you earlier that we'd have time to walk and talk together. I want you to use this time to ask me any questions you wish. After all, you're home with me forever. I want you to enjoy the bounty of my kingdom, which has no end."

"Before we go," Rachel said. "I'd like to ask you one simple question while we're here at the top of the mountain."

"Go right ahead."

"Why did you choose a mountain to teach me about real love?"

Jesus grinned. "Parables are a great way to illustrate important spiritual truths."

"Oh, I realize that, Lord. But why a mountain?"

"I chose a mountain because it vividly demonstrates what your life should look like. Every person has differing responsibilities and circumstances in their life. But none of it should block my real love from cascading down onto you. In the case of idols, all they do is create a cloud cover that blocks the top of the mountain, which is where I am. After all, that's what I want for everyone—to repent of their sins and trust alone in me."

"Oh, I see," said Rachel. "So once I visited with each sister who shared with me their specific sins of idolatry, I was then able to walk above the clouds and visualize the truth that you are the only true God in existence."

Jesus nodded. "Now that you understand all of that, I wish to discuss a wonderful surprise I have in store for you as we walk back down the mountain."

"A surprise? For me?"

"Indeed. Just for you."

"What is it, Lord?"

"I don't want to ruin the surprise just yet."

Rachel grinned. "After all you've done for me, why in the world would I try to argue with you?"

Jesus laughed. "Indeed! Come, now. Walk back down the mountain with me. I think you're really going to like what I have to share with you. Oh, and you're going to just *love* your surprise."

PART 3

EYES OF THE HEART

18

Jefferson, GA
October 10, 2007
"And if I go and prepare a place for you, I will come back and take you to be with me that you also may be where I am"
John 14:3

The funeral home in Jefferson quietly sat perched atop a small hill across from a lovely lake, which lay peacefully across a two-lane street. Located near the confluence of two primary roads in this quaint northeast Georgia town, a sparse gathering awaited the funeral service for Rachel Green to begin.

"So how's your dad doing?" Vanessa Hunter asked PJ, standing inside the foyer adjacent to the chapel. "He and I haven't spoken much since Rachel passed away last week. He was the first person I called after she died, you know."

"Oh, I think he's doing okay," PJ said. "Your husband Wyatt has been a huge big help to him the last few days. I'm just glad Wyatt's not out of town on business this week and could be here today. As you can see, there isn't exactly a throng of people attending the service."

"Thanks, PJ. Even though she was elderly and sick, Aunt Rachel's passing was still a bit of a shock to us all. As I shared with you, I'm the first family member who arrived at her house after the fella who was working in her yard called 911. This whole thing has been more difficult than I could've ever imagined."

"I understand."

"Anyway, while I'm glad Aunt Rachel is finally at rest, I do hope she turned to Christ before passing. This has been bothering me all week."

"I have that very same hope," PJ said. "Dad said they had a great talk about Jesus after yours and her discussion of the same subject last week. He has great hope that she turned to Christ before she died."

Rachel forced a grin. "Thanks."

PJ nodded, slightly. "As a pastor, I deal with the subject of death all the time, Vanessa. So please let me give you a little bit of advice. I suggest you not spend much time trying to predict where your aunt is right now. In truth, none of us knows what happens in the last moments before someone enters eternity. That's strictly a transaction between each person and their Creator."

Vanessa shrugged. "Then what should I do? I have a lot of conflicting feelings going on."

"Death is out of our hands. It belongs to God, so leave it with Him. In the meantime, I believe moments like this service today are great opportunities to tell others about the importance of trusting alone in Jesus Christ—"

She shook her head. "Yeah, but with some people, you just know they'll be in the immediate presence of the Lord when they die. For example, someone like … your father Harvey. There's no way you can convince me he isn't headed right into the presence of Jesus Christ when he leaves this life."

"I understand what you're saying, Vanessa. And I don't disagree with you. The point I was driving at is that we cannot pretend to have the knowledge of God when it comes to those who may or may not have repented of their sins and received Christ's forgiveness. For those who bear the obvious fruit of repentance and salvation—like my father—it's far more obvious and therefore very comforting."

"So in the situation of my Aunt Rachel—?"

"In her case, there's always the hope in Christ for where she is right now. So let's honor Rachel today with that wonderful hope. Between you and me as fellow followers of Jesus, we really can't be sure if Rachel turned to Christ or not. So what do you say? Can we just honor her?"

Vanessa lightly squeezed PJ on the arm. "I agree, yes."

They were quiet for a few moments.

"So where is—?" PJ began.

"There they come," Vanessa said, pointing over at Harvey and her husband Wyatt as they approached them.

"Are you ready, son?" Harvey asked PJ when they arrived. "Did you go over what we discussed last night?"

"Yes, I've got it dad," PJ said. "And thanks to you, Wyatt, for spending some time with my dad this week. You've been a big help."

Wyatt nodded. "The pleasure's all mine."

"Okay then," PJ continued. "It's time to get the service started. Dad—as we discussed, I'll do the preliminary intro for a few minutes and then turn the floor over to you. Please remember to take your time, breathe, and most importantly, honor Rachel from your heart."

"Don't worry, son," Harvey said. "I've got a real sense of peace about everything. I know you may not believe me, but trust me on this. The Holy Spirit is with me. Thanks to Wyatt, I'm not thinking about how to deliver fancy words or impress anyone with my biblical knowledge. I'm just going to speak to the attendees from my heart today. While I plan to honor my dear friend Rachel, I also have an important message to share with everyone. God has made that clear to me."

"Good, dad. Let's get started."

****

After the service's early arriving attendees filed into the chapel along with some late arrivals, PJ spoke to the group of about forty people with some opening prayer and Scripture. After giving some basic background information on Rachel, he was then ready to turn the pulpit over to his father. After he called Harvey to the stage, PJ prayed silently for God to anoint his dad with the strength to emotionally hold up and deliver a two-fold message: one that honors Rachel, and one that honors God.

Harvey stepped up to the lectern and opened his Bible. He then put on his glasses and opened a piece of paper, which had been folded neatly in half and tucked into his Bible. These were his notes. Harvey was dressed in a typical black suit with a dark tie. The suit was very loose on his frame due to his recent weight loss.

He cleared his throat.

"Good morning everyone," he said, somberly. "As a lifelong friend of Rachel's, and on behalf of the entire family, I want to thank you all for coming today. Now what I have to say to you will probably be unlike anything you might be expecting. That's very much by design. In my various experiences in life, I've unfortunately attended far too many services like this. It goes without saying that days like today are profoundly sad. But days like today can also serve to shake us out of our false comfort zones to face the sobering reality that the specter of death is always near to all of us. Death always summons an understandable sense of dread in our souls. I don't think I'm stretching the truth to say that death is as unnatural as it is frightening.

"With that in mind, what I first want to share with you is something simple and quite obvious: Death is the great divider. Death is obviously a very serious and terrifying subject. However, we cannot simply ignore it and expect it to go away. Without question, death looms over all of us like a vicious raptor circling overhead, during all of our days in this life. No matter what we think, or like, or say, or do, death is indeed a reality for our brief time here on Earth. It is the great equalizer for every single living thing.

"At first, this may seem to be cruel of the Lord for death to be such a prominent and foreboding element in our lives. But it really isn't—at least from His eternal perspective. I've been a follower of Christ since I can remember, and there's one incredibly important thing I've come to realize and want for all of you to hear right now—real love endures hardships and momentary pain. Our tribulations can, should, and absolutely will be replaced one day with God's eternal glory, but it can only happen through the person of Jesus Christ."

Harvey took a breath.

"I've known Rachel Green for as long as I can remember. Our special friendship goes back to a time so long ago; neither of us could remember when we first met. I can tell you with complete honesty that Rachel has always been an important part of my life. She was very much like family to me. Rachel is often in my thoughts and prayers, and I actually feel like she is a part of my soul. Although we never married or even dated, I know our destinies have always been indelibly intertwined. From the bottom of my heart, I say this to you now … I hope my life is always connected with Rachel's.

"Like I said, throughout my seventy-five years, Rachel has always been a big part of me. This was so, even when I was angry at her for some of what I consider to have been some very poor choices in her life. I understand the fact that we all make mistakes, but Rachel seemed to be unusually attuned to falling into worldly traps. She always had a great big heart, but in my loving opinion, her head wasn't always as discerning as it should have been. Having said that, however, the bottom line is that I have always loved Rachel ... and I always will.

"She and I grew up in a small community named Cottondale, which is not too far from Ft. Worth, Texas. After we finished school, we both went out into the world to pursue our destinies. Somehow, perhaps through the providence of God, we both ended up here in Northeast Georgia, many years later. Now don't ask me how this happened, because I really don't know. Only my heavenly Father knows the answer to that question. But honestly, God's strong presence in my life has always given me great comfort; knowing He is leading me towards His will, not my own. Although following God's will for my life is the only way I can imagine living, sometimes it's also painful to my human nature.

"Honesty is very important, and days like today are a good time to be completely transparent with both God and with others. As I stand here now over the deceased body of my beloved Rachel, I can tell you I have no regrets about anything in my own life. Although it certainly hasn't been the script I chose for myself, I know my Savior has been with me throughout all of the good times—and certainly through the bad ones. I honestly couldn't have survived all this time without the Lord. I pray that all of you feel that same way about God.

"I have a few passages I want to share with you today to express how I'm feeling inside about our loss of Rachel. I hope all of you will glean something of eternal value as I share them with you."

He paused, catching his breath. It was now difficult to hold back a sudden torrent of tears, which were absolutely desperate to escape.

"The first one I'd like to share with you is from *3 John 1:4,* which says ... *I have no greater joy than to hear that my children are walking in the truth.* Now what I mean is simply this ... I can spend all day telling you about how wonderful Rachel was, but those words would ultimately fade like smoke on the wind. What really matters here today is that every single one of you understands that death is real; death is imminent; and death is emphatic and painful. Before we die, we all need forgiveness for our sins. This can only come through the person of Jesus Christ.

"Going back into biblical history, we learn something very important from King Solomon in *Ecclesiastes 3:1-2 ... There is a time for everything, and a season for every activity under the heavens: a time to be born and a time to die, a time to plant and a time to uproot.* I've always believed that even though this statement in Scripture is absolutely true, that's not all there is to our lives. Some say that love is the most important thing we leave this world with, but that's not entirely true. You see, the human version of love must line up with God's version, or it's not real love; it's not a love that lasts forever. And to be honest, a love that doesn't last forever isn't really all that wonderful when you really think about it. Other than salvation being only through the person of Jesus Christ, what I wish to impart to you today about the subject of love is the most important thing I want you to leave here with.

"God tells us something wonderful, that's as pure as it is short and sweet in *1 Corinthians 16:14 ... Do everything in love.* Now this may sound good to all of us—even unbelievers. But what exactly is love? How can we push ahead in life with something most everyone in this world agrees with, but something which is so vague? Today, my friends, just like the youngsters say, I hope to unpack this subject for you. I don't believe it's good enough to just say how important or wonderful love is. I feel that a much deeper definition of real love and what it entails is critically important to understanding what God means in that passage."

Harvey paused.

"When I got the call last week from Vanessa that her Aunt Rachel had suddenly passed away, I felt very much like a prophet in the Old Testament named Nehemiah. In his opening comments, we see this interesting passage in *Nehemiah 1:4 ... When I heard these things, I sat down and wept. For some days I mourned and fasted and prayed before the God of heaven.* This, my friends, for a different reason than the prophet experienced, is exactly how I felt when I heard that Rachel had passed away. I was overcome with shock and an emptiness that defies words.

"The good news is that it didn't take long for God to begin to soothe my soul with His blessed words of comfort. Chief among the passages I studied after hearing of Rachel's sudden passing is an interesting one in *1 Corinthians 15:55 ... 'Where, O death, is your victory? Where, O death, is your sting?'*

"At this point, I think it bears noting that God sent Jesus to take the punishment for our sins. When you look at the next two important verses in that overall passage, we see the completion of an incredibly important message. It continues in *1 Corinthians 15:56-57 ... The sting of death is sin, and the power of sin is the law. But thanks be to God! He gives us the victory through our Lord Jesus Christ.*"

When Harvey paused this time, he waited for several moments as he scanned the entire group of people assembled before him. The gravity of the moment coupled with what he felt was an important message to at least one person in the audience felt heavy on his shoulders. Perhaps there was even more than one person who needed to hear the importance of the Gospel message, so he continued with what God had placed on his heart.

"I'd like to now share with you some attributes of what I see as God's version of real love. Throughout my nearly seven decades of studying the Bible, I feel that mankind has kidnapped and corrupted the definition of love. I think it's important to now delineate these differences.

"To begin with, I feel that mankind's version of love is flawed and incomplete. Benjamin Franklin is quoted as saying, 'half a truth is often a great lie.' To my way of thinking, it's always a great lie.

"Because of the magnitude of our loss of Rachel, I believe the world has nothing substantial to offer when it comes to our grief. There's really nothing in the natural world which can effectively deal with something unnatural like death. Because of this, I feel that the world is completely deficient and desperately incomplete when it comes to losing a loved one. In other words, the world has absolutely nothing to offer my soul.

"We read something interesting in *Mark 8:36 … What good is it for someone to gain the whole world, yet forfeit their soul?* This sobering passage doesn't sugar coat the truth that death is the great divider. Chasing after the world is a path to nowhere, my friends. Actually, check that. It's the road to perdition.

"So let me tell you some of the things I wrote down that I feel represent what real love is. From an old man's perspective like mine, I feel like these things very much compliment what we're told about love in *1 Corinthians 13:4-8*. As many of you know, that passage is often recited at many weddings. I truly hope you'll hear me today, because I've given all of this a lot of thought before speaking with you. These thoughts are very much based on my own experiences in life.

"Okay, here goes. I believe that real love is a decision and a choice; I believe it's sacrificial, and when it's used properly, it's godly; I believe real love is both strong and discriminatory; it's not based on mere feelings or emotions; real love stands alone and above the world; and real love brings about real love. It all starts with God, and there can be no real love apart from Him.

Harvey paused again.

"On the other hand, let me share with you a few things I feel that real love is *not*. Real love is not to be confused with lust; real love is not about your longings or who makes you feel a certain way; real love defies logic and is above all things in this world because it is borne of God; real love is not strictly about romance and sex. Real love is not about how you feel—it's about what is righteous.

"In speaking about the different kinds of love, CS Lewis is quoted as saying that 'Eros will have naked bodies; friendship naked personalities.' In order to experience real love, one must transcend the body, mind, and soul into something far greater than anything imagined by a mere human being.

"Please hear me when I tell you that passionate or eros love is absolutely important in a marriage—but it cannot sustain a relationship without some help. Yes, eros love stirs our emotions like nothing else, but it cannot stand alone. In other words, eros love can only be an ingredient; not an entire meal. Far too often, people get this concept wrong.

Harvey paused and quickly scanned the room again. Every single person seemed to be riveted to his every word. Normally this might be a bit disconcerting. But he was in the wheelhouse of the Holy Spirit and he felt calm and amazingly powerful due to God's presence and guidance.

"In the romance book of the Bible, we see this powerfully emotional passage. It's in *Song of Songs 8:6 ... Place me like a seal over your heart, like a seal on your arm; for love is as strong as death, its jealousy unyielding as the grave. It burns like blazing fire, like a mighty flame.* Indeed, eros love motivates the human heart like nothing else. It can feel like a veritable bonfire of passion.

"But is that all there is to love? Are human feelings strong enough to carry the load for an enormous concept like real love? Am I wrong about all of this???

He paused for only a moment.

"Certainly not. If God isn't involved, love will inevitably fail. Like I said, the human version of love, which is largely based on feelings, isn't designed to stand alone. Although it feels incredibly powerful, it's incomplete without the Creator of all things. It's like trying to bake a cake with only the flour and none of the other key ingredients.

"So why am I telling all of this to you today? Why am I speaking about what real love is at the funeral service for my dearest friend? It's because I want every single one of you to consider what the world would look like without God. That, my friends, is what Hell must be like. Can you imagine a place without faith, hope, or love? Personally, I cannot.

"The reason I'm speaking about real love today is that I feel it's the best way I can honor Rachel. How so? Because I tried as hard as I could to demonstrate real love to her throughout our lives together, even when some might say she didn't deserve it.

"Does it surprise you to hear me say that? It shouldn't. My role model is Jesus Christ, so I'm always trying to mirror the real love He showed mankind by dying for our sins. In my own small life, I felt that God taught me early on that real love isn't about getting what you want all the time. No, real love is based on agape, sacrificial love. Agape love is the real deal. It's the one that lasts.

"Before I close today, I'd like to encourage all of you to consider what you think real love is all about. Is it centered on you and your feelings or dreams, or is it about God and His plan for you? When I was a young adult, I was fortunate to have learned how to abandon my search for the life I *desired*. Instead, I actually discovered the life I *recognized*. At first, this may seem a bit complicated, but it's really not.

"The life I wanted so badly was to marry Rachel, but she didn't want that from me. From the time I can remember, I thought she and I would get married and live happily ever after. But like I said, that didn't happen. So … should I feel sadness that this plan didn't go my way?

"Certainly not. God provided a way for me to show Rachel real love by being patient and by persevering; by having the opportunity to continue showing her a caring type of love, while at the same time, praying for her salvation in Christ; and by sticking with her when my feelings told me to just run away. That, my friends, wasn't the life I wanted. But it's very much the life I recognized. It was my purpose in Christ.

Harvey paused for the final time.

"I've been blessed in both my personal and business life to a degree I never could have imagined. For example, I was able to watch my beloved son PJ start our service today. And trust me, there's nothing more that warms my heart than to see my children loving and trusting alone in Jesus Christ. What more could a father ask for?

"Could I have lived my life just as happily if Rachel and I had married? Perhaps ... and perhaps not. Only God knows this. But I will tell you that after Rachel and I met for the last time a few days ago, I felt God working on her heart to a degree I hadn't ever seen before. I take great solace in the hope we will be reunited in Heaven one day. What a glorious day that will be.

"I have one last word for you, before PJ comes back up and continues with the service. It's in *2 Thessalonians 3:5 ... May the Lord direct your hearts into God's love and Christ's perseverance.*

"As you hear my words today, please know that God desires for everyone to repent of their sins and trust alone in Jesus Christ for their salvation. It is my great hope that all of us in this room will be in Heaven together one day, reminiscing about this very moment. Wouldn't that be an incredible thing?

"May the real love of Jesus Christ be with all of you always...."

19

"Jesus replied: 'Love the Lord your God with all your heart and with all your soul and with all your mind.' This is the first and greatest commandment."
Matthew 22:37-38

Harvey's beloved English bulldog named George sprawled across the floor of his screened-in back porch, panting steadily in the unusually warm night. Once again, as was their tradition, PJ sat with his father on the porch, staring out into the woods beyond the yard. Since the night time sky was pitch black, the stars and half gibbous moon shined an exceptionally bright contrast to the dark canvas they appeared to be painted upon.

"I have to say, dad," PJ said. "Your eulogy yesterday really stirred my heart. Although it wasn't the usual funeral fare, it was honest and it had a great message. I've done a fair number of funerals in my day, so I can say with confidence—that was a unique approach, for sure."

Harvey shrugged as he petted George's floppy ears. His beautifully pudgy companion lay comfortably at his feet.

"I don't know, son. Part of me feels like I should've done the usual thing and just said a few kind words. I certainly didn't want it to come across in any way as being about me—"

"Trust me, it didn't come across that way. I've always believed that funeral services are the best way to present the Gospel because you have such a captive audience. So many people live their lives with their head in the sand when it comes to the inevitability of death. The truth is, we'll all live forever. But not everyone will live in the same house after death."

"We both know that, son. Honestly, I wanted to bring a much stronger message than what I actually delivered. At my age, I don't feel like tip-toeing around the truth anymore, just to appease someone's entrenched humanism. Every single day is a ticking clock and our time left in this temporary life is short. I really feel like time's-a-wastin'. We all must tell the truth all of the time."

"I agree, but it's not easy. There's no singular way to share the Gospel."

"I understand that. Listen, it's been a strange week for me, son. This may sound a little odd, but I feel like I've now accomplished everything I'm supposed to do while I'm still on Earth. I certainly don't want to die, but—"

"No one really wants to die," PJ said. "God designed death to be a very serious event in one's lifetime."

Harvey nodded. "That's true. But PJ, trust me on this. There comes a time where really ardent followers of Christ just can't stand to live anymore in the death-ridden environment Earth has to offer. I mean, think about it. Even with something as common as our dinner of juicy hamburgers tonight, it involved an animal having to be sacrificed for us to eat. Although meals like that are fairly common to those who are blessed like us, it remains a type of sacrifice. God didn't originally design animals to become food, you know."

"True."

"Oh, perhaps I'm getting soft in my old age, but I'm telling you this again, right now—death is imminent for all living things. We all know that. However, death is very, very unnatural—especially to the soul of the Christian who longs so much to be in Heaven, where death doesn't happen. In God's presence, death is swallowed up in victory."

"That's in *1 Corinthians 15:54*."

"You are correct."

PJ shrugged. "So what are you getting at?"

"Just this—death is the great schoolmaster for ontology."

"What—?"

"Since Adam and Eve were cast out of the garden, our existence has always stood in the shadow of death. Well … to be perfectly honest with you … I'm sick and tired of dealing with death down here on Earth. I'm not saying I want to die, but I just feel mentally and spiritually exhausted with always having to deal with the shocking reality of death. It truly makes me sick, but there's not a whole lot I can do about it."

"I see. Since we're both big Star Trek fans, are you saying that your soul's deflector shields are breaking down when it comes to the subject of death? Are you tired of death being like a series of phaser blasts from the Klingons?"

Harvey laughed. "Indeed, son. That's pretty much it. I'm just tired of it all. I can't stand to see so many people—and even animals—die anymore. It actually hurts my soul in ways it never did when I was younger."

"That's interesting. I'll have to give all of that some thought. And speaking of thinking, I actually have a proposal for you tonight."

"Oh—what's that?"

"I had a type of a vision last night, after the funeral," PJ said. "When I woke up this morning, I found a passage that literally jumped out of my Bible at me. It's in *Daniel 2:19 ... During the night the mystery was revealed to Daniel in a vision. Then Daniel praised the God of heaven.*"

"Ahhh, so you had a vision from God, huh? You have to be careful about something like that. Sometimes, people get alleged visions that are either from themself ... or even worse ... from the enemy."

"No, dad. It's not like that at all. I'm very familiar with how Satan launches fiery darts at us, and I'm at peace with what I'm about to tell you. I've actually been praying about it all day."

"You certainly have my curiosity piqued. What's on your mind?"

"I think you need to go back home to Cottondale for a visit."

"Cottondale?"

"Yes, Cottondale. I think you need to go home to see what God has to say to you. I sense He will reveal something very important to you, but only if you go home."

"Hmmm. That's certainly an interesting prospect."

"I know your appointment with the heart doctor isn't until the week after next, so I think you should hop on a plane in the next few days and go to your original hometown. You haven't been out there for awhile, and I'll be more than happy to watch George for you. I feel strongly that this trip is what God wants you to do, but I honestly don't know why."

Harvey pondered this.

PJ continued, "I think it's ironic that the growing up in the small town of Cottondale ended up launching you into the world with the one value that has nothing to do with money, education, or intelligence. This one thing actually prepared you to learn both intellectually and spiritually, and it's always stuck with you. I believe this one element is what Jesus has used to bless you with such a wonderful life—beyond what most people ever experience."

"Wow," said Harvey. "Maybe you *did* get a vision. So what's this one thing you're speaking of?"

"Humility."

"Humility?"

"Yes, dad. True humility. It's the absolute enemy of pride. Without humility, you would've probably followed a worldly path like poor ole Blaine Billings did. On the couple of occasions I met him, Blaine came across as a self-absorbed, hedonistic scoundrel."

"Whoa, son. Those are some mighty strong words."

PJ shook his head. "You know what's interesting? I feel totally ambivalent about how he treated Rachel. On the one hand, like we joked about the other day, if he hadn't kept Rachel's attention for all of those years, you would've never met mom and I sure wouldn't be here today. I feel that you and Rachel would've ended up getting married, if not for Blaine."

"Perhaps…."

"On the other hand, there's no way I could've sat there yesterday and not seen just how profound your love for Rachel is. What person wouldn't be retroactively rooting for y'all to have gotten married and to have lived a long life together after that speech? After all, isn't a love that deep the goal of true human-to-human romance? Shouldn't that be the goal of every marriage?"

Harvey grinned. "You're very kind for saying that, PJ. I'm grateful that our relationship allows us to be so honest with each other."

"Me too, dad."

"You know something? I still remember that autumn day when Blaine rode off with Rachel, just like it was yesterday. Although I really wish otherwise, that event is forever galvanized in my soul. To me, it seemed like Rachel was trying to reach the nearby town of Paradise like it was the real paradise in Heaven. I feel like she somehow thought her pathway there was somehow her salvation. Unfortunately, she didn't bring her humility and focus on God with her, so she never really made it to the adjacent town of Paradise. I just hope she's in the real paradise in Heaven, waiting for me."

"We'll see. I sure hope so."

"Anyway, I know you're kicking off a small group with Wyatt and Vanessa next week, which is good. If I end up taking your advice and head out to Cottondale, I'll miss the first meeting. Can you give me an overview of what y'all are going to study?"

"I'd love to," PJ said. "Our tentative topic is about possessions."

"Possessions? Do you mean like exorcisms and the like?"

PJ chuckled. "No. I mean possessions ... as in what we own. In my vision last night, God also directed me towards studying our possessions and how they sometimes become false idols in our life. Do you know what I mean?"

"Oh, yeah. That's a worthy topic to discuss, all right. Actually, you and I touched on idols just last week—didn't we?"

"We sure did."

"So what passages have you chosen so far?" said Harvey, opening his Bible. "I have a few verses highlighted on that topic. That is, if I can still find them."

PJ shook his head. "There are so many biblical warnings about idols, it'll make your head spin. You can almost open your Bible anywhere and blindly point down at one."

"I'm with you on that. I have one right here: *Psalm 97:7 ... All who worship images are put to shame, those who boast in idols—worship him, all you gods!*"

"That sounds like a good passage to start off our discussion on earthly possessions. But before I get started down the road of sharing the tsunami of biblical warnings about idols with the group, I found three wonderful passages that should make a person actually not want to put their possessions ahead of God in their life."

"Oh—what are they?"

"It starts with some wisdom in *Proverbs 21:21 ... Whoever pursues righteousness and love finds life, prosperity and honor.*"

Harvey nodded. "Nice."

"The next one is *2 Peter 1:3 ... His divine power has given us everything we need for a godly life through our knowledge of him who called us by his own glory and goodness.*"

"Yeah, it's all about God's glory, not earthly possessions. No doubt about that."

PJ nodded. "And the third one is *Ephesians 1:4-5 ... For he chose us in him before the creation of the world to be holy and blameless in his sight. In love he predestined us for adoption to sonship through Jesus Christ, in accordance with his pleasure and will.*"

"Like we've talked about on many occasions, the whole crux of the Bible gets down to one simple concept—you cannot have any other gods before the real God. The Lord just won't stand for it. Jesus came to atone for sin, but sin wouldn't have happened if mankind hadn't decided to elevate itself above God by its disobedience."

"That's true, dad. But there's actually some great news in those passages. The last one shows that we're adopted as children through Jesus Christ. That's a very significant distinction. We're not slaves of God; we're sons and daughters of God—if we choose to be."

"Since there's only one spirit of God in this world, there can only be one real love. That's how God designed our universe. It's similar to a huge orchestra where you can only have one conductor; and that's Jesus Christ. No other godship can exist in God's world because that's how He ordered all things."

They were both quiet for a moment.

"So what further thoughts do you have about our small group subject?" said PJ. "What else can you give me from your many years of gaining wisdom on this topic?"

Harvey chuckled. "No pressure or anything."

"Oh c'mon, dad. You know what I mean. What do you think about the subject of our possessions?"

"I think possessions are like food, sex, money, and other double-edge swords that can either be used correctly or incorrectly. The sad part is when people elevate their possessions to idol status—that's when it goes off the rails and becomes serious sin. One cannot elevate their possessions or they're in for a severe disappointment on many levels."

PJ nodded. "I know when Jane and I were young, you and mom had to sacrifice many things to take care of us. I'm grateful that your desire for possessions didn't overtake your instinct to be a good, sacrificial parent. Sadly, I know of some folks where that didn't happen."

Harvey shook his head. "You don't get extra credit for sacrificing for your children. It's just what you do if you're going to be a parent. To do otherwise is incredibly selfish."

"I just love how old school you are."

"There's nothing new under the sun, my boy. Human selfishness has been around for a *looong* time. And it's very much a road to nowhere."

PJ nodded. "Selfishness sure won't survive the grave."

"The only thing that survives the grave is the real love which can only found in Jesus Christ. He's the one who conquered the grave."

"Nice one. Can I quote you on that?"

Harvey laughed and gave PJ a playful shove on the arm. "Your sermons can only benefit from an old geezer like me, son. I'd be a little more appreciative if I was you."

"Okay, fine. Since you're on such a roll, what else can you tell me about possessions for my sermon series and small group study?"

"Real love sacrifices. If you're not willing to sacrifice things you want for those who you love and who need you, then you cannot find real love. It will always elude you because self-love just doesn't work."

"Good thought," PJ said. "What else do you have?"

Harvey sighed. "Well ... this isn't an easy thing to admit ... but my love for Rachel was a personal idol for me for many years. Embarrassingly, I was already married to your mom before it began to subside."

"Really?" said PJ. "Please go on."

"There's really not much more to it than that. I'd be a liar if I didn't admit that my early eros love for Rachel had to evolve into agape love or I would've just abandoned her as a friend and moved on. My desire for passionate love with her had to change, or our relationship would have disappeared."

"Really? So in a way—"

"Yes, eros love is oftentimes an idol. True agape love cannot be, because it comes from God. But passionate love can and often does become an idol. It's based on feelings, not truth."

PJ continued writing some notes.

"While you're writing," Harvey continued. "I have something to confess to you. I've been waiting for the right moment to do so."

"Oh—what's that?"

"I've already made arrangements with Vanessa for Rachel's body to be shipped out to Cottondale to be buried out there near her parents. Not only that, but I'm going out there also."

"Really?"

"Yup."

"Why didn't you tell me?"

"I was getting ready to, but you then shared your vision with me and I didn't want to interrupt you."

PJ chuckled. "Ironically, part of my proposal tonight was that I'd watch George for you as an enticement for you to go."

"And one of the reasons I invited you over for dinner was to ask you to watch my little buddy while I'm gone. I was actually afraid you'd think me silly because I wanted to go home for a few days."

PJ shook his head. "Of course not."

"It's absolutely fantastic how God works."

"No doubt about that. Okay, then. It's all set. Have you looked online for—?"

"I've already purchased my tickets and made my arrangements," Harvey interrupted. "The last piece was what to do with George."

"You're covered, dad. I'd love to watch the ole boy for you. Something about your destiny lies out in Cottondale, and I really want you to go. When do you leave?"

"In a few days. Rachel's body is on its way out there as we speak. I'll oversee her burial."

"I'm really glad to hear this," PJ said. "I'll be praying that God will be with you during your travels."

"Thanks, son. Something really tells me I need to go home for some odd reason."

"Then home, you're going."

20

Cottondale, TX
October 16, 2007
"'Return home and tell how much God has done for you.' So the man went away and told all over town how much Jesus had done for him."
Luke 8:39

The unpretentious Jericho Mart grocery store sat directly across the gravel parking lot from Jerry as he loosened his black tie and sat quietly in his rental car with the windows down. He was absolutely mesmerized with the profound serenity in his home town as memories of it came rushing at him from all sides. Though it had lain dormant in him for many decades, today, Harvey rediscovered just how much his heart yearned for once again connecting with Cottondale's intangibly refreshing solitude. This lovely community's tranquility stood in stark contrast to the overbearing turbulence of living in the sprawling Atlanta metro area, which Harvey had endured for most of his life.

Although Harvey was enjoying the brief peace of mind from being home, he was also very tired. He was tired of fighting against the world. He was tired of living in a domain of imperfection. He had always sensed that many years ago, God had purposely stationed him near Atlanta. He felt like God did this because Harvey was a loyal soldier who would fight against the fast pace of the world, which Atlanta so aptly embodied. To him, Cottondale always felt like the world's remedy because it was so close to Paradise; both physically and spiritually. Now that Rachel was gone, Harvey wanted to go home; also both physically and spiritually. His soul ached as he sat there, feeling totally depleted in every way.

It was mid-afternoon and overcast as Harvey sighed, not sure what to do next. The Jericho Mart was located on the exact footprint of Jerry's General Store, which was now long gone. In a stroke of incredibly good fortune, however, the immense, sprawling tree next to the store was still alive and thriving. It was so vibrant; it almost seemed like it was human.

The Jericho Mart was more modern in appearance than Jerry's store had been, but it was similar in size. The only other vehicle in the parking lot was an old white Ford F150 pickup truck. Harvey thought it was ironic that old Jerry used to also have a white pickup truck back in his childhood.

Harvey stared down at the clock within the modern vehicle's numerous dials and sighed. He felt something gnawing at him to exit the car and go inside. But for some intangible reason, he didn't want to. At this very moment, Harvey felt like a man without a country. Annoyed at his ambivalent feelings, he finally relented and headed that way, entering the store with an odd sense of anticipation.

"Howdy neighbor," a voice from behind the counter said, on the left. The man had his back to Harvey and was tending to something on an upper shelf. "I'll be right with you."

"No hurry," Harvey said. "I'm just browsing."

"Then you go right ahead and make yourself at home. I'll be here if you have any questions."

"Will do."

Harvey proceeded to the right and began perusing the aisles with nothing in particular in mind. He really just wanted to clear his head from the various emotions that were borne of just leaving Rachel's grave site. This whole business of burying his beloved friend, which he had mistakenly thought would be routine to accomplish, left him feeling listless and empty—even grumpy.

After lollygagging around the store for several minutes, Harvey decided he should at least purchase something to justify his presence there. He selected a large bottle of water and a bag of potato chips, and then continued to look at various items on each aisle.

As he finally approached the counter, but before he saw the face of the man behind it, Harvey heard the man say, *"Joshua 5:15* says …

The commander of the Lord's army replied, 'Take off your sandals, for the place where you are standing is holy.' And Joshua did so."

Good deal, Harvey thought. A man of God still owns this store.

"Sir, you remind me of—" Harvey began, but instantly stopped dead in his tracks, a few steps from the counter.

He was speechless; dumbfounded.

"Hello Harvey. Long time, no see, huh?"

"But ... that's ... *impossible....*"

"Not really," the man at the counter said. "You know what they say—with God, all things are possible. Am I right?"

"Jerry???"

"That's me."

"But how—?"

"How about if I let some Scripture answer that question for you. What do you say?"

"Uhmmm ... sure."

"Let's start with *Psalm 103:20 ... Praise the Lord, you his angels, you mighty ones who do his bidding, who obey his word."*

Harvey moved forward, slowly approaching the counter.

"Wait a minute. Are you claiming to be an angel or something?"

"I sure am. You never figured that out?"

Harvey shrugged. "I know angels exist, but I never thought—"

Jerry shook his head. "Hang on. Do you mean to tell me you've also not figured out just how important you are to your heavenly Father? *Tsk, tsk, tsk,* Harvey. God has had countless angels stationed around you for all of your life. Trust me, without God's protection, you wouldn't have gotten this far. No offense, but Satan really hates your guts."

"Really???"

"Really."

"Even when I was living here in little ole Cottondale?"

"Especially when you were living here in little ole Cottondale. God's ways are far different than those of mankind. It shouldn't surprise you one single bit that the Lord has used your talents and efforts for His kingdom for a long time now. Just look at the fruit of your whole life, Harvey. Think about that for a moment...."

Harvey did so. He considered the way he had both treated and loved people, and the sacrificial nature of almost everything he did. Harvey's humility wouldn't allow him to boast about his actions, but somehow, this situation felt different. Now that he was face-to-face with an angel of the Most High God, being completely honest about who he was seemed to be the only sensible thing to do.

"Okay, Jerry. Let's just pretend for a moment I'm not dreaming. If that's the case, I still think you have a lot of explaining to do about some things."

"Such as—?"

"How come you haven't aged? You look the same as you did back in the forties."

"Angels don't age, Harvey. C'mon, now. I didn't think you'd be throwing softballs at me for questions. Try digging a little deeper."

Harvey sighed before accepting the challenge. "Okay, fine. Then how come there's no one else around here right now? Has God somehow kept everyone away so you and I can talk? And what's this stuff about holy ground? Were you serious about that passage in Joshua?"

Jerry shook his head. "One thing at time. First, let me address the reason why no one else is around. Once again, you're missing the obvious. Let me ask you this—was the airport and highways unusually busy when you came into DFW the other day?"

"Uhmmm … yes."

"The Texas State Fair is still going on over in Dallas. Lots of folks from these parts are actually over there this week."

"Hmmm," Harvey mumbled. "I did notice how busy it was near my hotel near the Stockyards in Ft. Worth last night."

"Bingo," said Jerry. "Good job. Stay with me, now."

"So what about this being holy ground?"

"I'll get to that one in a moment."

"But why—?"

Jerry's eyebrows rose. "All in good time. Just keep digging."

"Okay, okay. I'm just a little flustered with this revelation. I don't know whether you know this or not, but your influence on me has been profound throughout my entire life. This is just a bit of a shock."

"God sent me to look after you when you were a wee lad, Harvey. After you left Cottondale, you had enough spiritual strength to face the world, so God kept me on other assignments so you could fulfill your destiny. That's why it's been so many years since I've seen you."

Harvey shook his head. "I don't get it."

"It's simple. God ordained that I'm to personally minister to you during a couple of major events in your life. When you were ten years old and Rachel drove off with Blaine, God knew you needed me—"

"But what about this afternoon? Why today? Up until now, today has actually been pretty boring. Other than the local cemetery staff, I've not seen hardly anyone else ... except for Rachel's coffin and a few cars driving by."

"I'll also get back to why I'm here in a moment," said Jerry. "But first, I'd like to see if you can figure it out by me giving you three passages of Scripture. Are you game?" Harvey shrugged. "Suit yourself. But before I leave this store, I want some real answers. This whole thing is unbelievably surreal."

Jerry nodded. "The first one is *Psalm 139:17 ... How precious to me are your thoughts, God! How vast is the sum of them!*"

"I have no clue—"

"The next one is *1 John 3:20 ... If our hearts condemn us, we know that God is greater than our hearts, and he knows everything.*"

"Of course God knows everything. I'm still not following you."

"Patience, Harvey. Let me go ahead and give you the last one. It's in *Deuteronomy 32:16 ... They made him jealous with their foreign gods and angered him with their detestable idols.*"

"Now *that* sounds familiar."

"Why is that?"

"Because PJ and I have been discussing idols lately. My son is working on a curriculum for his church on this subject."

Jerry nodded. "We're well aware of that, and we love PJ and what he's doing. The point I'm trying to make here is that first, you've always kept God on His proper throne in your life. This is *very* important. You've also continuously conducted yourself in a way that acknowledges that God's heart is greater than your own. This is also an uncommon thing among so many selfish people down here on Earth. The third thing is that you've never elevated anyone or anything in your life to true idol status. Here again, this is uncommon for so many people. Angels like me constantly deal with humanity's idols in our largely covert ministry efforts."

Harvey thought for a moment before saying, "I have to admit something to you. My love of Rachel was a bit of an idol for many years. In fact—"

223

"Hang on," Jerry interrupted. "Do you remember that Saturday back in 1942 when you and I had that little chat after Rachel drove off with Blaine? It was right here, in this very spot."

"Of course I do. It sort of changed my life."

"It didn't 'sort of' change your life. It absolutely changed your life, but for reasons you may not fully understand."

"What do you mean?"

Jerry nodded. "Were you aware of the fact, that fateful day was almost sixty-five years ago? Tomorrow will actually be the exact day."

"Seriously?"

"You bet. Anyway, that day changed your life because you allowed God to begin to heal your little broken heart instead of selling out and continuing towards your own selfish feelings at any cost. You see, so many people abandon God when He doesn't deliver the things they demand. After they don't get what they want, they often claim they don't believe in Him anymore. This attitude is as childish as it is sinful and foolish."

"I agree," Harvey said. "I've always understood that. No one should believe in a false god who is only there for showering you with gifts of your choosing whenever you want them. That god really doesn't exist."

"Exactly. In your case, you allowed God to mold you into the image of His son Jesus Christ, day by day, week by week, and year by year. The key part to all of this is that you were available for God to work on. You must remember, the Lord doesn't force Himself on anyone. He generally will only help you if you allow Him to. God desires to have sons and daughters, not slaves or robots."

"Indeed."

"So Harvey, please ask me another question. You seem to be on a roll, now."

Harvey thought hard for a moment. "Okay then, Jerry. Is Rachel in Heaven with Jesus Christ? Did the Holy Spirit penetrate her heart before she died so suddenly?"

Jerry shook his head. "I'm sorry, but that's a question I'm not permitted to answer."

"Why not?!?!?!"

"I think Jesus wants to answer that one, Himself—"

The door to the store suddenly opened and a man in a pony-tail, worn jeans, and a warm smile walked inside. He appeared to be a real Texan.

"Hello, Mick," Jerry said. "C'mon in. You're just in time."

"Howdy Jerry," Mick said. "And howdy Harvey. How's it going, dude?"

"Who are—?"

"I was the last one who was with Rachel before she died."

"And you flew all the way out here to Cottondale?" said Harvey, incredulous. "Rachel never mentioned you before."

"Oh, you've got me all wrong," Mick said. "I'm also an angel—just like ole Jerry, here. We actually work together all the time. But no worries. My form of transportation is a little ... let's say ... *above* yours."

Harvey sighed. "I must be going nuts."

The angels looked at each other and laughed heartily.

Mick then spoke, "This is a cool moment for angels like Jerry and me. We've been working in the shadows of your life for quite some time now, performing different functions."

"What kind of different functions?"

"Jerry is essentially a teacher. His classes focus on faith, hope, and love, as are mentioned in *1 Corinthians 13:13*. Your education in Jerry's class on love actually started way back when you were a boy."

"Seriously?" Harvey mused. "And I'm supposed to believe you?"

"We're not lying," Jerry said. "Please trust me. This is a very special day for you."

"Fine," Harvey said. "So what about you, Mick?"

"My functions are primarily centered on watching over a few special families. Included are Wyatt and Vanessa's family. So by association, since Rachel and you were essentially family to each other, you get lumped in with the rest of them and fall under my ministry responsibility."

One of Harvey's eyebrows rose. "Lucky me."

"Oh, c'mon," Jerry said. "Don't be such a putz. It's like you're surprised that angels are engaged in God's work down here on Earth. As a man who's studied the Bible for so long, you really should know better than that."

Harvey was quiet as he sized up the two angels.

"Okay, guys," he said. "I'll stop pulling a Jacob and won't keep wrestling with you anymore. For argument's sake, let's just say you're indeed real angels. So why are you here? Why are you revealing yourselves to me today? There must be a good reason for this."

Jerry leaned in and said, "There is. You don't know this right now, but today is a very special day in your life, Harvey. It's kind of like a birthday of sorts."

"Why do you say that?"

"You were born and raised in a place that is so close to Paradise; you can hardly tell where Cottondale ends and Paradise begins. The same is true of your life on Earth."

"I'm not following you."

"Please bear with me. You see, relationships die when trust is either gone, or is not there at all. In your case, you've known for many, many years exactly where you're going after you die. It's all because you've trusted alone in Jesus Christ for your salvation and forgiveness of sins. As for our recently departed friend Rachel ... well ... she had a much more tumultuous ride in her life—spiritually speaking and otherwise."

"Wait a minute," Harvey said. "Why did you imply this grocery store is somehow hallowed ground a few minutes ago? Can you at least tell me that?"

"Hang on," Mick said. "Take a look at all of the evidence before you. This is the Jericho Mart and Jerry quoted you a verse from the book of Joshua, which happened just as the Israelites were claiming the Promised Land. There's more going on today than meets the eye. I think you need to consider the big picture of everything we're saying."

"But—?"

"Deep down, I think you already know the answer to your question. We've been giving you some rather good clues as to what's about to happen, and why a couple of angels have appeared to you today. Use your heart to figure it out, not your head."

Harvey looked down as the realization of what was happening fell upon him like a ton of bricks. Jerry and Mick saw the light bulb come on and that he was now on board with them.

"Let's see," Harvey said. "I'm very close to Paradise ... I'm on hallowed ground in the Jericho Mart, next to what looks like it might be the Tree of Life ... and I've returned to my home for what appears to be a very good reason. Also, Jerry mentioned that he only comes to see me on significant events in my life. Well, I can certainly think of an impending significant event for a seventy-five year old man with a growing heart condition."

"Don't be sad," Jerry said, quickly. "Today is a day of incredible victory for you. Mick and I are here to gently hand you over to those in the spiritual realm who will escort you into the very presence of Jesus Christ himself. You should feel honored because the Lord sent us to be here with you today for this triumphant departure. This kind of thing really doesn't happen very often, and it almost always happens for someone who has pleased God with their life's accomplishments."

"I see. So angels are going to escort me into Heaven, just like the Scriptures say?"

"Indeed," Mick said. "Harvey, believe it or not, this is a real honor for Jerry and me."

"Why is that?"

"We deal with a lot of wicked people down here on Earth. It's absolutely awesome when we're given the rare mission of escorting someone on this side of death into eternal life. Basically, we're seeing you away from this life and into the most incredible place you can ever imagine. What you're about to experience is far beyond your previous expectations of Heaven. You and I will chat about this later on, but please trust me on what I'm sharing with you."

Harvey was quiet as ambivalence ruled his soul.

"But I really don't want to die," he said. "I mean, I don't want to live here on Earth anymore, but I don't want to die either."

"Take heart," Jerry said. "Jesus didn't want to die either. You're in good company."

"We each have one last thing to tell you, before you leave," Jerry said. "Both Mick and I have given our parting comments to you a great deal of thought."

"Oh—what's that?"

Jerry nodded. "What I have to say is this: real love survives death. Please remember this fact during your journey into the real Paradise, which is closer than you may think."

Harvey nodded. "And you, Mick?"

"All I have to say is summed up in a wonderful little gem. It's in *Numbers 6:24 … The Lord bless you and keep you.*"

And with that, Harvey slowly slumped over as his heart gave out and he passed from this world.

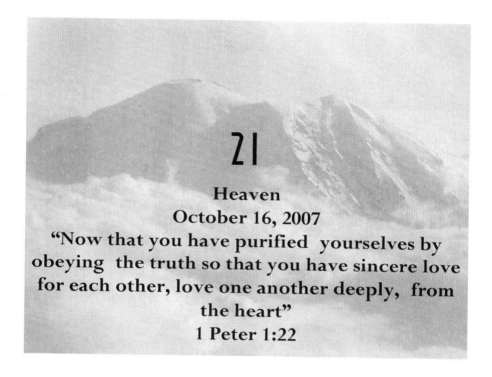

21

Heaven
October 16, 2007
"Now that you have purified yourselves by obeying the truth so that you have sincere love for each other, love one another deeply, from the heart"
1 Peter 1:22

A great realization gently descended upon Harvey as he gleefully stood in the center of the forest lodge at the edge of Heaven. This compelling wisdom settled into his soul like the last piece of an enormous jigsaw puzzle; one he had been working on for the past seventy-five years. This realization was as incredibly powerful as it was simple—Harvey now fully understood the fruit of real love.

Since he had just broken loose of the shackles of living on Earth, Harvey now understood the meaning of the concept that real love is eternal. Knowing the only one who is truly eternal is God, he now grasped just how important it is that real love can only be attained when God is involved. Apart from the Lord, real love isn't real at all. It's merely an imposter posing as God.

In other words, love without God is a liar.

After being escorted by a series of angels to this very spot not long ago, Harvey finally met his Savior, face to face. After falling to his knees in gratitude during this poignant moment, he then met several people who had been a big part of his life for so many years. It was a reunion like no other.

"So Harvey, are you enjoying this joyous moment?" someone said, placing their arm around his shoulders.

Harvey looked over. It was Jesus once again.

"Oh, yes!" he said. "I thought you left already, Lord. I was just looking around the room for you."

"No, I haven't left yet. Actually, I have some things on my mind we still need to discuss."

"That's great. Listen, do you mind if I ask you a very important question? This is something Jerry and Mick weren't permitted to—"

A sudden knock at the door grabbed their attention and they both looked that way. Jesus smiled knowingly. One of the angels near the entrance opened the door and Jerry and Mick entered.

Harvey smiled and waved at them. "Speaking of angels. I didn't expect to be seeing you guys again so soon. Thanks for the lovely send-off from Earth."

The angels waved back, but quickly turned their attention back to the doorway they had just entered through. Harvey thought this was a bit odd, until he saw the reason why.

"Welcome, Rachel," Jesus said, above the celebration's gleeful din. To Harvey, His powerful voice sounded like it had just thundered throughout the universe. "Please join us over here," the Lord said.

Rachel Green entered the forest lodge wearing an expression of great anticipation. When her eyes locked-in with Harvey's, the exhilaration of the moment exploded with a unique array of powerful emotions for both of them.

As Rachel arrived at the center of the lodge, she and Harvey first embraced, then joined hands and faced each other.

"Harvey, it's so wonderful to see you," Rachel said. "As it turns out, you are indeed my real love. In fact, you always have been. I just didn't know it until I arrived here. My own sin kept me from seeing it."

"But—?"

"You're my real love—besides Jesus, that is," she added, winking.

Harvey was quiet before stating, "I'm not sure what to say. I honestly didn't know if you'd be here when I died. I'm afraid these two fellas wouldn't tell me."

He nodded towards Jerry and Mick, who had followed Rachel to the center of the lodge.

"They weren't permitted to, Harvey. But let's not do what we're told in *Joel 1:8 … Mourn like a virgin in sackcloth grieving for the betrothed of her youth.*"

Harvey chuckled. "Okay, let's not do that. Mourning seems to be non-existent up here, anyway. Besides, our human youth is far behind us now. I wouldn't want to go back to it, even if I could."

Rachel smiled. "All pain, suffering, and death are also gone forever. That's the one thing about Heaven I think you're going to love the most."

"I have an appropriate verse for the both of you," Jerry said. "We see this in *Ecclesiastes 11:10 … So then, banish anxiety from your heart and cast off the troubles of your body, for youth and vigor are meaningless.*"

Harvey nodded. "Yes, indeed. All of the powerful feelings of my youth now seem pretty silly when compared to what I'm experiencing right now."

"It was all just an appetizer for this moment," Rachel said. "All of our struggles down on Earth now seem well worth it. Although I haven't been here for very long, I've learned a lot since I died. I think you'll be pleasantly surprised by what God has done for me since arriving in Heaven."

Rachel and Harvey locked eyes once again as they continued to face each other. Jesus now put His mighty arms around both of them. This was the love of total unity and fellowship between God and humans. Harvey was spellbound with the magnificence of this incredible moment.

"I'm so excited to have you both here together," the Lord said. "I've been waiting for this moment for quite some time now. You both belong to me."

Jerry quickly added, "I think now's a good time for *Jeremiah 31:3,* which says … *The Lord appeared to us in the past, saying: 'I have loved you with an everlasting love; I have drawn you with unfailing kindness.'*"

"Amen," Harvey said. "Do you know something odd, Rachel?"

"What's that?" she said.

"I know people aren't married in Heaven like down on Earth, but this feels like the most incredible thing that could have happened to me. My best friend in the world repented of her sins and made it to Heaven. And here we are, being embraced by the King of kings. It just can't get any better than this. It just can't."

"Hang on a minute," Mick said. "You need to have some of Heaven's awesome coffee before you say it can't get any better. It's outstanding."

Harvey laughed. "What's so good about it?"

"Well, for one thing, the actual inventor of coffee has His arm around you at this very moment. That should tell you something."

Harvey looked at Jesus and they both burst into laughter.

"Indeed!" Harvey said. "I guess things really are different up here."

Jesus patted Rachel and Harvey on their backs and said, "Please excuse me for a moment. I need to speak to someone in the kitchen. But before you go, I would like to speak with the both of you, alone. Okay?"

"You bet, Lord," Harvey said, and Rachel nodded her agreement.

Jesus made his way through the crowd as Mick stepped a little closer to them. "Harvey my friend," Mick said. "We have another little surprise, just for you."

At this, Jerry disappeared towards the back of the lodge and opened a beautiful wooden door.

Mick winked. "You're really gonna like this, dude."

"What could it be?" said Harvey.

Suddenly, he heard a bark he had not heard in many decades. Although time had temporarily healed his pain of their separation, that familiar bark was an unmistakable part of Harvey's life. It was indelibly etched into his very soul.

"Is that——?" he began.

Harvey's dog Pumpkin came running towards him like a runaway freight train. The little schnauzer jumped into Harvey's arms with a glee that cannot be described.

Harvey wept openly as Pumpkin licked his face; her little nubby tail wagging into overdrive.

"This is soooo unbelievable," Harvey said. "I just want to shout the name of the Lord! I'm so grateful that He loves me so much, He's giving me my little furry friend from so long ago."

Rachel put her hand on Harvey's back and joined in the joyous reunion with Pumpkin.

"Actually, I've been hanging out with Pumpkin the past few days," Rachel said. "Although Jesus didn't tell me when you were coming, I felt like it was going to be very soon."

"That's wonderful. It really is."

"In anticipation of your arrival, I chose three things that I think demonstrate how both of us feel right now."

Harvey shrugged. "Oh—what things are those?"

"I'll start out with *Isaiah 42:8 … I am the Lord; that is my name! I will not yield my glory to another or my praise to idols.*"

"Why would anyone in the world want a mere idol when you can have all of this?"

"I agree," she said. "Next, I have *Psalm 103:11 … For as high as the heavens are above the earth, so great is his love for those who fear him.*"

"That's so true," Harvey agreed.

"And the last one is *Lamentations 3:22 … Because of the Lord's great love we are not consumed, for his compassions never fail.*"

"Amen, Rachel," Jerry said. "Very well done. I can see that I trained you well."

Rachel chuckled and nodded.

They were all quiet for a few moments as Pumpkin continued to lick Harvey's face.

"I have a question for you angels," Harvey said. "This may seem to be a bit off the wall, but why do evildoers down on Earth always seem to win? For example, ever since Blaine drove off with Rachel that fateful day, this question has always vexed my soul. Although I ultimately found peace with it when I was down on Earth, I'd very much like to hear Heaven's perspective on this subject."

Jerry nodded. "If it's okay with you, I'll be glad to answer you with the Word of God. That's kind of my thing."

Harvey laughed. "I'd expect no less."

"We see the answer in *Psalm 92:7 … that though the wicked spring up like grass and all evildoers flourish, they will be destroyed forever.*"

"Ahhh," said Harvey. "That makes sense. I was right. Evildoers will ultimately get their punishment."

Mick shook his head. "That's not something anyone should be happy about. Those who don't make it to Heaven to enjoy this incredible place are destined to a place of eternal separation from God. That, my friends, is the tragedy of Hell."

Harvey turned to Rachel, "I asked God to save you and give you to me—and He did. It just wasn't when I was expecting Him to."

"And I was a fool for chasing after a silly pipe dream," Rachel said. "I was blind back then and I couldn't see the top of the mountain of my own life."

"What do you mean by that?"

Rachel grinned. "I'll explain the details to you later. It's a long but wonderful story."

"I see. I'll look forward to it."

"A brief overview would be that I allowed a cloud cover of idols to block my view of Christ, who is at the top of everyone's mountain of life. After all, He is our God and Savior."

"How true."

"Thankfully, the clouds in my life were moved aside just before I died and I saw the extended hand of Jesus Christ waiting for me to reach out to Him."

"Indeed," said Jerry. "Your mountain of life starts on Earth. The sooner you can see above the cloud cover of sin, temptation, and idols, the more quickly you can experience real love and clearly see into an eternal life with Jesus Christ."

A group of about eight people suddenly descended on Harvey and Rachel, obviously with a specific purpose.

"So who are you folks?" said Harvey. "No offense, but I'm not sure I recognize any of you."

The leader of the group said, "You don't know us Harvey, but my name is Jimmy. On behalf of the others, we just wanted to thank you for something important you did for us."

"Wait—since I don't know you, how can I have done anything for you?"

Jimmy smiled. "You raised a wonderful son, that's what. PJ is the one who showed all of us the way to eternal life through his pastoring. Every single one of us used to hate church in varying degrees, but PJ helped us through that. Although it was Jesus who saved us, PJ did his job in fulfilling the great commission as he shared the Gospel with us. As you can see, it worked."

Harvey nearly fell to his knees once again. The gravity of seeing the fruit of sharing one's faith nearly shook him to his core. He was overcome with joy. He almost felt like his brand new heart would explode.

"I ... I ... I don't know what to say, Jimmy. I suppose I never thought about what might—"

"You don't need to say anything at all," Jimmy said. "Jesus asked us to be here today to help you celebrate the wonderful life you lived. Now that your job on Earth is done, welcome to your eternal home. I think you'll be very pleasantly surprised by how many people were positively affected by both yours and PJ's efforts to share your faith. Well done, Harvey. Enjoy the celebration. We'll catch up with you later."

Jimmy and the others all waved good-bye and folded back into the crowd.

"That was unbelievable," Harvey said to Mick. "Are there more surprises like that in store for me?"

"You betcha," Mick said. "Life with Jesus is like Christmas morning to a kid. The only difference is that in Heaven, every single day is like Christmas morning—full of celebration and family."

"Wow."

"I'd like to talk about something Mick said to me before I died," Rachel said. "Mick—do you remember telling me that it was possible that God sent Harvey to the Atlanta area well before either I or Blaine moved there? You indicated it was sort of like a covert missionary journey that would pay off later on."

"I sure do, milady."

"Now that I can more clearly see the beginning of my life from the end of it, I feel that you were absolutely right. Since Harvey and I are experiencing real love and will never have to face anything painful ever again, it's easy to see how God moved the pieces into place to ultimately help me. Every single thing I see here in Heaven every day reminds me of who God really is."

"Well said," Jerry added. "In a way, I think you can say that Harvey allowed God to use His agape love to ultimately help you, Rachel, arrive here, many years later. That's part of the exhilaration you're feeling. Being one with the Lord and doing things His way always ends up being the right thing to do."

"Thank you, Jerry," Jesus said. He had just walked back to the group. "I now need to have a little chat with Harvey and Rachel before I go tend to some other matters. I have something I'd like to discuss with them."

"Of course, Lord," Jerry said.

"Listen, folks," Mick said. "We'll have that coffee ready when you get back from taking a stroll with Jesus. It seems He has something in particular He wants to discuss with you."

"Very well," Rachel said. "We'll take you up on that coffee offer when we get back."

Jesus proceeded to walk arm-in-arm with Harvey and Rachel as they left the forest lodge. After they had made their exit, Jerry asked Mick, "What are they going to talk about?"

"I'm not exactly sure," Mick said. "But it probably has something to do with what His perfect will for their lives would have looked like if Rachel had married Harvey down on Earth."

"Oh. That makes sense. Only Jesus knows something like that."

"Anyway, it's back to work for you and me, amigo."

"True."

Mick nodded. "I'm excited because I have a big project coming up with some of Rachel's relatives, starting next year."

"Yes, I remember," Jerry said. "That whole project will certainly change things down on Earth, won't it?"

"It sure will. Anyway, I'll catch you later."

"You sure will."

It was indeed, another spectacular day in Heaven.

22

Jefferson, GA
November 22, 2007
"A person's days are determined;
you have decreed the number of his months
and have set limits he cannot exceed."
Job 14:5

"I certainly didn't expect my dad to die when he went home to Texas," PJ said to Wyatt and Vanessa Hunter. They all sat comfortably in the Hunter's living room on a cool Thanksgiving morning. PJ had arrived around ten thirty a.m. to go over some things for their small group's big outreach event the next day, on Black Friday.

PJ continued, "To be honest, I'm still feeling a little bit guilty for how it all went down."

"You shouldn't feel guilty at all," Vanessa said. "I think you know it was God's plan was for Harvey to fulfill his destiny by going back home to Cottondale to pass into eternity. We may not understand the reason for it now, but deep in my heart, I know it was what the Lord wanted."

"I sure hope you're right."

"We all know that God's will for your dad's life is what was important," Wyatt said. "It wouldn't surprise me one single bit if Harvey's soul quickly eroded when Rachel passed away last month. I may be off base, but it seems like his life's mission was somehow completed."

"Since I'm a pastor, I shouldn't feel this way, but having two significant funerals within a few weeks of each other is a bit much for even me. Honestly, I need a break from dealing with so much death."

Wyatt nodded. "I understand, but I still think it was a good idea to have two services for your dad—one here, and one out in Texas."

PJ shrugged. "Not many people showed up at the graveside service out in Cottondale. As you know, the funeral here was very well attended. But the one out there only had a few distant relatives from the area."

"I think it was also a great idea for Harvey to be buried next to Rachel, near her folks out there," Vanessa said. "It just seems fitting."

PJ was quiet for a few moments before saying, "I suppose y'all are right. It was time for dad to go home—both physically and spiritually."

"I keep wondering if Aunt Rachel made it to Heaven," Vanessa said. "I mean ... I feel like she did ... I *hope* she did."

"I hope so too," PJ said.

Vanessa held back a tear. "Anyway, if Aunt Rachel is in Heaven right now, we know that she and Harvey are together. For some reason, I can just picture them experiencing the fullness of God's real love right now."

PJ opened his Bible. "My response to that is in *Malachi 1:5 ... You will see it with your own eyes and say, 'Great is the Lord—even beyond the borders of Israel!'*"

"Hey," Wyatt said. "You used that verse the other night at group, didn't you? I think I recognize it."

"Good catch," PJ said. "And speaking of God's greatness, if you'll remember, I also used this little gem on our group: *2 John 1:2 ... because of the truth, which lives in us and will be with us forever.*"

"Speaking of our last meeting," Wyatt said. "I love the verse we're using on our outreach event tomorrow: *Psalm 103:8 ... The Lord is compassionate and gracious, slow to anger, abounding in love.*"

PJ nodded. "Giving out bottles of water and Gospel tracts to Black Friday shoppers is a good opportunity to share God's great love for the world."

"It's just like we said the other night when we decided to do this outreach to the community," Wyatt said. "Real love is fearless."

"It sure is," said PJ. "But we have to remember that we're going to run into many idolaters at the mall tomorrow."

"Idolaters?" a voice said from behind them. "Really?"

Wyatt and Vanessa's son Danny came bounding down the stairs.

"Hey Danny," PJ said. "How're things going at UGA? Is college life treating you well?"

"It sure is. I only have a couple more semesters before I graduate."

"Good deal."

"So what was that about idolaters?"

"Oh yeah," PJ said, chuckling. "Idolatry is a general term used in the Bible for things that people elevate to god-like status. I think they're best described as the fruit of temptations and sin."

"Okay, I'm with you," the tall, handsome young man said. "I run into idolaters at school all the time. They're actually all over college campuses everywhere."

"They sure are," Vanessa said. "Idolatry is a sin of the heart and it usually indicates a huge propensity towards self focus. I'm just glad you understand that, son."

Danny shook his head. "I'm not sure how I could've gotten through college to this point without my foundation in Christ. I've seen a lot of peer pressure on my fellow students—especially the underclassmen. They constantly try to fit in with the culture of binge drinking, promiscuity, and the like. You know ... stuff of the world."

"Yeah, but it's not all bad at school," Wyatt said. "At least you have the Dawgs to root for."

They all laughed.

"And speaking of bulldogs," PJ said. "Since dad passed away, I suppose I've now inherited his bulldog, George. He's actually a great dog."

"I heard that," Wyatt said. "George is lucky to have you."

"Not that I was eavesdropping," Danny said. "But what was the point of all of that talk y'all were having about sin and idols?"

"We started a study of earthly possessions and biblical idolatry a few weeks ago," PJ said. "It started out with discussing my father's interesting relationship with your mother's Aunt Rachel. Both of them have passed on recently, as I'm sure you've heard."

"I did," Danny said. "Were they married at one time or something?"

"No, they weren't. They just had an interesting relationship."

"I see."

PJ nodded. "Anyway, what we've actually been studying is what the real love of God is, and how the human version is typically so different."

"I hate to ask you to repeat yourself, but can you give me an example of what you're talking about?"

"Sure," PJ said. "As an example, let's look at *1 Corinthians 12:2 … You know that when you were pagans, somehow or other you were influenced and led astray to mute idols.*"

"Pagans worshipping idols?" said Danny. "Isn't that just biblical history?"

"Not really, son," Wyatt said. "Pagan worship still exists today—albeit in different forms."

"For example—?"

"For example … the whole idea of human progressivism. What people today refer to as being a progressive is actually quite regressive from a biblical perspective. While progressives generally look down their noses at people of faith in Christ, the fallacy is that they consider themselves to be moving forward. I'm afraid that's nothing but short-sighted foolishness. Those of us who cling to the truth of Christ see progressivism as actually being regressive in nature; meaning it has turned away from God, who is immutable."

"To Wyatt's point," PJ said. "King Solomon said something spot-on in *Ecclesiastes 1:9 … What has been will be again, what has been done will be done again; there is nothing new under the sun.*"

"I see," said Danny. "So what are the alleged 'progressives' actually missing in all of this?"

Wyatt leaned in. "Like I said, what some consider to be 'progress' is actually moving away from the Lord. So to us, it's very much regress, instead. I'm afraid there's nothing new in this world. Progressives arrogantly think they're creating something new, but it's far from that. Sodom and Gomorrah were the fruits of human progressivism, and look what happened to those cities."

Danny shrugged. "Yeah, but if the modern progressives are following in the same path as the inhabitants of those evil cities, I'm sure the ancient progressives have got to be similar to the modern ones in some way—right? Is there some kind of common thread?"

"Actually, there is," said PJ. "All of the progressives espouse the virtues of love, but there's something very significant missing from their flimsy version of it."

"What's that?"

"God's version of real love also includes His hatred of sin. Therefore, God's wrath, anger, and judgment of sin are most definitely included in the mix as it relates to what real love is."

"Yeah," said Danny. "I think you're right about that. The progressives I know all think they can do whatever they want—"

"Exactly," Wyatt said. "They're missing the fact that God is our Creator and this is His world. Bad behavior and sin are up to Him to define and judge; not any of us."

Danny considered this for a moment.

"So PJ," he said. "What's the story with Aunt Rachel and your father Harvey? Were they in love or something?"

"We all think so," PJ said. "They were just never quite able to get it together while they were alive."

"Pay attention, Danny," Vanessa said. "This is a great example of how you should treat your wife when you get married one day."

"How's that, mom?"

"You should learn about the real love Harvey showed to Rachel."

"In what way?"

"I feel that Harvey grasped what divine, sacrificial love was when he was young. Fortunately for Aunt Rachel, he stuck to that during his entire life. Early on, I believe he knew Rachel didn't understand this type of love and that she needed him to demonstrate it to her."

"So what's your point, mom?"

"For a man to truly love a woman, he must model what Christ did and sacrifice everything for her. In the end, I feel that Harvey led Rachel to Heaven because he loved her in a way that many people today simply cannot understand. People today define love as something you feel."

"So love isn't about how you feel?" said Danny.

"Feelings are certainly a part of it," Vanessa said. "But there's a whole lot more to real love than merely how you feel about someone."

"Why is that?"

"Sometimes, feelings are liars; other times, feelings fade away with time. Real love lasts forever."

"Okay, mom. I believe you. That makes sense to me."

Vanessa smiled. "I'm glad you're listening."

"Anyway, folks," Danny said. "I have to study for awhile. Mom— what time is our Thanksgiving feast today?"

"About four pm. I'm sure you and your dad will watch some football and whatnot before supper, so you go study so you can relax later on."

Danny nodded and got up and kissed his mother on the cheek. He then shook hands with PJ and patted his dad on the back before heading back upstairs.

Vanessa then said, "I can't help shake this funny feeling that funerals come in threes. I hate to sound like a superstitious pagan, but I hope I'm wrong and we don't have to deal with another funeral service for awhile."

"Amen to that," PJ said. "But even if we do, those who love Jesus have nothing to fear."

"How true," Vanessa agreed. "How true."

EPILOGUE

Heaven
August, 2008

Now that the celebration at the forest lodge for one of Heaven's newest citizens was near its end, it was time for her eternal life to begin. Rachel and Harvey stood in a semi-circle with the angels Mick and Jerry as they prepared to speak with the newest guest of honor. With all of the celebration's guests now either headed home or on their way out the door, it was time for some important matters to be discussed.

"Will I see Jesus again soon?" Vanessa asked. "It was so incredible finally seeing Him face-to-face."

"Of course," Mick said. "But first, we have some things we need to cover with you. Think of it as the beginning of your orientation in Heaven."

"Sounds good," Vanessa said. "I suppose it's been quite a whirlwind since I arrived here not long ago. There's so much I still need to learn."

"And like I said a minute ago," Mick said. "Wyatt will be just fine. Although my time to speak with him hasn't arrived yet, I did see him down at the accident scene a little while ago. Fortunately, some good law enforcement officers are taking him home."

Vanessa shook her head. "But what will he do? My death was so sudden and totally unexpected."

"There's really not a lot I can tell you about the overall plan right now. But one thing I can share with you is that your departure from Earth has started a chain reaction of events which will involve Wyatt and your son Danny for quite some time."

"Really?"

"You bet. It's a wonderful new project God has given me to oversee. Sometime in the near future, everything will start to happen. The new project will ultimately be called the Flaming Sword Communications Group."

"That's an interesting name."

Mick nodded. "The group's focus will be based on the flaming sword concept mentioned in *Genesis 3:24.*"

"What exactly—?"

"While I can't divulge any details at this time about it, I can assure you that God has a wonderful plan to use your husband and son for His kingdom's business before they arrive here in Heaven one day down the road."

"Sounds good to me."

"Trust me," Mick said. "Every follower of Christ should passionately serve Him until they are brought home. Wyatt and Danny will be given an incredible opportunity to do God's bidding. An enormous spiritual war is on the horizon, and it's all hands on deck."

Vanessa was quiet for a moment before saying, "I still can't believe a freaky car accident just ended my life on Earth. Not that I have any regrets, but it was very strange how it all happened. It was like the driver of the car that hit us did so intentionally."

Mick nodded. "I'll keep you tuned into the nefarious details of that fiasco as God allows me to share them with you. That's kind of what we-angels are here for."

"What's that, exactly?"

"Among other duties, we deliver messages."

"Oh," said Vanessa. "So Aunt Rachel," she said, turning towards her beautiful, red-headed aunt. "It appears that we have much to get caught up on."

"We sure do," said Rachel. "Seeing you walk into Heaven a little while ago was glorious beyond words. Since I never had any children of my own, it was like seeing my very own daughter arriving home."

Vanessa smiled. "I just knew you'd be here when I arrived. Somehow, I felt like your heart was primed for a big change when I left you, just before you passed away."

"Actually," Rachel began. "I think it was the rapid-fire visits I had with you, then Harvey, and finally, Mick. Right after that my heart was convicted and I prayed to Jesus to forgive me for my sins. Very soon thereafter, I passed away. It was very strange how it all happened; but it was wonderful."

Jerry quickly added, "All that matters is this: *1 Samuel 12:21 … Do not turn away after useless idols. They can do you no good, nor can they rescue you, because they are useless.*"

Rachel laughed. "You've made your point a thousand times over since I arrived here, Jerry. And I thank you again for all that you've done for me … and Harvey."

"It's been my pleasure," the angel said.

Rachel looked at all of the others. "All of you played such an important role in my salvation and new life in Heaven. For all of my earthly life, I actually felt like I was living-out my own dreams. It's funny how I can now clearly see how so many people on Earth fail to treat death in the right way; as if it's not real. Somehow, they think it won't happen to them. Deep down, death is indeed the great divider."

"Yes, but it's also the great unifier," Mick said, pointing at everyone.

Jerry quickly added, "Indeed, Mick. I think now is a good time to give you folks this appropriate gem: *Psalm 89:48 … Who can live and not see death, or who can escape the power of the grave?*"

"The wages of sin is death," Vanessa said. "I'm glad I learned that a long time ago."

"You got that right," Mick said.

"You know something?" Vanessa continued. "Wyatt and I lived a great life on Earth together as husband and wife. But when he arrives here one day, I know our relationship will somehow be different and that our marriage will be with our bridegroom, Jesus Christ—"

"But what you probably didn't realize," Rachel said. "Is just how much better your relationship up here will be."

"Well, I'm kind of new, so please help me understand what you're saying."

Rachel smiled. "You know the story about Harvey and me pretty well. For three quarters of a century, he and I danced around the flawed, human version of love—mostly because of me. All along, I think God was planning on showing us what real love is by how I made it to Heaven. Although Harvey and I never married down on Earth, we're enjoying what real marriage in Heaven is—being in total unity with Jesus Christ. One day, you and Wyatt will be reunited here in

Heaven and will enjoy all of eternity with all of us and our Lord. In the end, this is the most important thing in the universe."

"By the way, Vanessa," Harvey said. "After Mick and Jerry cover some things with you, Rachel and I would like you to come visit us in our village, which isn't far from here. Oh, and since Jerry has us continually thinking about the Word of God, I'll give you the invitation this way: *Zechariah 3:10* says … *In that day each of you will invite your neighbor to sit under your vine and fig tree,' declares the Lord Almighty."*

Jerry laughed. "Well done, Harvey."

Everyone chuckled and smiled.

"So Rachel," Vanessa said. "You used the term 'real love' a moment ago. Since I'm a newbie up here, can you explain exactly what you meant by that?"

"Certainly, dear," Rachel said. "Real love is all about God's uncaused love. Really and truly, from the human perspective, God's real love is not fully understandable. On the other hand, human love is drawn out by something in the object of their love. That's the basic difference. God's love is real and it's free; human love isn't free at all."

"And only in Heaven can God's real love be fully realized," Harvey added. "Don't forget that part."

"Why is that?" said Vanessa.

"It's because down on Earth, sin, pain, and death are everywhere. Up here—as you'll soon discover—those things are behind you forever. Essentially, real love cannot abound when it's separated from Jesus."

"Well said," Mick added. "So Vanessa, I want you to know that sometime in the future when I go back down to see Wyatt and reveal God's plan for him and Danny, many things will begin to unfold as a tremendous spiritual war will rage on for many years. Wyatt's family has played a large role in many battles for God in the past. This trend will not only continue, but it will actually increase dramatically. But don't worry, I'll be overseeing your boys and will guide them towards God's will for their lives and for the kingdom."

"That sounds wonderful, Mick. I'll continue to pray for them."

"As well you should," Jerry said. "And to that end, I'd like to leave you with this simple word to all who can hear my voice; to all who can hear my words today. It's in *Jude 1:2* … *Mercy, peace and love be yours in abundance."*

PRAYER OF SALVATION

I am excited that even seekers of biblical truth who are not yet committed to Christ would be drawn to this novel, and I pray that your heart would be open to salvation. The amount of information now available for those seeking to find answers to their questions is nothing short of amazing. Finding faith in Christ is not about acting religious or having to dress a certain way. It's about surrender to the Creator of all that we see; the One who loves us more than we can imagine; the One who died for our sins; and the One who loves you, no matter what you have done.

It's important for you to know that it's absolutely normal to have questions and objections regarding matters pertaining to life in Christ. However, failing to truly seek the answers to your questions is extremely inadvisable. I ask you to consider going into an investigative mode, and to not let previous potentially false paradigms about matters of faith corrupt your journey. In other words, please go into your investigation with an open mind. I believe it will not be hard for you to find the answers to what you seek.

You must remember that only the Word of God is inspired by the Holy Spirit. Therefore, even though there are tremendous ministry tools available to aid you in your quest, they must always be synchronized with the Bible. If they fail to do so, they're absolutely false.

If you find yourself ready to find true joy for the first time in your life; if you're ready to change your days from hopelessness to hope; and if you're ready to secure your future for eternity; then please consider praying this simple prayer. If you pray this prayer in earnest sincerity, please understand that it's just the *beginning* of a long and incredibly enjoyable walk with the LORD. You'll need help along the way, so finding a local, Bible-based church with strong Christian leadership to disciple you in your walk is the next step.

Jesus,

I confess that I have sinned and fallen short of your glory.

I believe that you suffered and died on the cross for me,

And when you did that,

You paid the full price for the punishment due me, for my sins.

Please forgive me for my sins,

And accept me into your kingdom.

Until right now,

I have only lived for myself.

From now on,

I will only live for you.

Thank you for your incredible sacrifice,

And please also show me

How to help others.

When it is my time,

I look forward to being received

Into your glorious presence.

Please come into my life

Now,

And forever …

Welcome to the family!
Don't stop now, there's work to be done.

BIBLICAL VERSES USED OR REFERENCED

GENESIS

Genesis 1:27 p.105
Genesis 3:5 p.170
Genesis 3:6 p.77+78
Genesis 3:24 p.244
Genesis 25:29-34 p.94

EXODUS

Exodus 20:3-4 p.14

LEVITICUS

Leviticus 19:4 p.100

NUMBERS

Numbers 6:24 p.227

DEUTERONOMY

Deuteronomy 1:6 p.196
Deuteronomy 32:16 p.223

JOSHUA

Joshua 5:15 p.220-221
Joshua 6:27 p.147

JUDGES

Judges 8:23 p.129

RUTH

Ruth 1:16 p.70

I SAMUEL

1 Samuel 2:7 p.120
1 Samuel 12:21 p.245
1 Samuel 15:23 p.183

2 SAMUEL

2 Samuel 6:14 p.80

SONG OF SONGS

ISAIAH

JEREMIAH

LAMENTATIONS

EZEKIEL

DANIEL

HOSEA

JOEL

AMOS

OBADIAH

JONAH

Made in the USA
Columbia, SC
31 October 2017